Porter-Tingley Debate

Birmingham, Alabama, February 24-March 1, 1947

Between

W. Curtis Porter, Monette, Arkansas

and

Glenn V. Tingley, Birmingham, Alabama

Speeches Recorded and Manuscripts Prepared by
George W. DeHoff

Subjects: The Direct Operation of the Holy Spirit; The Necessity
Of Baptism; Are We Saved By Faith Alone?

© **Guardian of Truth Foundation 1947.** All rights reserved. No part of this book may be reproduced in any form without written permission from the publisher. Printed in the United States of America.

ISBN 1-58427-045-4

Guardian of Truth Foundation
P.O. Box 9670
Bowling Green, Kentucky 42102

INTRODUCTION

The Porter-Tingley Debate was conducted in Birmingham, Alabama, for six nights—February 24 to March 1, 1947—between W. Curtis Porter of Monette, Arkansas, representing the Churches of Christ, and Glenn V. Tingley of Birmingham, Alabama, representing the Christian-Missionary Alliance. Both men are well and favorably known among their respective brethren.

The first three sessions of the debate were conducted at the Central Church of Christ and the last three at the Birmingham Gospel Tabernacle. Twelve to fifteen hundred people crowded into all available space every night at both places—there simply was not room for any more—and many heard over the loudspeakers placed in basements and class rooms. From first to last the deportment of audience and speakers was marvelous and hundreds of visitors from distant states left "singing the praises" of the good which can come from debating of this kind.

I recorded the entire debate with my own Soundscriber equipment and with an auxiliary machine borrowed from Freed-Hardeman College, Henderson, Tennessee. My thanks are due the following people who assisted with the recording: Loyce L. Pearce, Flavil H. Nichols and A. E. Emmons Jr. My thanks are also due the following for valuable assistance rendered: Mr. and Mrs. A. E. Emmons Jr., Franklin T. Puckett, W. Curtis Porter, Glenn V. Tingley, Emerson J. Estes, Mary Bryan, Mrs. Claudie Hibdon, Mrs. George W. DeHoff and Richard C. Bell of the Mid-South Publishing Co.

Both Mr. Porter and Mr. Tingley have cooperated splendidly in correcting transcripts of their speeches and assisting with publication of the debate. It is their desire and mine that our Blessed Lord may use this book to His honor and glory in enlarging and extending theh borders of His kingdom among men.

The entire work of recording, transcribing, printing, binding and circulating has been done by me without profit and without pay as a labor of love because of the good which I believe such debates will do.

GEORGE W. DEHOFF

October 1, 1947.

CONTENTS

FIRST NIGHT

Subject: Holy Spirit

	Page
Tingley's First Speech	7
Porter's First Speech	15
Tingley's Second Speech	27
Porter's Second Speech	35

SECOND NIGHT

Subject: Holy Spirit

Tingley's First Speech	47
Porter's First Speech	56
Tingley's Second Speech	68
Porter's Second Speech	79

THIRD NIGHT

Subject: Baptism

Porter's First Speech	92
Tingley's First Speech	103
Porter's Second Speech	113
Tingley's Second Speech	126

FOURTH NIGHT

Subject: Baptism

Porter's First Speech	136
Tingley's First Speech	148
Porter's Second Speech	158
Tingley's Second Speech	170

FIFTH NIGHT

Subject: Faith Alone

Tingley's First Speech	180
Porter's First Speech	192
Tingley's Second Speech	204
Porter's Second Speech	215

SIXTH NIGHT

Subject: Faith Alone

Tingley's First Speech	227
Porter's First Speech	238
Tingley's Second Speech	251
Porter's Second Speech	263

PORTER - TINGLEY DEBATE

First Session: 7:30 P. M., February 24, 1947

Central Church of Christ—Birmingham, Alabama

Chairman: Emerson J. Estes — Birmingham, Alabama

Announcements and welcome to visitors: A. E. Emmons, Jr.,— Birmingham, Alabama

Singing directed by: H. A. Sikes — Birmingham, Alabama

Prayer: I. A. Douthitt — Hohenwald, Tennessee

Moderators: Gus Nichols, Jasper, Albama, for Mr. Porter; Millard Cairns, Decatur, Illinois, for Mr. Tingley

Proposition: The Scriptures Teach that in the Conversion of Alien Sinners the Holy Spirit Operates Directly Upon Them as Well as Through the Word of Truth or Gospel of Christ.

Glenn V. Tingley, Affirms

W. Curtis Porter, Denies

(Affirmative Address by Glenn V. Tingley)

Dr. Glenn V. Tingley

Mr. Chairman, Worthy Opponent, Ladies and Gentlemen:

I am very happy to be here in what I believe to be the clear defense of the truth of God. The question as stated should be carefully defined so there will not be misapprehension in the mind of any of us. "The Scriptures," that is the Word of God, the sixty-six books called the Bible. "Teach that in the conversion," that is the turning around of the sinner whereby he ceases to be a sinner and becomes a child of God. In the conversion there is included the justification, regeneration, the turning around, the new birth, the making new—the "converto" of the sinner. Whereas he was a sinner away from God, now is a child of God in fellowship with his Lord. "The Scriptures teach that in the conversion of alien sinners the Holy Spirit," the third Person of the Godhead, "operates directly," the question is not how He operates, the question is: does He operate in any way directly upon a sinner as well as the word of truth or the Gospel of Christ?

The question briefly stated is does the Holy Spirit operate directly upon sinners? My opponent denies this. I affirm this.

I have never been interested nor would I hold a debate where any vote is taken because so-called winning is not the purpose of debates from my viewpoint. I want the truth. Years ago I broke with man's shibboleth's and forms, and ceremonies and sought and wanted the truth of God. And tonight we want the proof of God as it is found in the Word of God.

Now in order to understand whether the Holy Spirit does operate, there are three things. First, who is the Holy Spirit? Second, can He operate? Third, Does He operate directly upon the sinner? My worthy opponent contends that an individual does not have any direct operation of the Holy Spirit upon him in the matter of conversion; that conversion is a mechanical matter like purchasing out of a gum vending machine a package of conversion. I contend that conversion is something infinitely more than a mechanical operation, that it is something infinitely more than accepting just a word or a receipt, that it has to be accomplished by divine power—a divine operation, every bit of the nature of the sinner whereby the sinner is born from above by direct operation of the Holy Spirit.

Who is the Holy Spirit? Well, the Holy Spirit was present in the Old Testament. The Holy Spirit was sent by the Father in Christ's name. John 14:26, "But the comforter which is the Holy Ghost which the Father will send in my name." The Holy Spirit was sent by Christ, John 16:7, "It is expedient for you that I go away for if I go not away the comforter will not come unto you. If I depart I will send him unto you." John 15:26, "The Holy Spirit came from the Father, "When the comforter is come whom I will send from the Father." The Holy Spirit is of Christ, the Holy Spirit is of God, therefore a person, the third person of the Godhead, a personality operating in the world today. For instance, Romas 8:9, "Ye are not in the flesh but in the Spirit if so be the Spirit of God dwell in you." "Now if any man have not the Spirit of Christ"—the Spirit of God, the Spirit of Christ, a Person Himself, the Holy Spirit.

We are told in Matthew 3:6 that the Father spoke from heaven, Jesus was baptized and the Spirit descended—the Trinity. If the Holy Spirit is part of the Trinity, if He is God, if He is a Person, then He can—with God all things are possible—He can operate directly upon the sinner. The Holy Spirit is very God. Who is He? He is very God. Matthew 28:19, the name of the Holy Spirit is coupled in equality with the name of God and of

Christ in the apostolic commission. In the apostolic benediction in 2 Cor. 13:14, the Holy Spirit is coupled with Christ and God. He is the third Person in the Trinity. In 1 Cor. 12:4-16 there the Holy Spirit is coupled with God and Christ in administering the work of the church. If the Holy Spirit is God, how dare anyone deny that God can operate directly upon the sinner.

The Holy Spirit can be worshipped. He is not an influence, not an "it". In 2 Cor. 13:4, "The grace of our Lord Jesus Christ, the love of God and the communion of the Holy Ghost be with you all." He can be worshipped. He can return communion directly to a worshipper. In 2 Cor. 3:17 and 18 we find He is called God and Lord. "Now the Lord is the Spirit and where the Spirit of the Lord is, there is liberty." If He is Lord and God, He can operate directly upon man.

The Spirit is a person with names. He is called "the Spirit." In 1 Cor. 3:16, He is called the "Spirit of God." In Isa. 11:2, "the Spirit of Jehovah." 2 Cor. 3:3, "the Spirit of the living God." Rom. 8:9, "the Spirit of Christ." In Gal. 4:6, "The Spirit of His Son." In Phil. 1:19, "the Spirit of Jesus Christ." In Luke 11:13, He is "the Holy Spirit." Isa. 4:4, "the Spirit of burning." Rom. 1:4, "the Spirit of Holiness." In John 14:17, the "Spirit of truth." Rom. 8:2, 'the Spirit of life." Heb. 10:29, "the Spirit of Grace." Heb. 9:14, He is the "eternal Spirit." In John 14:26, He is "the comforter." The Holy Spirit is: who He is—God, the third Person of the Trinity. If He is a Person He can operate directly upon the sinner.

The Holy Spirit is a Person, further, because personal pronouns are applied to Him. John 15:26, "When the comforter is come whom I will send from the Father, the Spirit of truth he shall testify." John 16:7-14, over and over "He," "Him." Since He is a Person of the Godhead then he who denies the ability of a person of the Godhead to operate directly upon men limits God, denies God His divine perogrative, and abuses God Himself.

The Holy Spirit does things that only a person could do. Romans 8:26, He intercedes directly for men. In John 14:26, He teaches directly to men. In Acts 16:6, He guides directly for men. In 2 Cor. 13:14, He communes directly with men. In Acts 8:39, He works miracles directly upon man. He can be lied to. You can not lie to a book or to a word. You lie to a person. He is God—a Person. In Acts 5:3, Ananias lied. You can not insult a word, a paragraph or a book. Yet, the Holy Spirit in Heb. 10:29 can be done despite to. He can be wrongfully treated, ill treated, personally insulted, done despite to—the Spirit of grace.

Divine works are ascribed to Him. In Job 33:4, the breath of Almighty God comes in life to men by the Spirit of God. He is life giving in Genesis 2:7 and in John 6:63, the Spirit quickeneth. Romans 8:3, "The Spirit of life." He is life giving. Yet my worthy opponent says: He can not operate directly upon an individual; He can not operate upon a sinner; there is no way for Him to operate upon a person, upon a poor lost sinner.

The Holy Spirit prophesies. 2 Samuel 23:2-3, "The Spirit of the Lord spake by me." Since He is a person and operates directly to, for, with and upon men, then my worthy opponent is attacking the third Person of the Godhead in denying Him His divine perogative.

He has personality, He is God, omnipontent, omnipresent, onmniscent, eternal.

The Holy Spirit cries out. My worthy opponent contends the Holy Spirit can not operate directly upon you as a sinner, there is no contact. He has accepting words, yet, the Holy Spirit cries out. In Gal 4:6 and in other scriptures. In Heb. 9:14, He is eternal and in Isa. 63:10 He is vexed. In John 15:26 He gives testimony. Words can never be vexed. Acts 13:2, He commands men. He has a will. 1 Cor. 12:11. He has love. He has knowledge, He has grief. He searches and He speaks now. Who is He? If He is God, then all things are possible. If He is man, then we are fools and the Bible is a lie. If the Holy Spirit is an influence, then the Godhead is untrue and there is no Spirit, there's an influence. He must be a Person. If He is the printed or spoken word then He is the letter that killeth, He is omnipresent. There are five thousand languages and dialects in this world. The Bible has only been translated into a little over one thousand. Yet the Bible plainly declares that the Holy Spirit is omnipresent in the world.

If He is the third person of the Trinity and if He is God's administrator in this age, then He blesses the Word, convicts the sinner, fills the church by the direct operation of the Holy Spirit upon men. Therefore, who is He? The third Person of the Godhead. Can He? With God all things are possible.

Now, does He? If I only had one scripture to read tonight, I would read to you 1 Corinthians the second chapter. That's enough. "And I, brethren, when I came to you, came not with excellency of speech or of wisdom, declaring unto you the testimony of God. For I determined not to know anything among you, save Jesus Christ and him crucified. And I was with you in weakness, and in fear, and in much trembling. And my speech and my preaching was not enticing words of man's wisdom, but in the demonstrations of the Spirit and of power; that your faith should not stand in the wisdom of men, but in the power of God. Howbeit we speak wisdom among them that are perfect; yet not the wisdom of this world, nor of the princes of this world that come to naught, but we speak the wisdom of God in a mystery, even the hidden wisdom, which God ordained before the world unto our glory; which none of the princes of this world knew: for had they known it, they would not have crucified the Lord of glory. But as it is written, Eye hath not seen, nor ear heard, neither have entered into the heart of man the things that God hath prepared for them that love him. But God hath revealed them unto us by his Spirit, for the Spirit searchest all things, yea, the deep things of God. For what man knoweth the things of man, save the spirit of man which is in him? Even so the things of God knoweth no man, but the Spirit of God. Now we have received, not the Spirit of the world, but the Spirit which is of God; that we might know the things that are freely given to us of God. Which things also we speak, not in the words which man's wisdom teaches; but which the Holy Ghost teacheth; comparing spiritual things with spiritual. But the natural man receiveth not the things of the Spirit of God for they are foolinshness unto him; neither can he know them, because"—why does not the nautraJ man understand the word of God? Why can he not grasp the truth of God? Why is it his ears are dull? Because they are spirtually discerned! Unless the Spirit operates directly upon the sinner, the sinner is helpless to understand the way of salvation and the thing of God. "But he that is spiritual judgeth all things, yet he himself is judged of no man. For who hath known the mind of the Lord, that he may instruct him? But we have the mind of Christ." Now, there can be no reception or understanding of the word of salvation except cooperative with and accompanied by the Holy Spirit. The Holy Spirit must open the eyes of the sinner to receive the word. We have not received the Spirit of the natural man but the Spirit which is of God. Why? Why do men receive that? "That we might know the deep things of God!" Does the Holy Spirit operate directly upon the sinner? He must before he can receive and and understand the Word of God.

If I only had one scripture, Romans 8:9 would be adequate. "But ye are not in the flesh but in the spirit if so be the Spirit of God dwell in you." If any man have not the Spirit, he is not converted, he is none of His. The Holy Spirit must operate directly or he can not be converted. If the Spirit did not operate directly upon him, you then are none of His.

If I only had one scripture, Romans 5:5 would be enough. "And hope maketh not ashamed because the love of God is abroad in our hearts by the Holy Ghost which is given unto us." Now what is conversion? Conversion is the turning a man around who loves the world. At conversion, in conversion, in the act of conversion the love of God is shed in his heart otherwise he never is converted, never can be. Converted means a complete turning around. Who sheds the love of God in the man's heart and causes him in the act of turning around to become a born again child of God? The Holy Spirit sheds abroad the love of God in the sinner's heart.

God made us by direct operation. Christ redeemed us by direct operation, the Holy Spirit converts us by direct operation.

If I only had one scripture, Acts 7:51 is enough. "Ye stiffnecked and uncircumcised in heart and ears, ye sinners. Ye do always resist the Holy Ghost." How can men resist one who does not operate directly upon them? "As your fathers did so do ye." The Holy Spirit pleads, convicts, entreats, He brings men to the word. He works with and in addition to the Word. How can you profess to believe the Word and resist the Holy Glost? Those who take the position of my worthy opponent, as Jesus said to the Pharisees, "Ye search the scriptures for in them ye think ye have eternal life, they are they that testify of me and ye will not come unto me that you might have life." Mark this. The scriptures over and over emphasize the direct operation of the Holy Spirit in the conversion of the sinner. Over and over, yet with all the searching He can not be found. My worthy opponent says He does not operate directly.

If I only had one scripture, John 16:7-11 is enough. It is said to the disciples, "Nevertheless I tell you the truth. It is expedient for you that I go away, for if I go not away the comforter which is the Holy Spirit will not come unto you, but if I depart I will send him unto you. And when he is come he will convict the world,"—the world of sinners, the world of wicked men. The Holy Spirit will convict them by direct operation— "Of sin of righteousness and of judgement." What does the Holy Spirit convict the world of? Of sin! "Of sin because they believed not on me. Of righteousness because I go to my Father and ye see me no more, of judgement because the prince of this world is judged." The world is all flesh. He comes to reprove "the world." Operating directly upon all men, upon sinful men. The Word plainly declares it. My worthy opponent denies it. Men can never be convicted of sin without the Holy Spirit, said Jesus. The Word, said Jesus, is powerless unless accompanied by the Holy Spirit. The writing of John of the words from the lips of Jesus. In the Old Testament age the story was the same. In Genesis 6:3, the Lord said "My Spirit will not always strive with man." Repentance must be of God inspired by the Holy Spirit.

If I only had one scripture, John 3:1-8, is enough. "There was a man of the Pharisees named Nicodemus. A ruler of the Jews. The same came to Jesus by night and said unto him, Rabbi we know that thou art a teacher come from God for no man can do these miracles that thou doest except God be with him. Jesus answered and said unto him, Verily verily I say unto thee, except a man be born again, he can not see the kingdom of God. Nicodemus saith unto him, How can a man be born when he is old? Can he enter the second time into his mother's womb and be born? Jesus answered, Verily, verily I say unto thee, Except a man be born of water and of the Spirit, he can not enter into the kingdom of God. That which is born of flesh is flesh; and that which is born of the spirit is spirit. Marvel not that I said unto thee, Ye must be born again. The wind bloweth where it listeth, and thou hearest the sound thereof, but canst not tell whence it cometh and whither it goeth: so is every one that is born of the Spirit."

The birth of the Spirit is spoken of three times. There are two agents. The word and the Spirit direct from God to operate upon the sinner. The Word and the Spirit as well as the Word. The other day I was in the hospital where my oldest daughter had given birth to her first baby. That baby was born of my daughter. No one else was its mother. It was a matter of direct operation. The Word of God says that if a sinner is born again he is born of the Spirit. My worthy opponent says that He can not operate, does not operate, directly upon the sinner.

Now, I have proven the scriptures teach that in the conversion of alien sinners the Holy Spirit operates directly upon them as well as the word of truth or the gospel of Christ—because: the Holy Spirit was omnipresent in the Old Testament age; He has come from the Father in Christ's name; He is the third Person of the Trinity; He is diety and can not be limited; He is God and Lord and is a Person; He is a Person with personal names, and personal pronouns are used to describe Him. Therefore, if He is God, He can operate directly upon the sinner. The Holy Spirit does things only a person can do. He does divine works, gives life, prophesies, has all the attributes of personal deity. Therefore He can operate directly upon the sinner. The Holy Spirit invites the sinner to Christ. Man's sinful nature can be changed only by a divine miracle of the Holy Spirit. Man only receives the witness of salvation and is damned in rejecting the Holy Spirit, therefore the Holy Spirit does operate directly upon the sinner. The Holy Spirit is the One who convicts the sinner and alone produces repentance. The New Birth is wrought by the Holy Spirit. The Holy Spirit does operate directly upon the sinner.

One can resist the pleading of the Holy Spirit. Ye become epistles of Christ by the Spirit and the love of God is shed abroad in our hearts by the Holy Spirit. Therefore the Holy Spirit operates directly upon the sinner.

If I only had one scripture I would give this one: Acts 10:44, "While Peter yet spake these words, the Holy Ghost fell on them which heard the word." In the conversion of Cornelius he heard the Word and as well as the Word—which my opponent denies—and while the Word was preached, the Holy Ghost descended upon them, personally fell, and He can and does operate directly upon the sinner because of Cornelius' household. Thank you.

FIRST NIGHT — PORTER'S FIRST SPEECH

Mr. Chairman, Gentlemen Moderators, Respected Opponent, Ladies and Gentlemen:

I am indeed glad for this privilege which I now have of coming before you at this time in the negative of the proposition which my friend, Mr. Tingley, has been affirming for the past thirty minutes. I appreciate also the confidence which my brethren placed in me in calling me to engage in this discussion with Mr. Tingley, on these propositions which will be studied during these six nights of the discussion.

I assure you of the fact, at the very beginning, I am seeking to get before you the truth; and it is not a matter of winning a victory but getting before you the truth of God Almighty. I shall endeavor to do that as best I can as the discussion goes on.

But before I reply to the speech that has just been made I have just a few questions that I want to present to my opponent. These questions are not presented for the purpose of diverting attention from the question before us, or turning aside your minds from the issue of the discussion; but for the purpose of focusing the issue and getting before you just the things that are involved in this discussion tonight and the position which my friend must occupy in order to sustain the position which he has maintained for the past thirty minutes. These questions are not given for the purpose of taking up time, but I simply want to get before you the truth of God Almighty upon these matters; and so these questions I shall expect my friend to answer.

First, Is it possible for the direct operation of the Holy Spirit to save a sinner without the preaching of the word?

2. Is it possible for a sinner to be saved by the influence exerted through the word without the direct operation of the Spirit?

3. Does the direct operation of the Spirit precede or follow the preaching of the word?

4. What does the direct operation of the Spirit do for a sinner that can not be accomplished by the preaching of the gospel?

5. Is the miraculous outpouring of the Holy Spirit the same as the direct operation of the Holy Spirit in conversion?

6. Does the Holy Spirit in its direct operation on the sinner speak to the sinner?

7. If the Holy Spirit speaks to the sinner what does He say that He has not already said in the word of truth?

8. If the Holy Spirit does not speak to the sinner, then in what way does he exert power upon him?

9. How does the sinner know the Spirit is operating directly upon him?

10. What does the sinner do when he resists the direct operation of the Holy Spirit?

(Mr. Porter hands the questions to Mr. Tingley. Mr. Tingley: Thank you).

(Mr. Porter continues:)

I call your attention next to the definition which my opponent gave concerning the proposition. He mentioned the word "direct." That's the thing that's concerned in this question tonight. "The scriptures teach that in the conversion of alien sinners the Holy Spirit operates directly upon them as well as through the word of truth or gospel of Christ." Now the word "directly" simply means "immediately," and the two words may be used interchangeably. Those two words have to do either with time or method. If we use them with respect to time and say that a certain thing will occur directly or immediately, we mean without delay, that it will soon be accomplished. Certainly, that is not the meaning of the word as my opponent uses it in his proposition. In the second place, the words indicate without medium or with nothing intervening. When we are talking about a thing being done directly or immediately, we mean without means; there is no medium through which it works. It works directly, without means. That's the meaning of the term as used in this question tonight and which my opponent shall have to sustain as the discussion goes on.

Now, then, just briefly, before I notice his arguments, I want to introduce just a few counter arguments with a few negative thoughts; and then I shall take up his speech.

I am contending, of course, that the Holy Spirit operates upon the sinner through the word of truth. I call your attention to a statement made by Paul in 1 Cor. 1:21, in which it is said, "It pleased God to save them that believe through the foolishness of preaching." Now that, according to friend Tingley, can not be. Men can not be saved through foolishness of preaching. The thing that pleased God didn't please Elder Tingley at all. But it pleased God to save them that believe through the preaching of the gospel, the foolishness of preaching. The question arises, How do men believe? How does faith come about? How is faith produced? I call your attention to these thoughts upon that point. In John 17:20, Jesus prayed for them "That shall believe on me through their word," referring to the preaching of the apostles for whom he had just prayed. He prayed for those that believe on him through their word. He did not say "through a direct operation of the Holy Spirit" but for them that believe on me "through their word." In Romans 10:17, Paul said, "Faith cometh by hearing and hearing by the word of God." Elder Tingley would have to say, "No, Paul, you are mistaken about that. Faith comes by a direct operation of the Holy Spirit away from the word of God." But Paul says, "Faith comes by hearing the word of God." Then in John 20:30-31, we are told that "Many other signs truly did Jesus in the presence of his disciples, which are not written in this book; but these are written that you might believe that Jesus is the Christ; and that believing ye might have life through his name." That shows, again, that faith comes as a result of the things that are written. My opponent insists that the things that are written can not produce faith; that there must be a direct operation of the Spirit before the sinner can even know anything about it, much less believe anything about it.

Again, in Acts 4:4 we are told that "Many of them which heard the word believed," showing that their belief came as a result of hearing the word. In Acts 15:7, Peter said, "God made choice among us that the Gentiles by my mouth should hear the word of the gospel and believe," and that they should believe as a result of hearing the word.

In Romans 10:13-14 Paul declared, "How can they believe in him of whom they have not heard?" In Luke 8:12 we have a statement made which shows that even the devil knows that the word is able to save men. Referring to the seed that fell by the wayside, Jesus said, "The devil comes, catches the word away." He comes and removes the word, "lest they should believe and be saved." Of course, that could not be, according to friend Tingley; the word could stay there forever, and if there was not a direct operation of the Holy Spirit upon the person, he just would not be saved at all. So the devil was concerned about a thing that he needed not have been concerned about at all. He should have tried some way to prevent a direct operation of the Holy Spirit instead of removing the word, because removing the word from his heart would have nothing to do with it. Just keep the Holy Spirit from operating directly, and that would get the job done, according to friend Tingley.

I call your attention now to what the gospel does. Romans 1:16. Paul said, "I am not ashamed of the gospel of Christ: for it is the power of God unto salvation to everyone that believeth; to the Jew first, and also to the Greek." I know that God has power which is not exerted through the gospel. God has power as the Creator; God has power to do many things that are not involved in this question tonight. The power of God to save is exerted through the gospel, because Paul said the gospel is the power of God unto salvation. In 1 Cor. 4:15 he said, "I have begotten you through the gospel." Of course, Mr. Tingley would have to add, "No, not through the gospel but through a direct operation of the Holy Spirit."

Notice what the law of Christ does. In Romans 8:2, "The law of the Spirit of life in Christ Jesus has made me free from the law of sin and death." The word law means "rule of action." Why, my friend introduced this passage awhile ago in connection with what the Spirit did. It tells us how the Spirit did it; that the Spirit did it through His law. "The law of the Spirit of life in Christ Jesus hath made me free from the law of sin and death," and Elder Tingley says, "That can not happen. The law of the Spirit can not do a thing of that kind." But Paul said it did. You may take your choice.

In Psalms 19:7, it is said, "The law of the Lord is perfect, converting the soul." The word perfect often means complete. The law of the Lord is complete, converting the soul. No, it isn't complete, according to my friend; there must be something else.

In the fifth place, I call your attention to what the word is said to do. James 1:18. It is said to beget. James said we are begotten with the word of truth. In Psalms 119:50 it is said to quicken. In John 17:17 it is said to sanctify. In Psalms 119:9—it cleanses. In James 1:21—it is able to save. Acts 20:32—it is able to give you an inheritance among them that are sanctified.

In the sixth place, note what the truth does. 1 Pet. 1:22 says "purified your souls in obeying the truth." John 8:32 says, "Ye shall know the truth and the truth shall make you free."

I give those as negative thoughts showing that God operates upon men—the Holy Spirit operates upon men—through the word, through the gospel of Jesus Christ; and that through that operation He is able to save the souls of men.

Now, then, to the speech which my opponent just made. About half of it was unnecessary and altogether wasted effort on the part of my friend. He wasted about half his time endeavoring to prove to you that the Holy Spirit is a person; that he is not simply an influence or something of that kind; but that He is a person. He gave a great number of scriptures along that line. He said, "Who is the Holy Spirit?" and gave John 14:27 —"The Father sent the comforter," and John 16:17, Christ said, "I will send him." John 15:26—He came from the Father. Rom. 8:1—the Spirit dwells in you. Matthew 3:16—the Spirit descended. He said all of this shows that He is operating directly. And Matthew 28:19, the three mentioned there in connectioin with baptism in the name of the Father, the Son and the Holy Spirit; the Holy Spirit being the third person in the Godhead. 2 Cor. 13:14—the Holy Spirit is coupled with God and with Christ. 1 Cor. 12:4-6—He is connected with God. And 2 Cor. 13:14—he can be worshiped. And, then, he said, "He is called the Lord." 2 Cor. 3:17, 18. He gave a list of scriptures to prove what the Spirit's names are. 2 Cor. 3:16; Isa. 11:2; 2 Cor. 3:3; Rom. 8:9; Gal. 6:6; Phil. 1:19; Luke 11:13 Isa. 4:4; Rom 1:4; John 14:17; Romans 8:2; Heb. 10:29; Heb. 9:14. All of these are referring to it as the Spirit of the Son and the Spirit of God and various other terms that are used describing the Spirit—all proving that the Spirit is a person.

He came on down to some other things in that connection —the personal pronouns used in referring to the Spirit. John 15:26—referred to as "he"—the personal pronoun. John 16:7-4— the personal pronoun "he" again being applied to him. And so he declares that this proves that He is a person.

The next argument he made was that he does what a person does. Rom. 8:26—he intercedes. John 14:26—he teaches. Acts 16:6—he guides. 2 Cor. 13:14—he communes.

Then he can be lied to as Ananias did in Acts 5:3. He can be despised. Heb. 10:29. All of this, he claims, proves that the Holy Spirit is a person. Then Gal. 4:6—he cries out. Isa. 63:10—he is vexed. John 15:26—he gives testimony. 1 Cor. 12:11—he has a will. All of these things he introduced to prove that the Holy Spirit is a person, as though that were involved in his proposition tonight. I want to tell you, my friends, tonight, that not a single, solitary thing in this proposition gives any reason beneath the stars for the introduction of such arguments as that.

Mr. Tingley, I agree with you whole-heartedly, and I could have made that speech with all the sincerity of my soul that you made for the first fifteen minutes of it, endeavoring to prove that the Holy Spirit is a person. I believe that as well as you do; and I think you knew that I believed that He is a person. I just feel sure that that is right. And so you wasted half of your speech proving that the Holy Spirit is a person when there is no issue between us on that whatsoever. Certainly, I believe the Holy Spirit is a person. I can make every argument that you have made along that line, proving it to the audience just as you did. I can shake hands with you upon that, my friend Tingley, and just let that pass, because we both agree wholeheartedly upon that point. That's not the point involved in the discussion at all tonight.

The proposition does not say, "The Scriptures teach that the Holy Spirit is a person." Friend Tingley, if you had written a proposition like that I would have affirmed it instead of denying it.

You said, "The question is not how does the Spirit operate?" but "Does the Spirit operate?" No, that's not the question at all. There is no difference between my opponent and myself as to the operation of the Spirit—that is, as to whether the Spirit operates. I certainly believe that the Spirit operates. It is a question of how it operates and not whether it operates. And so you're side-stepping the issue. Come up and face the music and let's get going on this proposition—not whether the Spirit operates but how it operates. I am contending that the Holy Spirit operates through the word, through the preaching of the gospel. Friend Tingley says it operates directly—without means, without a medium, upon the alien sinner. So it is a question of "how" and not "whether."

Again, he said he was going to prove the Spirit could do so and so. He said there are three things involved: Who is the Spirit? Can he operate directly? And does He operate directly? He spent a great deal of his time endeavoring to prove that the Holy Spirit can operate directly. In fact, these arguments he made upon the personality of the Spirit were used to prove that the Spirit can operate directly. Friend Tingley, will you take this proposition and show me where there is anything there about whether the Spirit can operate directly? Is that what you are affirming? If you had written a proposition saying "The scriptures teach that in the conversion of alien sinners the Holy Spirit can operate directly." I would have affirmed it, Elder Tingely, and not have denied it. I would have affirmed that instead of putting my name to the negative of it. Why, certainly, I believe the Holy Spirit can operate directly. It is not a matter of what the Holy Spirit can do. It's what the Holy Spirit does. That's the point. It's not whether he can do it but whether he is doing it.

Elder Tingley, God can feed you with bread direct from heaven, but he is not doing it, is He?

Mr. Tingley: Yes.

Mr. Porter: Getting manna down from heaven just like the Israelites did?

(Mr. Tingley nods his head for "Yes.")

Mr. Porter: Physical food? Physical food direct from heaven? You go out in the morning and gather it up just like the Israelites did?

Mr. Tingley: He gathers it for me.

Mr. Porter: And who feeds you?

Mr. Tingley: His disciples.

Mr. Porter: And he puts it in your mouth? Well, that's going. Now, then, my friend says he does not have to work for food. He does not even have to gather it up. God sends it down directly from heaven. What does he send you—manna, fish or what?

Mr. Tingley: All of it.

Mr. Porter: Do you get all of it the same day?

Mr. Tingley: No, I get it whenever I need it.

Mr. Porter: Whenever you need it? How do you know when you need it? Now, that's the position to which this thing has driven him this early in the debate. He has taken a position now that God sends him food directly from heaven—without any medium, without any means. He does not have to have anybody to plow the corn. It does not have to be reaped; it does not have to be threshed; it doesn't have to be taken to mill or anything else. He gets it direct from heaven; already baked; already cooked; ready to eat. I suspect God forces his mouth open and crams it down. Now, that's where it goes when he goes to a thing of that kind. God can do things that He is not doing. He is not feeding Elder Tingley direct from heaven with fish or any other kind of material food. If he gets his food, he will have to work for it like any other man gets it. It is not a question of what God can do, or what the Holy Spirit can do, but it is what the Holy Spirit does. He says if you say the Holy Spirit cannot do it, you limit the power of the Spirit. All right; if you say the Holy Spirit can not save a man through the word, you have limited the power of the Spirit. Can God save a man through the word without a direct operation? Can the Holy Spirit save a man without directly operating upon him? Can he? Tell me, Tingley, can he?

Mr. Tingley: I'll tell you.

Mr. Porter: He will tell me. All right; you wait and see whether or not he will tell me if the Holy Spirit can save a man through the word without the direct operation. If He cannot, then you limit the power of the Spirit. If you say He can, you give up your proposition. Now just take either horn of it you want, and we will see how the goring goes on.

He said, "There are five thousand languages on the earth, and the Bible has been translated into only one thousand of them." Wonder just what he intended by that? I suppose he meant that God could save just the one thousand; and so the four thousand of them would have to remain unsaved, according to my position. If that is what he wants to say about it, we will be glad to have him say it in his next speech. So I wait further development upon that point.

Then he came to his third point and says, "Does the Holy Spirit operate directly upon the sinner?" He affirms that He does. He gave a number of passages proving that the Holy Spirit operates. Not a single one of them contained anything about "directly." The word directly or its equivalent is not found in a single one of them. Friend Tingley simply assumes that there is something there that isn't there. He bases his whole contention upon his assumption. That's all.

Now then let's get at the scriptures he gave. 1 Cor. 2. He read the entire chapter to prove that the Holy Spirit operates directly on sinners. Now, the second chapter of 1st Corinthians— I do not want to read the entire chapter but just a few things that my opponent read to prove that the Holy Spirit operates directly upon sinners. Now, he read this verse right in connection with the others. Verse 12, "Now we have received, not the Spirit of the world, but the Spirit which is of God." He applied that to alien sinners. Here's the Holy Spirit operating upon alien sinners in conversion; but Paul is referring to the revelation of God to them who are already saved, including himself. To whom does "we" refer? "That we might know the things that are freely given to us of God." Friend Tingley, tell us, does that mean alien sinners? If it doesn't, your whole argument is lost. If it does, then Paul was an alien sinner, because he included himself in the expression "we." In this same connection he came on down to the fourteenth verse. "But the natural man receiveth not the things of the Spirit of God; for they are foolishness unto him; neither can he know them, because they are spiritually discerned." So he said the natural man can not receive the things of the Spirit; so there must be a direct operation. Well, is a "direct operation" a thing of the Spirit? Is that power which you say the Spirit works upon a man one of the things of the Spirit? If it is, your passage says he can not receive it! So it cuts you loose from that because he can not receive the things of the Spirit; and the operation of the Spirit is one of the things of the Spirit. How about conversion? Is that one of the things of the Spirit? This says he can not receive the things of the Spirit, So he can not receive conversion, according to your application of the passage. We will have more to say about that later.

He also said, "The sinner must receive the Spirit before he can receive the word." He said, "I give Romans 8:9 as the passage." "Ye are not in the flesh, but in the Spirit, if so be that the Spirit of God dwell in you." Here's the passage that proves, according to friend Tingley, that an alien sinner must receive the Spirit before he can receive the word. Now, then, what about it? When he receives the Spirit, Paul says he is not in the flesh. "Ye are not in the flesh, but in the Spirit, if so be that the Spirit of God dwells in you." Now, when the Spirit dwells in you, you are not in the flesh, but in the Spirit. He said that refers to alien sinners. All right; then alien sinners are not in the flesh when they receive the Spirit prior to receiving the word. Then, they must be out of the flesh, and, they are no longer sinners. The passage does not do him any good at all, because even by his application, we have shown that they are not in the flesh, but in the Spirit, when they receive the Spirit; and all of that, he says, before they can receive the word. That being true, they are out of the flesh when they receive the Spirit and have never yet heard the word of God Almighty.

In Rom. 5:5—the love of God shed abroad in our hearts by the Holy Ghost. Yes, and that did not say "directly." It did not say a word about a direct operation. We learn in 1 John 4:19 that we love God because He first loved us; and the love of God is revealed to us through the testimony of the Spirit revealed in the gospel. Certainly, through that it is shed abroad in our hearts through the Holy Ghost.

He came to Acts 7:51. If he needed just one passage, that would be it. "Stiff-necked and uncircumcised in heart and ears." "Ye do always resist the Holy Ghost. As your fathers did, so do you." Now, what did those men resist when they resisted the Holy Spirit? Read right on down through the following verses and you will find they "stopped their ears"! They stopped their ears and rushed upon Stephen with one accord. When they stopped their ears they resisted the Holy Spirit. My friend says it must be otherwise. That is not the passage he wants. He will have to find something better than that. That shows they resisted the Holy Ghost by resisting the preaching of Stephen. Even as their fathers did. When you turn back to Neh. 9:30 you will find how their fathers did it, when they refused to hear the testimony of the Spirit of God in the prophets. It was in that way they resisted the Spirit.

Note, now, John 16:7-11. Here he said, "Now the Spirit was going to reprove the world of sin, of righteousness and of judgment." Yes, but it does not say he will reprove them or convince them directly. That's the thing he has to read into it. We turn to Acts 2 and we find the fullfillment of that promise. The Spirit came. How did the Spirit, on that occasion, reprove the world of sin? Through the preaching of the apostle Peter. He preached to them, and when they heard this they were pricked in their hearts and cried out unto Peter and the rest of the apostles, "Men and brethren what shall we do?" They were convinced by the Spirit through the preaching of the word on the day of Pentecost.

Mr. Nichols: You have four minutes.

Mr. Porter: Thank you. Then he said, "The word is powerless unless accompanied by the Spirit," said Jesus. We want the passage where Jesus said that. That's just Tingley's assertion; and we are not taking his assertion for it. We must have the passage that said so.

He came to John 3:1-8—"born of the Spirit" and the case of Nicodemus. He said, "The other day there was a baby born of my daughter in the hospital by a direct operation; and so the birth of the Spirit must be a direct operation." Well, Tingley, is the Spirit your mother? Is that what you're getting at? Is the Spirit your mother? Be careful or you are going to have a "he" becoming your mother, the first thing you know.

He gave another, "If we have not the Spirit of Christ we are none of his." But if we have the Spirit of Christ we are his, according to that passage; and he says you have the Spirit before you hear the word. Then, you are his before you hear the word.

In Acts 10:44, "The Holy Spirit fell on all them which heard the word." This is the case of the conversion of Cornelius. He said here we have both the word and the Spirit. While Peter preached the Holy Spirit fell on them that heard the word. There's the word and there's the Holy Spirit's part. There are two things. Yes. There was a miraculous outpouring of the Holy Spirit that enabled them to speak with tongues. Is that what you mean by a direct operation of the Holy Spirit on sinners? Tell me, please, in your next speech—was Cornelius a sinner when the Holy Spirit fell on him? Was Cornelius an alien sinner when the Holy Spirit fell on him? You have given it to prove your proposition. We are going to demand that you come up and tell us whether he was an alien sinner when the Holy Spirit fell on him. If he was not an alien sinner when the Spirit fell on him, then this case is not going to do you any good, because your proposition says an alien sinner. If he was an alien sinner when the Holy Spirit fell on him, and that is what you mean by a direct operation of the Spirit, then you are going to have to have a visit of angels, a vision, and tongues and all of those things accompanying the conversion of all sinners by the outpouring of the Holy Spirit. He can just take whichever he wants to take on that. We are going to insist that he take one of them, because he will have to do that to stay with his proposition and to get before you the things that he is contending for. I believe that just about covers his speech. If I have overlooked anything, I have done is unintentionally. I certainly thank you for your patient hearing during this thirty minutes' speech.

FIRST NIGHT — TINGLEY'S SECOND SPEECH

Mr. Chairman, Worthy Opponent, Ladies and Gentlemen:

I appreciate very much my worthy opponent. He has done exactly as I expected him to do. I was greatly interested in his being perturbed over my losing time. Why should he be so concerned about my wasting time. Did you ladies and gentlemen notice the time he wasted in answering the arguments I presented while I wasted my time? Certainly, if I wasted time in presenting the arguments—he knowing full well what he did—deliberately wasted time to answer or explain my wasting time.

My proposition does not have a thing in the world to say about who the Holy Spirit is in actual words. I know that. The question does not have anything to say actuall..y about does or can the Holy Spirit operate. I recognize that. One of the laws of logic is that any individual in debating a point has a natural and a perfect right and it is obligatory upon him to deal with the fundamental basis. The fundamental basis is my worthy opponent's dishonor of the Holy Ghost.

My worthy opponent accepts intellectually what I said about who the Holy Spirit was. I knew that before I said it. I wanted him to admit it. My worthy opponent said that he accepted the fact that the Holy Spirit could operate directly upon the sinner. I knew he would have to say that. My worthy opponent, is as nimble as a monkey, said that He does not. He can. He is God. But He does not do it.

I have instance after instance of where the Holy Spirit did do it. That's whole issue at stake, ladies and gentlemen; and I'm not here just to debate, I'm not here just because some proposition was agreed upon. I believe in this audience there are earnest seeking men and women who want to know how to know God. You are the ones I'm after. I want you to find peace and rest within your soul. I read to you a number of instances where the Holy Spirit does operate on a sinner. I will read them again for the further information of my opponent, but the Word of God and the Spirit of God are able to do something definite and positive in making you a new creature in Christ Jesus.

My worthy opponent reminds me of a story I heard. A colored fellow attended one of these big modernistic churches in the

North where a modern preacher did away with the New Birth and did away with the Holy Spirit operating in the New Birth and did away with anything miraculous in the New Birth. (Ladies and gentlemen, the whole issue at stake is that my worthy opponent does not believe that the Spirit of God in conversion actually directly changes the nature—the nature and mind and heart of the sinner. He'll beg that question and argue that question and sidestep that question and quote scripture after scripture but he does not believe in the direct operation of the Holy Spirit in changing the heart and nature of the sinner in conversion). The darkie listened to the preacher do away with the things that he loved. After the service was over he came up and said, "Doctor, that was a beautiful sermon. It was wonderful language. And doctor, you proved with words that there was not such a thing as the new birth. You proved to yourself that there was not such a thing as the new birth. There was only one mistake." "What was it?" "You should have added, 'As I knows of.'" As sure as anything in the world, an individual who has ever had God speak to him knows the Holy Spirit operates directly upon the sinner.

I would like to have my worthy opponent bring a definition of the word directly. He said it means immediately. I ask him to bring in the definition of directly from Webster's unabridged dictionary and read it to you. He again is begging the question.

He said I did not believe in conversion wrought by the word. He quoted scripture after scripture—1 Cor. 1:21, John 1:20 and a great host of them. I will not take your time to read the list of them. You heard them. This one for instance, 1 Cor. 1:21, "For after that the wisdom of God the world by wisdom knew not God, it pleased God by the foolishness of preaching to save them that believe." He paused after every one and said, "Tingley does not believe that." "That could not be according to friend Tingley." I do believe it! I believe all the Word! I read those scriptures to you to establish the fact that a man is converted, born again of incorruptible seed by the word of God which liveth and abideth forever. Let's be honest. Ladies and gentlemen, above everything else be brutally honest. Write down on one side where the Word is the direct agent in conversion. Be honest and write down on the other side where the Spirit is the direct agent in conversion and you will find they balance the one the other continually. It is the Word! It is the Spirit! Both of them operate in saving the sinner. Without the Spirit a man can never have a witness of the Spirit within him and know that he has passed from death unto life. Ladies and gentlemen, that is the issue.

I want to make it very clear: the Holy Spirit is God. The Holy Spirit can operate. The Holy Spirit does operate. Now, I call your attention to something. He will watch it from now on. I counted until I lost count. Over and over and over again my worthy opponent betrayed the real thought of his heart and what he believes by referring to the Holy Spirit as "It." "It." "It." That's what my worthy opponent believes. If I can get him to honestly open up to you, he does not believe that God has anything directly to do with changing a man's nature, renewing a man's mind, shedding the love of God abroad in his heart in the matter of conversion at all. It is a mechanical matter! Purely of the head!

Now, let me turn back to I Corinthians 2. He complained that I read all of it. It's the Word of God any how. He complains greatly about verse 14 and well he might. "But the natural man receiveth not the things of the Spirit of God." They can not be accepted by his reason. I would call his attention to the fact the apostle Paul has said, "I don't come in words of man's wisdom. I don't come with enticing words. I don't come with human persuasive power. I do not come appealing to the intellect." Over and over throughout the chapter he said "It is not a matter of the intellect." "For the natural man can not receive." I would ask him to tell us, in all honesty what is meant by not receiving and what the commentators say. I will tell you now. He will beg the question. It means intellectual assent, intellectually receive. He can not receive with his mind the things of the Spirit. They are received only by spiritual revelation, they are received only by spiritual operation. Now, They are discerned, they are understood by the Spirit.

Let me answer very briefly now. Tomorrow night we will deal with them far more fully.

"Is it possible for the direct operation of the Holy Spirit to save a sinner without preaching the word?" "Is it possible for a sinner to be saved by the influence exterted through the Word without the direct operation?" I would say, with God all things are possible but this is not God's program. God demands both Spirit and Word.

"Does the direct operation of the Spirit precede or follow the preaching of the word?" It may precede, it always must accompany.

"What does the direct operation of the spirit do for the sinner that can not be done by preaching of the gospel?" I read to you from I Cor. 2:14, that "The natural man can not receive the things of the Spirit of God." It is utterly impossible for just the Word. Let me pause and give you an illustration. Lew Wallace, an agnostic, was drafted by a group of men to write a story about Jesus to prove he was not the Son of God. Lew Wallace began to study the accounts of the gospel. He became convinced that Jesus was the Christ. Somehow, it did not have any effect upon him. One day, very humble he went to a simple old godly soul who said, "It's got to be the operation of God. It's got to be God revealing His word." He very humbly said, "Oh God, reveal thy word to me. Let thy Spirit reveal thy word to me." And God did. Before he left that humble cottage, he wrote a letter to his agnostic friends who had drafted him to write the story now known as "Ben Hur." He told them that God had revealed Christ to him as his personal Lord and Savior.

"Is the miraculous outpouring of the Holy Spirit the same as the direct operation of the Spirit in conversion." It is the same Spirit but not the same operation. That was one for dispensational fullfillment. The Holy Spirit operates today directly upon any individual heart.

"Does the Holy Spirit in its direct operation on the spirit speak to the sinner?" He may or he may communicate with the spirit in various ways.

"If the Holy Spirit speaks to the sinner what does he say that is not already said in the word of truth?" For one thing the Holy Spirit opens up the heart of the sinner. The Holy Spirit opens up the mind of the sinner that is closed by his stubborn resistance to God.

"If the Holy Spirit does not speak to the sinner, then in what way does he exert power upon him?" My worthy opponent is doing exactly the thing that he will do in his next speech (if he is not guarded now) and will do tomorrow night. He will keep crying out "How." The question is not "How?" but "Does the Spirit operate?" I could give you any number of ways both from the Word and from human experiences how the Holy Spirit operates and I'm not going to be drawn off into needless and foolish questions.

"What does the sinner do when he resists the direct operation of the Spirit?" Well, my worthy opponent, ought to know what the sinner does when he resists the Holy Spirit. Genesis the sixth chapter tells us exactly what he does. They hardened their hearts. They resist the Holy Spirit by hardening their hearts and rejecting the Spirit's word to them and the Spirit's entreaty.

Now let me deal further with some of these scriptures and give you some additional scriptures. My worthy opponent dealt at great length . . . (By the way, did you note that he did not deal with this: Rom. 5:5, "Hope maketh not ashamed because the love of God is shed abroad in our hearts by the Holy Ghost." How does the sinner become converted, how does he change from loving the world to having the love of God within him? What happens? The Word of God says it is shed abroad by the Holy Ghost. There is no mention of the word. There is no mention of any other—it is the Holy Ghost). . . . Again note this please. He quoted at great length and dealt with it—Rom. 8:9, "But ye are not in the flesh but in the Spirit if so be that the Spirit of God dwelleth in you. Now if any man have not the Spirit of Christ he is none of His." Ladies and gentlemen, this says that a man is not converted if he does not have the Spirit of Christ. If he does not have the Spirit he isn't converted. My worthy opponent does not believe in a spiritual experience whereby you know in your heart by the voice of the Holy Spirit that you are a child of God. My worthy opponent does not believe that. Mark this, the Bible says, "If any man have not that Spirit, he is none of His." He gets that Spirit in conversion by the Spirit communicating directly to him.

Now, let me note this. Man is damned not only by refusing to receive the Word but also by rejecting this Holy Spirit. My worthy opponent asks "How may he reject it?" John 4:24, says, "God is a Spirit and they that worship him must worship him in spirit and in truth." Not only in hearing—it will be through the mind, it will be through the heart, it may be through the body on the knees but the communication to God is to be in spirit. Gal 5:17, for the flesh lusteth against the Spirit. There is a warfare going on between man's flesh and man's spirit. The Spirit against the flesh—they are contrary one to another. Hebrews 10:29 says, "Of how much sorer punishment suppose ye shall be thought worthy who hath trodden under foot the Spirit of grace and of the son of God and counted the blood of the covenant wherewith he was sanctified an unholy thing and hath done despite unto the Spirit of Grace." Mark this my friends. Man is lost and pushes aside the Spirit of grace and thrusts him out. 1 Cor. 2:14, The naural man can not intellectually receive, cannot "cognize" is a good word, can not recognize, can not with his mind get the concept of the Spirit of God for—get this—it is foolishness to the natural man. Neither can we know them for it has to be a spiritual perception. Jude 19, these be they who separate themselves, sensual, fleshly, feeling with human feelings and human things having not the Spirit.

Now in regard to the word directly. We are going to have a good bit to say about that tomorrow night. What is meant by directly. My worthy opponent does not believe that by communicating to the heart, communicating to the mind, communicating by circumstances, communicating by providences, the Holy Spirit communicating directly, then my worthy opponent is not debating the subject and is begging the question.

If I take a pencil out of my pocket and write, I am writing directly on the paper. Yet my worthy opponent will endeavor, in order to confuse the issue, to throw up a smokescreen so you will not see that there is a divine spiritual reality whereby you can know you are born again by a change inside. He will do all he can to do away with that by throwing smoke in the air. He will tell you I am not operating directly, I'm operating through a pen. Now, ladies and gentlemen, I am operating directly in writing the word. If I feed myself I am operating directly. I am feeding myself and yet it is my arm or my fork or my spoon. It's begging the question simply and only to try and say if there is any agent the Holy Spirit uses, He is not doing it. If I take an ax to cut down a tree, I examine the tree, I examine it very carefully. I tie ropes to it. I'm cutting down the tree. I hack it on one side for awhile, then I go around and hack it on the other side, I watch it, tighten two or three ropes. My worthy opponent and I are debating about how that is done. I am operating directly upon the tree. When my worthy opponent is driven into the corner that he is being driven into, he will come back and say, "No, you're operating through the ax, through the ropes, through the chopping on various sides." That's begging the question! That's being dishonest! That's not being square with this intelligent audience. It is the ax that I am using. That ax is helpless without me. Ropes—I use them. I tighten them. The tree falls where I want it to fall. I, by direct operation, chop down that tree.

If you have rejected the Holy Spirit of God, if you have rejected that voice of God that's revealed Himself to you, you are not a child of God. He operates directly upon the sinner and he can accept him or reject him.

Well, my worthy opponent asks, "How?" If I only had one scripture, Acts 9:6 would be enough. "He trembling and astonished said, Lord what wilt thou have me to do." Now Paul did not have the word preached unto him. Paul was on his road to Damascus to bind Christians and haul them to Jerusalem to slay them. A light above the light of a noon day sun shone around this alien sinner. God's power by direct operation to Paul caused him to say, "Lord what wilt thou have me to do?" When was Paul saved? Any man who confesses Jesus as Lord is saved. Paul confessed Jesus as Lord on the Damascus road. The Holy Spirit operated directly upon Paul. He had a vision before he heard the Word and he was saved! The Holy Spirit operates directly upon sinners since He operated directly upon Paul.

If my worthy opponent wants to get into Acts, that's good. Acts 16:25-30 is sufficient scripture. "At midnight Paul and Silas prayed, and sang praises unto God; and the prisoners heard them. And suddenly there was a great earthquake, so that the foundations of the prison were shaken; and immediately all the doors were opened, and every ones bands were loosed. And the keeper of the prison awakening out of his sleep, and seeing the prison doors open, he drew out his sword and would have killed himself, supposing that the prisoners had fled. But Paul cried with a loud voice saying. Do thyself no harm for we are all here. Then he called for a light, and sprang in, and came trembling and fell down before Paul and Silas, and brought them out and said, Sirs what must I do to be saved?" What startled him? The earthquake. Who brought the earthquake? The Holy Spirit. The Holy Spirit is God's agent in this world. I write. I write directly. The message I want to give. The Holy Spirit directly shook the earth. Who convicted that jailer?

Honesty, if my worthy opponent will face it, honesty will compel him to admit that the Holy Spirit convicted the jailer directty and there is not any record of Paul and Silas preaching the word to the jailer until after he was convicted by the Holy Spirit. When did he hear the Word? After he was convicted. After the Holy Spirit had operated dirctly upon him. The Holy Spirit does operate directly upon sinners.

2 Cor. 3:3 is a good scripture. "Forasmuch as ye are manifestly declared to be the epistles of Christ ministered by us, written not with ink but with the Spirit of the living God; not in tables of stone, but in the fleshy tables of the heart." How are ye become epistles of Christ? How are you become epistles of Christ? "Ye are become epistles of Christ by the Spirit." The Word, the message of God and the nature of God, the new nature apart from the law that I could not keep, is written within my being on the fleshy tablets of my heart by the Spirit. The Spirit operates directly upon the Corinthians in converting them.

1 Cor. 12:3 is another good one. "Wherefore, I give you to understand that no man speaketh by the spirit of God calleth Jesus accursed. And that no man can say Jesus is Lord but by the Holy Ghost." No individual can say in saving confession that Jesus is Lord except by the revelation directly to his heart through the Word and other instruments that Jesus is Lord by the Spirit of God. Jesus is Lord. By reason men can not receive it. It's got to be spirtually discerned, spirtually received, spiritually understood. My friend, that is conversion. No man can confess Christ unto salvation except the Holy Ghost operates directly upon him.

In my last moment that remains, I would ask you very earnestly as one who must acount to God—do you know you are born again? One day I was—by the Spirit of God and by the Word of God. I have known it from that day to this, by His Spirit within my heart. You, too, can know it. I thank you.

FIRST NIGHT — PORTER'S SECOND SPEECH

Mr. Chairman, Gentlemen Moderators, Respected Opponent, Ladies and Gentlemen:

I am delighted for the privilege of coming before you again at this time to continue my denial of the proposition which friend Tingley has been affirming for another thirty minutes, to the effect that there must be a direct operation of the Holy Spirit upon sinners in conversion, or there can be no conversion.

Now, as to whether the Spirit operates through the word—through the truth—my opponent affirms that it does in his proposition. He has been having a great deal to say about my contending that it operates through the truth; and he insists that that's the same as no operation, because it's a mere influence or something of that kind. Since his proposition says that it does operate through the truth it comes back to him with all the force that he has tried to put into it, because his proposition says that it operates directly "as well as through the word of truth, the gospel of Christ," thus indicating that the Holy Spirit does operate through the truth. And that's the thing I'm contending for and denying another operation referred to as a direct operation of the Spirit.

He said he was rather amused at me because I told you about his wasting half of his speech in dealing with certain scriptures and arguments regarding the personality of the Holy Spirit; and said if he did so, he did it ignorantly; but I came along with my eyes open and wasted half my time in replying to him. Well, it's certainly the duty of the negative to reply to what the affirmative says, whether it is wasting time or not. It's my duty to show that he is wasting his time in giving something that has no connection with the proposition. I'm doing the very thing that the negative requires me to do when I take up whatever you introduce, Mr. Tingley, regardless of whether it is anywhere close to the proposition or not, and show the audience that it is not. That's how I wasted my time.

Well, he said again that the proposition does not say anything about who the Spirit is, or whether he can operate, but he was simply giving the basic truths upon which these matters rest. Therefore, he endeavored to prove that the Holy Spirit is a person; and he said, "I knew that Porter would agree with me on that—I knew that he was going to say that; I knew that he believed that: but I just wanted him to come out and say so." I do not know whether he thought I would come out and say so, or just what he thought about it; but at least he knew that I believed that. After having said he knew that I believed that — that I believed in the personality of the Holy Spirit—before he got through with that speech he turned around and said that Porter betrayed his actual belief about it when he referred to the Holy Spirit as "it", contending that I did not believe in the personality of the Spirit. Yet, he said that he knew that I did believe it. Now just which way is he going to have it? Elder Tingley, if you knew that I did believe in the personality of the Holy Spirit, then why did you turn around and say that I betrayed my feelings and my faith in saying that it was not a person at all? Maybe I did use the pronoun "it". If I did, I certainly did not intend to indicate that he was not a person. I have always believed the Holy Spirit to be a person; and friend Tingley says that he knew that I believed that. He knew that I agreed with him perfectly on that, and yet I turned around and betrayed that I did not believe what he knew that I did believe. So that's that.

He said also he knew that I would say that he could operate directly. Yes, he knew I would say that. I am certainly not endeavoring to limit the power of God, the power of divine beings, the persons of the trinity. It is not a question of whether or not they can do so but whether or not that is their program. (I believe that's the way Elder Tingley referred to it when he answered my question).

We are going to notice what he said about one or two of these questions right here. My first question: "Is it possible for a direct operation of the Holy Spirit to save a sinner without the preaching of the word?" And the second, "It is possible for a sinner to be saved by the influence exerted through the word without the direct operation of the Spirit?" He said concerning both these questions, "Yes, all things are possible with God; but it is not God's program." Well, he is insisting that when I deny the Holy Spirit is operating directly, I am denying that he can do it. If I admit that it is possible for him to do so, then I must admit that he does so. It comes right back to Elder Tingley. If he admits that it is possible for God to save one without the direct operation of the Spirit, then he is going to have to say that He does it that way, or he is limiting the power of God, you see, according to his own argument. Or if he says that it is possible for God to save one with the direct operation of the Spirit without the word, then he must say God does it that way; for if he can do it that way, that's the way He does it. That's the way he reasoned about this proposition. If the Holy Spirit can operate directly, then the Holy Spirit must operate directly. That's his conclusion. If it works in one case, it will work in both cases.

By the way, I'm still interested about that fish, eggs, ham and everything coming directly down from heaven. I just wonder if God is feeding him that way. He promised to tell us something about it, but he did not seem to remember it; so we are still wondering about that. Does he have to get it through some medium or does it come directly—without means? Does God feed you, Elder Tingley, like He fed Israel in the wilderness on that journey from Egypt to the land of Canaan? I want you to come up and face that. Does God feed you like he fed them? Speak up and tell me if you want to. I would not object. We want to know whether God is feeding Tingley like he fed the Israelites in the wilderness. God can do it, can't He? And if He can do it, He must do it, according to your argument. If the Holy Spirit can operate directly, you say He must do it. If he can feed you like he fed Israel, then He does it, doesn't He? Is that the way you get your food? Now, come on and tell us. That proposition on can is just about torn up. His "can" has exploded.

As to what God can do, and what the Holy Spirit can do, that, after all, is not in the proposition. The proposition does not say "that the Holy Spirit can operate directly, but is says the Holy Spirit does it that way—the Holy Spirit operates directly. Now, I am not limiting the Holy Spirit as to what the Holy Spirit can do. The Holy Spirit can operate on a dog or a mule or a canary bird. That does not mean that he is operating on them. I recall a statement in the book of Matthew that God is able of these stones to raise up children to Abraham, but He did not do it, did He? Did God raise up children to Abraham through stones? Why, certainly, God is able to do so and so. God's power is unlimited. We're not talking about what God can do or what the Holy Spirit can do. The question is: What is God's program? Is God doing it that way? That's the question, and that's the issue. That's the issue my friend is side-stepping, and I'm sure the audience is beginning to see it.

He said the Holy Spirit must come and operate directly upon a man that he might know God. I want you to know God; I want you to be at peace with God, he added. But how can men know God? That's the question. I Cor. 1:21, Paul said, "After that in the wisdom of God the world by wisdom knew not God, it pleased God by the foolishness of preaching to save them that believe." Now Paul reasons that the world by wisdom did not know God, but they knew God through the foolishness of preaching. That's the way they came to know God. They learned of God when the gospel was preached to them.

He told the story of the colored person and then later on about Ben Hur as though that would sustain his proposition. The colored man who went to a meeting, where they did away with all miraculous work, said, "Doctor, that was a very beautiful sermon." He proved that there was no new birth, and so on, but, "You should have said 'As I knows of.'" Well, if Elder Tingley "knows of" some of these cases where the Holy Spirit operates directly, why, then, he ought to begin to tell about them. If he "knows of" them, let us have some of the information; and then maybe we will know something about them. As for the new birth, I'm not doing away with the new birth. I know that we are born of the Spirit—the book says so—but 1 Pet. 1:23 also says that we are born by the word, "being born again, not of corruptible seed, but of incorruptible, by the word of God, which liveth and abideth forever."

He reasoned awhile ago that to be born of the Spirit meant that there must be a direct operation of the Spirit, just as when the baby was born of his daughter by a direct operation. So he made the Spirit his mother; and we are still insisting that he tell us if he—the Spirit—is his mother of which he was born directly. If he is not, then he has the wrong parrallel—the wrong illustration—and ought to find something else.

As to the word "directly" he said, "Why doesn't Porter bring on Webster's Unabridged Dictionary and tell us what it means?" It's in your proposition, Tingley. You signed it. The rules that we agreed upon in this discussion say that the man who is affirming must define his proposition; that's the thing. Why don't you bring along Webster's Unabridged Dictionary and let us see what it means? Tell us what he says about it— whether "directly" means as he has introduced it tonight; or whether it means without means, without medium. Well, maybe he will bring it tomorrow night, and we will read it.

He came to the negative arguments which I introduced. He

said I gave a whole list of them and he did not have time to fool with them. He did not want to waste any more time, you see. He did not have time to fool with them, so he just referred to one—I Cor. 1:21. "It pleased God by the foolishness of preaching to save them that believe." He said, "Porter said Tingley does not believe that." He says, "Tingley does believe it." He said, "Yes, I do believe it." Well what about those four thousand tongues he talked about awhile ago out of the five thousand that had no Bible translated into their language? You indicated awhile ago that I could not reach those people because the Bible had not been translated into their language. You said—you promised me—you'd tell me something about it in your next speech. You did not say a word about it. He was just as silent as the tomb about it. Not a single, solitary word was uttered as to what he meant by the four thousand languages into which the Bible had not been translated. Does he indicate by that that it takes a direct operation of the Spirit to save these four thousand tongues? Is that what you mean, Tingley? Why didn't you tell us? I'm still insisting that you tell us in your first speech tomorrow night. Do you mean by that illustration that the Holy Spirit must operate on these four thousand tongues in order to save them when they can not hear the word? You get down to this and tell us about it. Do not forget it like you did tonight. You have such a marvelous forgettery. Please, do tell us something about it.

He said, "I believe in all of these because on the one side there is the word operating as a direct agent, and on the other side there is the Spirit." Well, you said you believed the Spirit operated through the word—or do you? Your proposition does. You signed it anyway. It says that the Holy Spirit operates through the word! And that He also operates directly. Now, then, will you please explain yourself. What do you mean by "directly" in contrast with "through the word?"

He turned around awhile ago and gave a number of arguments in which he tried to say that "directly" means through some means, through some medium, like he was writing on the paper directly with a pencil. Now that was through a medium. He said, "That's what I mean by 'directly'." All right; then if that's so, when the Holy Spirit operates through the word he is operating directly, isn't he? It he? Is he?

(Mr. Tingley nods, "Yes.")

Mr. Porter: The Holy Spirit operates directly through the word? Well, then you do not need any direct operation of the Holy Spirit apart from the word; it is already through the word. My opponent has reached the end of his trail! For he now says that when the Holy Spirit operates through the word that's a direct operation. Do you want to back out?

Mr. Tingley: "No."

Mr. Porter: He's not going to back out but stay with it. All right. He's going to stay put. Well, I'm going to see that he stays put.

The Holy Spirit operates through the word. Tingley says so. His proposition says so. He says, "That is a direct operation of the Spirit!" Well, then, how many direct operations of the Spirit must a sinner have? If the Spirit operates through some other means besides through the word, then what's the other means? What's the other agency through which he works besides the word? You say it's direct because it's through some medium, through some agency. Then, what's the other agency? This thing is going to get interesting before the next two hours are over. We are going to see what my friend Tingley will tell us about that tomorrow night.

He came back to 1 Cor. 2:14, "The natural man receiveth not the things of the Spirit; neither can he know them, because they are spiritually discerned." He said, "Paul is showing all through this chapter that it is not a matter of intellect." In other words, a man's intellect has nothing to do with it. I suppose that's the reason he is insisting on a direct operation of the Spirit. It does not appeal to man's intelligence; so he has some sort of direct, mysterious thing that does not appeal to the intelligence of man. Paul did not indicate anywhere in that chapter that it was not a matter that concerned man's intellect at all. Paul is showing that man, by his own wisdom, could not know God; and the natural man is the man who rejects divine revelation and depends on his own wisdom; and that man can not receive the things of the Spirit, because he rejects divine revelation. That's the natural man. (1 Cor. 2:14).

Now, back to the questions: "Does the direct operation of the Spirit precede or follow the preaching of the word?" He said, "It may precede but it must accompany." Well, if it does not precede, then the preaching of the word does not do any good, does it? Because you are reasoning that he can not do anything about it. He can not understand it. He can not know it. He can not learn it. He can not comprehend it unless the Spirit precedes it. So the Holy Spirit must precede in direct operation through some other medium beside the preaching of the word, through which he also operates directly in order to save the sinner. Friend Tingley has, I do not know, how many direct operations of the Holy Spirit to save the sinner.

"What does the direct operation of the Spirit do for a sinner that can not be accomplished by the preaching of the gospel?" He said, "It reveals the word." Tell us how it reveals the word. He is not concerned about the "how." That gets him into trouble, you see. He's not concerned about the "how." He just knows He does it because He does it! But he does not know how He does it or anything about it. That's the predicament of the gentleman brought about by his false position in this matter.

"Is the miraculous outpouring of the Holy Spirit the same as the direct operation of the Spirit in conversion?" He said "It's the same Spirit." I did not ask if it is the same Spirit. I did not ask that question at all. Certainly, it's the same Spirit. You're side-stepping, friend Tingley. You said, "It's the same Spirit but it is not the same operation." Then, Acts 10:44 does you no good, does it? He gave the case of Cornelius where the Spirit fell on all them that heard the word; and Tingley, was that a miraculous outpouring of the Spirit? Yes or no; shake or nod.

Mr. Tingley: "Yes."

Mr. Porter: That is not the conversion you talked about in your proposition, is it?

Mr. Tingley: I could answer but I think I better . . . . .

Mr. Porter: Yes, I think you better . . . .

Mr. Tingley: Mr. Moderator. I would ask your ruling on this matter. I would be very happy—time out please—if you would not ask the opponent any questions and force him to speak. If you will consult Hedge's rules, you will find that such is unparlimentary and improper tactics. If the opponent does desire me to speak, I should have adequate time to answer; and I will be very happy to answer. I will be very happy to answer all the questions tomorrow night. This is merely stage play, and I ask you to rule in regard to this.

Mr. Nichols: I would say to save time I believe it would be a good idea for the speaker to use his own judgement. He does not have to speak from his seat, if he does not want to; and I believe it is better not to until his time comes. Many times these questions are placed just to emphasize the point; and if that's it, why just wait until your time comes. I will say, use your own judgment so far as I am concerned.

Mr. Porter: When I asked these questions of friend Tingley, I did not expect him to speak from his seat, but he did that. Then, when he did that, why, that's perfectly satisfactory to me if he wants to do it.

Mr. Cairns: I beg your pardon. You almost forced him to do it. You just put him into a very embarassing position. Please don't do that again.

Mr. Porter: Well, he can force me if he wants to try it. I am perfectly willing to abide by that which I give him. If he wants to try forcing me, let him go ahead.

I simply asked in order to emphasize, and I am trying to emphasize that Acts 10:44 has no relation to the question under consideration, according to Tingley's own admission already made. He agrees that in Acts 10:44 we have a miraculous outpouring of the Holy Spirit. If he does not agree, let him deny it tomorrow night. He will not dare deny it because he has already committed himself tonight that the outpouring of the Spirit on Cornelius was a miraculous outpouring, because it enabled him to speak with tongues. Now, my friend introduced Acts 10:44 to prove a direct operation of the Spirit on the sinner. Yet he says the outpouring of the Holy Spirit in a miraculous form is not the same operation as that which takes place in conversion. Then, Tingley, will you please tell us why you introduced that passage? If you knew that that had no relation to the operation which you are contending for—that there's a difference between the operation on the sinner in conversion and the miraculous outpouring of the Spirit, why did you introduce a miraculous outpouring of the Spirit to prove your idea of the operation? If you knew it did not do it, why did you introduce it in the first place? I asked him awhile ago to please tell me, Was Cornelius a sinner when he received the Holy Spirit on that occasion?" And not a single word has he said. He's a promising fellow. He promises to do it in his next speech; he will not do it from his seat. He promises to do it in his next speech; and in his next speech he forgets about it. I am insisting that tomorrow night, friend Tingley, you tell us whether Cornelius was a sinner when the Holy Spirit fell on him. I'll tell you what I will do. I will put it in writing tomorrow night, and I will see that you answer it. I'll not let you forget it. Was Cornelius a sinner when the Spirit fell on him? Was it a miraculous outpouring? Tingley says it was. Then, he says the miraculous outpouring of the Holy Spirit is not the operation that's mentioned in my proposition. Why, then, did you try to prove your proposition by scripture that you say you knew had no relation to it? Let's see him "wiggle" out of that!

He came to Romans 5:5 again and said, "Porter did not deal with this—that "the love of God is shed abroad in our hearts by the Holy Spirit." Oh yes, he did! I referred to that and showed that in 1 John 4:19 we have the statement made that we love God because he first loved us. Where do we learn of God's love? Through the things in His word, and through the revelation of that word, we learn of the love of God; and we are made to love him because he first loved us. It has come through the Holy Spirit because the Holy Spirit dictated that word. The words of the New Testament are the words of the Holy Spirit.

Back to Romans 8:9. "Ye are not in the flesh, but in the Spirit if so be that the Spirit of God dwells in you." He said, "Now this says you are not converted unless you have the Spirit. You must have the Spirit or you are not converted." Well, do you have the Spirit before you are converted? That's what we are getting at. This refers to men who are already converted and who had the Spirit. But did they have the Spirit before they were converted? If they had the Spirit before they were converted, then they were not in the flesh when they were converted—they got out of the flesh before they were converted. Without conversion and without hearing the word they are out of the flesh! Saved—not in the flesh—converted—and never did hear the truth of God, according to friend Tingley's position.

He came to Jude 19—those having not the Spirit. Well, that does not say a word about the direct operation of the Spirit or any other operation of the Spirit on the sinner. So it has no relation to the question in hand. We are discussing the conversion of the alien sinner. Let him find something about that. That's what we want him to get at.

Then he came back to the word "directly." He said, "Now

I will show you what I mean by the word directly." He took his pencil and said, "I'm writing on this paper. I am writing directly on the paper—through a pen—through a pencil." Well, if that's what you mean by "directly" in your proposition, tell us what it is that the Spirit operates through when he operates directly. You operate through the pencil on the paper and you call that a direct operation; and your proposition says that the Holy Spirit operates directly on the heart of the sinner. Now, I want to know, through what? In order for you to have a parallel case, you must have the Spirit operating through something. One part of the proposition says, "through the word." I agree with that. What about the rest of it? Through what does the Spirit operate that compares with your operating through the pencil on the paper directly? Now, let us have the next scripture which he introduced along that line.

Then, the illustration about the ax and the tree. He takes the ax and goes out to cut down the tree. He cuts a little on this side and a little on that side. He hacks here and he hacks there. He tightens his ropes here and he loosens them over there. The first thing you know, the tree is down, and he has operated upon that tree directly through the ax. Now, if my friend could have just stood aside and thrown his ax away and have blown the tree down, he might have something corresponding to his proposition. As long as the man must operate through the ax, that's not direct. That's through means. That's through a medium, friend Tingley, that's not direct. "Directly" means "without means," "without any medium," "nothing intervening." So that's the thing you must have. You have not found that in these. The illustrations you have given prove my position. The man cuts the tree with the ax. He exerts the power on the tree through the ax. The Spirit exerts his power on the heart of the sinner through the word that's preached to the sinner. There you have your parellel—both of them through agencies, both of them through means. But that's not the direct operation of the Spirit. You must have your direct operation in some other way, because if you do get it that way, you have only half your proposition—the other half is left begging for support.

Well, he said if I were to tell Mr. Porter how, I'd just give him Acts 9:6, in which Saul of Tarsus is reported to have said, "Lord what will thou have me to do?" He said when Saul made that inquiry he had not heard the word. The word had not been preached unto him, and so there must have been a direct operation, because the word had not been preached to him. Well, Jesus had just said to him, "I am Jesus of Nazareth whom thou persecutest," and that convinced him. You claim the direct operation of the Spirit was not the speaking of Jesus but the light that shown about him. Jesus did speak to him before he made the inquiry. He heard the word of Jesus before he said, "What wilt thou have me to do?" That upsets his direct operation there; besides if that was the direct operation there, and he received the Spirit there, then tell me why Ananias came to him three days later and said, "The Lord sent me that you might receive your sight and be filled with the Holy Spirit." Tingley said he was filled back there when he saw the vision. Ananias said he had not been filled until three days later. So there's something wrong somewhere.

Then in Acts 16:25-30, in the conversion of the jailer, he says that the Holy Spirit operated directly—that the Holy Spirit directly shook the earth. Through what means? Through what agency, Mr. Tingley? You said "directly" means through some agency. Will you please tell me through what agency the Holy Spirit shook the earth that night. Furthermore, that earthquake, he said, was the operation of the Spirit on the jailer. When the jailer awoke out of his sleep, following the earthquake, and saw the prison doors open, what did he do? He got his sword and started to kill himself. That was the result of a direct operation. It almost led the man to suicide. But the preacher spoke and said, "Do thyself no harm. We are all here." Then, when he heard the words of the preacher, he came in and fell down trembling and brought them out and said, "Sirs, what must I do to be saved?" And the preacher preached the gospel to him and he obeyed it. There's your direct operation of the Spirit. The operation of the Spirit, according to Tingley, almost led the man to death. He was just about to commit suicide because the Holy Spirit operated on him! Well, now, that's proving his proposition with a vengeance.

Then in 2 Cor. 3:3, "Ye are our epistles, ministered by us, written not with ink, but with the Spirit of the living God; not upon the tables of stone, but upon fleshy tables of the heart." Notice Paul says, "Ministered by us." That's preaching, operating through the word. Now, where's your direct operation? In order for him to have a direct operation, besides the ink being "administered by us" he will have also to upset the ink bottle and pour it out directly upon the paper in order for his position to hold. He did not upset the bottle of ink. The ink was administered through the pen. "Ye are our epistles, ministered by us; written not with ink, but with the Spirit of the the living God." Friend Tingley, when you write an epistle, and you use the pen, and the ink comes through that agency (the apostles said we're the pens, it's administered by us) then do you turn around and upset the bottle of ink on the epistle when you get through, or before you start, or just when do you get your direct operation in there?

Thank you, ladies and gentlemen.

PORTER-TINGLEY DEBATE

Second Session: 7:30 P.M., February 25, 1947
Central Church of Christ — Birmingham, Alabama
Chairman: Emerson J. Estes — Birmingham, Alabama
Singing Directed by: H. A. Sikes — Birmingham, Alabama
Prayer: Franklin T. Puckett — Atlanta, Georgia
Moderators: Gus Nichols, Jasper, Alabama for Mr. Porter;
Millard Cairns, Decatur, Illinois for Mr. Tingley

Proposition: The Scriptures Teach That in the Conversion of Alien Sinners the Holy Spirit Operates Directly Upon Them as Well as Through the Word of Truth or Gospel of Christ.

Glenn V. Tingley, Affirms
W. Curtis Porter, Denies

(Affirmative Address by Glenn V. Tingley)

Gentlemen Moderators, Worthy Opponent, Ladies and Gentlemen:

Again I am very happy to stand tonight in defense of the truth of the gospel. I would take a moment of valuable time to commend the chairman on those words. I appreciate them very much. I am not here to be just speaking to people. I am not here to win some debate or surpass some man. I am here very desperately in earnest that people might know the Lord Jesus Christ as their Savior. That's my sole object in being here.

The question is: "The Scriptures," the Word of God, "teach that in the conversion," by that we mean the regeneration, the renewing, the justification, that which takes place in a man when he changes from a sinner into a saint, "of alien sinners." "The Holy Spirit," the third person of the Godhead, "operates directly upon them as well as through the Word of truth" or the the gospel.

The question is: Does the Holy Spirit operate. Last night my worthy opponent over and over cried out " How . . . how . . . how . . . how." That is not the question, does not enter into the question, has nothing to do with the question. The question is: Does the Holy Spirit operate directly?

The tactic of a debater in desperation is always to ask a multitude of questions which are incidental and not of primary importance to the question involved. This multitude of unimportant questions will tend to confuse the issue until the public loses sight of the point at issue so says one great manual on debating. My worthy opponent followed that tactic last night—leading us up blind alleys, but I refused to go. I will go with him for just a moment answering some of the questions that are incidental and have nothing to do with the debate.

1. Was Cornelius a sinner? 2. How does God give you fish and ham directly? 3. Does God feed you like He fed the children of Israel? 4. Is the Spirit your mother? 5. Through what agency did the Holy Spirit operate to produce the earthquake? 6. Explain what you mean by five thousand languages and the Bible in only approximately a thousand of them? 7. If Elder Tingley knows of any cases of where the Holy Spirit operated directly let him tell us some.

So that none of you will think that I am sidestepping in the slightest, I am going to take a moment to answer these. Now watch my worthy opponent dwell on the unimportant and irrelevant questions to confuse and becloud the issue and make you forget what we are debating. First, "Was Cornelius a sinner?" Yes, "All have sinned and come short of the glory of God." He was saved by the Word and the Holy Ghost falling upon him.

"How does God give you fish and ham?" I will give you one illustration. Eighteen years ago we lived in Ensley on rice for ten days. We ran out of rice. Tomorrow was Sunday—nine mouths to feed—not a solitary bit of money or food. I waited on the Lord from nine until approximately eleven. A knock came on the door and I went to the door. There was a bushel basket full of food for breakfast, dinner and supper and lasted us for several days. God can answer prayer by ravens, or jackasses, or man. That time He chose a man and a woman. They lived eighteen miles away, knew nothing of my need and only heard me preach once and never had spoken to me personally in their lives. I have a God whose Holy Spirit is in the world, who answers prayer. Let my worthy opponent now make light of miracles.

"Does God feed you like he fed the children of Israel?" He fed me just as miraculously as he fed them.

"Is the Spirit your mother?" That is begging the question. It takes a man and a woman to beget a child. It takes the Spirit and the Word to convert the sinner. My worthy opponent does not seem to know that with God there is no sex, that angels neither marry nor are given in marriage.

Five, "Through what agency did the Holy Spirit operate to produce the earthquake?" Through His divine perogrative as the Creator of the earth.

"Explain what is meant by five thousand languages and the Bible in approximately a thousand?" Jesus commanded us to go into all the world and preach the gospel to every creature. It is significant, ladies and gentlemen, (I did not want to say this, my worthy opponent begged for it, seven times in one speech last night, I give it to him now) the churches that believe in the direct operation of the Holy Spirit have been earnest to carry out the command of Jesus. The so-called churches of Christ are notoriously the slowest and most dilatory in carrying out His command, having the least missionaries of any body of people in Christendom out in the foreign fields. I challenge my worthy opponent to tell you how many languages his missionaries have translated the Bible into—even how many missionaries he maintains in the foreign lands. It is the smallest number not only pro rata but total of the 256 denominations in America. "By their fruits ye shall know them." Proselyting and confusing disciples is not the business of true Christians.

"If Elder Tingley knows of any cases where the Holy Spirit operates directly, let him tell us so." My worthy opponent thinks it light to poke fun at miracles. My daughter, now a mother of two children, when a baby of thirteen months was stricken with infantile paralysis and left with a twisted and deformed leg. Several months later, in answer to prayer, with no hope offered by the doctors at all, while playing in the yard, as amazed friends watched, the Spirit of life without human means of any kind straightened the leg of that fifteen months old baby. Now let him poke fun at a prayer hearing, prayer answering God, a miracle working Spirit of God.

The Holy Spirit does operate directly upon the earth and all men. The Holy Spirit operates upon matter—inanimate matter: Genesis 1:2, "The Spirit of God moved upon the face of the waters." On beasts: Psalms 104:29-30. "Thou sendest forth thy Spirit and they are created."

On babes in the womb: Luke 1:41-44, when Elizabeth heard the salutation of Mary, the babe leaped in her womb and Elizabeth was filled with the Holy Ghost and she spake with a loud voice.

The Holy Spirit operates directly in inspiration. 1 Sam. 10:10, The company of the prophets met him and the Spirit of God came upon him.

The Holy Spirit operates directly in dreams and visions. Gen. 28:11-17. Jacob's ladder at Bethel.

The Holy Spirit operates in demoniacial possession. Acts 5:3, Peter said to Ananias, "Why hath Satan filled thy heart to lie to the Holy Ghost and to keep back part of the price of the land" and lying Ananias dropped dead.

In preparing the hearts of sinners for the gospel. Acts 16:14. "And a certain woman named Lydia, a seller of purple, of the city of Thyatyra, which worshipped God, heard us whose heart the Lord opened, that she attended unto the things which were spoken of Paul." Two things: The Lord must open her heart, she must attend the message of Paul. People hear the message preached but there is no response of any kind. Their hearts are hard, they resist the Spirit, they can not receive, they cannot accept, they will not accept because they reject the Spirit which opens the heart.

My worthy opponent said quite a bit about Romans 5:5, when I pressed him last night. "Hope maketh not ashamed because the love of God is shed abroad in our hearts by the Holy Ghost which is given unto us." My opponent asked, "Did they have the Spirit before conversion?" I answer, they had the Spirit in the act of conversion. The proposition states the Holy Spirit convicted, the Word was received by Spirit operation through the love of God shed abroad in their hearts making them children of God in conversion by the Holy Ghost.

Last night in both messages I quoted and referred to John 16:7-11. I emphasized very strongly one word. My worthy opponent was as silent as the tomb about it. It is, "He (the Holy Spirit) will reprove the world," the world of sinners, the world of saints. "He will convict the world." He was upon the world poured out in the world, and will convict the world. I want him to deal with that tonight.

Again, he was as silent as a tomb last night about John 3,

"Born of the Spirit." You know "Born of the Spirit" is found three times in that scripture. There is no life without direct influence of a life giving agent. Matthew 1:2 uses the same word and it is translated, "Abraham begat Isaac." The same word as used in John 3, "Born of the Spirit." "Abraham begat Isaac." Matt. 1:20 is the same word. "That which was conceived in her is of the Holy Ghost." Exactly the same Greek word. In 1 John 5:18, "Whosoever is born of God." Same word. The individual is born of the Spirit. We perfectly agree that the Word must be preached, that the Word saves, that the Word brings men to life—but my worthy opponent insists on there being no life giving agency, no person of the Godhead. It takes a father and a mother to begat a child, it takes a positive and a negative to give life. It takes the Word and the Spirit to beget life. The Spirit must deal with the heart of a man.

1 Cor. 12:3. Again he was silent upon this scripture that Jesus is Lord no man can confess but by the Holy Ghost. A man can hear about Jesus and read the scriptures. Then he can say with his lips, "I believe Jesus is Lord." That does not mean he is converted. The Bible is very clear. It is not mental assent. He can say he is moved by the story of Calvary, but it does not mean emotional assent. No man can truly say so that he is a born again child of God—say it as a child of the Father, "Jesus is Lord" except it is the Holy Ghost which has wrought this within his heart.

My worthy opponent said I spilled a bottle of ink. I could not understand for the life of me what he was driving at. He was talking in regard to 2 Corinthians 3:3. I tried honestly to figure it out and I hope he will show me where the ink is spilled. Let me show you where he did upset the apple cart. 2 Cor. 3:3. If I could get my worthy opponent to read the verse before and the verse after there'd be no debate. But my worthy opponent will take a word, grab it out, put them all together and cry "See." I could prove the moon is made of cheese by that system. My worthy opponent absolutely ignores the clear statement of 2 Cor. 3:2, "For as much as ye are manifestly declared to be the epistles of Christ ministered by us." He dwelt at great length on the "ministered by us." See it is ministered by us! That's correct. Paul came and preached the gospel to the people at Corinth. They became epistles of Christ by the ministry of Paul. That's true! But how did they become the epistles of

Christ? It goes on to tell you. He did not read that to you. All he could see was "Ministered by us." There's something else. "Written not with ink!" It was not even the letter to the Corinthians, it was not even the words! What caused the change within them? The verse reads, "Written not with ink but with the Spirit of the living God!" Not in tables of stone, not on parchment, not on things but in the fleshy tablets of your heart by the Holy Ghost! The Holy Spirit accompanied Paul.

My worthy opponent dealt at some length with Paul's conversion. He said, "Paul was saved by preaching." That it was Jesus preaching that saved him. There has to be the Word but Paul was saved by miraculous operation of God and God not only operates now by the Holy Spirit—and then—and Paul was saved by the direct operation of the Holy Spirit. The word says so. Acts 22:8, "And I answered Who art thou Lord? And he said, I am Jesus whom thou persecutest." Paul said, "What wilt thou have me to do?" Listen, if you will read carefully Acts 25:14, Acts 9:7 you will note this fact that when the light shone they were all smitten; and when the voice spake the people with Paul heard a noise, the Book says, but didn't hear the word. There was no intelligent message for the natural man. The Spirit was operating upon him, and a man must receive the Holy Spirit, and Paul alone of all the crowd that travelled together received by revalation the fact that that was Jesus. Acts 22:9, "Them that were with me saw indeed the light and were afraid but they heard not the voice of him that spake to me."

My worthy opponent asked about the earthquake. I have already answered it. In Acts 16:25-30, but just a word. His argument is a specious argument. He said that the Holy Spirit there nearly killed the jailer. I did not say that nor suggest that. One of the tricks of debating for those who are seeking by subterfuge to confuse people's minds is to put in the mouth of the opponent things he did not say. The jailer almost did kill himself, not because of the Holy Spirit, but because of his danger and desperation and sins. Anyone, ladies and gentlemen, who has ever been under the presence and power and conviction of the Holy Spirit knows that they reach a point of desperation where desire for food leaves them, sleep may leave them, and their heart cries out for God. It is a war in the spiritual realm between the Holy Spirit and the soul bringing the soul to accept and receive the word. His heart was prepared for the

Holy Spirit—for his salvation—and he was saved by the Holy Spirit and the word.

Though it is not in the debate and does not enter into the question, my worthy opponent kept crying last night, "How? How? How? How? Tell me?" I could resort to stage play. I could nettle and needle my opponent. I could address him and pause. He is not allowed to speak yet I could say, "Speak. Answer me," and I could embarrass him, too. I was a gentleman before I was a Christian! But I will answer my opponent, "How?" I will give him eleven hows or all the time will allow. He wants to know how the Holy Spirit operates directly. I. Rom. 15:9, by mighty signs. II. by wonders. III. Acts 2, through foreign tongues. IV. tongues of fire. V. and mighty wind. VI. Acts 18:16, by bearing witness with our spirit. VII. Acts 16:25, by the earthquake. VIII. Acts 10:44, by the miraculous falling on Cornelius. IX. Luke 2:26, by revelation to Simeon. X. Acts 5:33, by killing lying Ananias. XI. Acts 16:14, by opening Lydia's heart.

Now to the arguments. If I only had one scripture, Joel 2:28 would suffice, "And it shall come to pass afterward that I will out my spirit upon all flesh." Good flesh, bad flesh, rich flesh, poor flesh. "All flesh." My worthy opponent will say the Holy Spirit is poured out upon saints and not upon sinners. "The Holy Spirit does not operate directly upon sinners," he says. God's Word says it is poured out upon all flesh including alien sinners. "Your sons and your daughters shall prophesy, your old men shall dream dreams, your young men shall see visions." The Spirit is upon all flesh.

If I only had one scripture, 1 Cor. 6:11 would be enough. "Such were some of you but ye are washed, ye are sanctified, but ye are justified in the name of the Lord Jesus and by the Spirit of our God." Now how were the Corinthians converted. They were washed. That's one thing. They were sanctified. That's another thing. They were justified. That's another thing. All going into conversion—washing, setting apart, justifying— that is the bundle of conversion according to this in Corinthians. How did this come about? It came about on the basis of the name of Jesus and in the name of the Lord Jesus. Who wrought this conversion? **"And by the Spirit of our God!"** Our God wrought the washing, the sanctifying, the justifying—the Spirit of God. My worthy opponent must meet these clear, unmistakable statements of the word of God. The Holy Spirit therefore operated directly upon the Corinthians.

If I only had one scripture, Titus 3:5 would be enough. "Not by works of righteousness which we have done but according to His mercy he saved us by the washing of regeneration," that is, the regenerating of the heart, taking the sinful nature and making it new again, "And the renewing of the Holy Ghost," the making new of our minds and hearts, regenerating our hearts. How? Who does it? Where does it come from? "Of the Holy Ghost." "The washing of regeneration and renewing of the Holy Ghost." Certainly the Spirit operates directly. Ladies and Gentlemen, there isn't one word in the Bible that says that the Holy Spirit only operates through the Word but for every scripture that my opponent can trot out, and were we to debate on this subject for six nights, every scripture he could stand and quote about the Word doing something in the new birth, I could stand and quote an equal scripture saying that the Spirit does the same thing. The Word operates directly upon the sinner and the Spirit operates directly upon the Sinner. It takes both.

Listen again. If I only had one scripture, 1 Cor. 12:13 would be enough. "For by one spirit are we all baptized into one body whether we be Jews or Gentiles, whether we be bond or free and have all been made to drink into one Spirit." How are men put into Christ? He is put there by the Spirit for "by one Spirit" we all were baptized into one body. None can become a part of the body of Christ unless the Holy Spirit operates directly upon them into Christ.

If I only had one scripture, Romans 15:18-19 would be enongh. "I will not dare t ospeak of any of those things which Christ hath not wrought by me to make the Gentiles obedient, by word and deed, through mighty signs and wonder, and by the power of the Spirit of God; so that from Jerusalem and round about Illyricum, I have fully preached the gospel of Christ." What is it? The gospel of Christ is fully preached everywhere? Why? Because Paul declared the whole counsel of God and the Gentiles were obedient. What was the power that gave the Word and Paul power and the Gentiles ability and power to receive it? "Mighty signs and wonders by the power of the Spirit of God." Yet, my worthy opponent says "That's not so." He says, "These signs and wonders and the power of the Holy Spirit. There are none. That's not so." The word says "It is so." Paul's preaching would be vain without the accompanying power of the Holy Spirit with signs and wonders. Why? To make the Gentiles obedient. How? By the power of the Spirit of God. The Holy Spirit operates directly upon the Gentiles—upon sinners—to convert them.

If I only had one scripture, Matt. 12-31 would be enough. "Wherefore I say unto you all manner of sin and blasphemy shall be forgiven unto men." An individual may blaspheme the word without being damned. The very next verse says an individual could blaspheme Jesus Christ and not be damned. The blasphemy against the Holy Ghost is an unpardonable sin. Why? The Holy Ghost is the only life giving agency that could put a new nature within a soul! The Word is powerless except when it is accompanied by and the Holy Spirit operates directly upon the sinner as well as the Word.

If I only had one scripture, Acts 2:4-5 is enough. My worthy opponent complained about my reading whole chapters last night. I'll give him the gist of it then tonight. "They were all filled with the Holy Ghost, and began to speak with other tongues, as the Spirit gave them utterance. There were dwelling at Jerusalem Jews, devout men, out of every nation under heaven." "Now when they heard this, they were pricked in their hearts, and said unto Peter and to the rest of the apostles, Men and brethren, what shall we do?" Where were they pricked? In their hearts. Where does the message come? To the head! To our intellect! What moves the inner being of a man? The Holy Spirit who was poured out. "Then they that gladly received his word were baptized. And the same day there were added unto them about three thousand souls." The Holy Spirit brought: the wind operating directly upon men, the fire operating directly upon men, the unknown tongues operating directly upon men. The Holy Spirit by the phenomena operating directly upon men convicted them in their heart. Operating directly upon men, He converted three thousand of them. The Holy Spirit as well as the Word operated.

Man's nature is a depraved nature. There must be a complete spiritual transformation in the man wrought by the Holy Spirit. John 3:5 says "Verily, verily I say unto you, except a man is born of water and of the Spirit he can not enter the kingdom of God." Is my time up?

Thank you, ladies and gentlemen.

SECOND NIGHT — PORTER'S FIRST SPEECH

Mr. President, Gentlemen Moderators, Respected Opponent, Ladies and Gentlemen:

I am glad indeed for this privilege to come again before you in the negative of the proposition which my friend Tingley has been affirming the past thirty minutes. The same proposition was affirmed during the session last evening. "The Scriptures teach that in the conversion of alien sinners, the Holy Spirit operates directly upon them as well as through the word of truth or the gospel of Christ."

While it is fresh on your minds I want to notice just briefly the last argument my opponent introduced; and then I will go back and review the statements that he made.

He was discussing the matter of the operation of the Spirit in Acts 2. Of course, if he "had only one scripture," any of these would do, because he gave a number of them and said either would be sufficient if he had just one. If he "had only one scripture," he said Acts 2:35, 37-41 would be it. He said that I complained last night because he read a whole chapter. So he would just give the gist of it tonight. I made no complaint whatsoever. I merely mentioned the fact that he read an entire chapter to prove the operation of the Spirit upon sinners, coming in a direct manner, when it had no reference to it, but referred to the revelation of the will of God to the apostles as they received it, and as it is there discussed by the apostle himself. I did not complain at his reading whole chapters. He can read all he wants to as far as that is concerned. I will be right on his track regardless of where he leads.

He spoke concerning this particular question: "When they heard this, they were pricked in their hearts, and said unto Peter and the rest of the apostles, Men and brethren, what shall we do?" He said note the fact "they were pricked in their hearts." He said that referred to the Spirit, because the word goes to the mind or the head or the intellect, while the Spirit goes to the heart. It could not refer, therefore, to an operation upon their hearts through the word, because the word is addressed to the head, and the Spirit goes to the heart. This was his argument. He said the word does not reach the heart; the word merely reaches the head. I wonder if friend Tingley will be so kind as to tell us in his next speech just what the heart is. We might have something interesting along that line if he will be so kind as to tell us—if he does not think the question is altogether irrelevant, and that it has no connection at all with the proposition or the issue under discussion.

I want to turn and read a passage. (I can tell you what it says, but I want to turn and read it in order that you may get the effect of it and know that I am reading from the book of God). I have turned to Luke 8:11-12, keeping in mind that friend Tingley says that Acts 2 can not refer to the word because it reached the heart, and the word simply reaches the head. Well, in Luke, the eighth chapter, the Lord gave the parable of the sower; and in explanation of that parable concerning the seed that fell by the wayside and was picked up by the fowls of the air, we have this statement, "Now the parable is this: The seed is the word of God. Those by the wayside are they that hear; then cometh the devil, and taketh away the word out of their hearts, lest they should believe and be saved." Now Jesus said, Elder Tingley, that the word reached the heart; that if that word were allowed to remain in the heart, the man would even be saved. The devil knew the only thing necessary to keep men from being saved was to get the word out of thetir hearts. Tingley says it is not so; the word does not reach the heart! It only reaches the intellect; it only reaches the head; and the Spirit reaches the heart. But here we find Jesus said the word was in their hearts. The devil took away the word out of their hearts, and did it "lest they should believe and be saved." Now, Elder Tingley, tell me: If the word had remained in their hearts, would it have effected their salvation?

I have two or three questions. My friend objects to the questions. He says they are incidental and unimportant. They becloud the issue and make people forget just what we are discussing. The fact is, they are focusing the issue too strongly for my opponent. They are getting down to the issue too well. That's where the trouble is, and that's why he is complaining. It puts him on the spot to have to tell what he believes about this or that, what position he is going to take relative to this matter or that. That's the reason why he is objecting so much. He must face them, anyway, regardless of his objections. I have here five questions:

The first one he answered awhile ago. I will read it. I am not expecting him to answer it again. Was Cornelius an alien sinner at the time the Holy Spirit fell on him? He can ignore that one when he comes to answer, because he has already given us his answer on that.

Second. Was the outpouring of the Spirit upon Cornelius a miraculous outpouring?

Third. Since you say that the miraculous outpouring of the Spirit is not the same operation as that used in the conversion of sinners, then is the case of Cornelius applicable to your proposition?

Fourth. If a direct operation means an operation through some means or agency, through what agency, besides the word, does the Holy Spirit operate directly?

Fifth. As there are four thousand tongues into which the Bible has not been translated, does the Holy Spirit operate upon and save the people who are identified with those tongues?

Now, then, one or two things. One passage I failed to get to last night; and he came along and said I was as silent as a tomb about that, and a number of others. Well, this particular one I said nothing about. It was the last one noted in my notes, and I was just ready to notice it when my time was called.

That was 1 Cor. 12:3—that no man can say that Jesus is Lord except by the Holy Ghost. Now, what my friend needs to find is that no man can say that Jesus is Lord except by a direct operation of the Holy Ghost. He does not find his direct operation there. It merely says he can not say it except by the Holy Ghost and does not say anything about a direct operation of the Holy Ghost. Well, over in the second chapter of Acts and verse 36, the apostle Peter, who was speaking by the direction of the Holy Spirit, said, "Let all the house of Israel know assuredly, that God hath made that same Jesus, whom you have crucified, both Lord and Christ." Every man who accepts the statement made by the apostle Peter on that occasion, and, in harmony with and in view of that statement, says that Jesus is Lord is saying it by the Holy Ghost, because the Holy Ghost revealed it through Peter. There is nothing at all in the text to indicate a direct operation of the Holy Spirit.

Now, then, my friend is coming and talking about how and insisting that the "how" is not the issue—that it is not in the proposition. Friends, it is the issue, and it is the only issue! He says the issue is, Does the Holy Spirit operate? That is not the issue. Both of us agree that the Spirit operates through the word. Friend Tingley agrees with that because he has it in his proposition that the Holy Spirit operates through the word. I agree that this thing is so. We both agree that the Spirit operates and, therefore, that is not the issue. When we say the Holy Spirit operates through the word, that is how, that is a manner. There's a method by which it operates. It operates through the word. That's how. We both agree on that "how" and both agree that the Spirit operates by that method. But in addition to that—besides that—friend Tingley says it operates directly upon sinners; and that's another method. It does involve the "how" and the "how" is the only point at issue in this discussion tonight.

Friend Tingley, you just as well come up and face the issue. You can not side-step in that way. You are going to have to face what your proposition says; and I am going to be right on your heels until we come to the close of this session, keeping before this audience the fact that the method, the manner, the "how" of the operation is the issue. It is not whether he operates—we both agree to that, Tingley. We both agree that the Spirit operates and that it operates through the word. We both agree on that method. But you say in addition to that method, it operates by another method—it operates directly; and that has to do with the "how."

You remember last night he asked me why I did not bring up Webster's Unabridged Dictionary and give him the definition. I said, "Why it's your proposition. You're the man who is obligated to define the terms of your proposition, according to the rules signed." But since he hasn't done it, I'm going to comply with his request tonight and give him the definition. I have here a definition copied from Webster's Unabridged Twentieth Century Dictionary, and it gives six definitions to the term "directly."

First. "In a straight line or course, rectilineally; not in a winding course; as, aim directly at the object; or gravity tends directly to the center of the earth." Now, is that the definition Tingley wants? We will wait and see.

Second. "Immediately, soon; without delay; as, 'He will be with us directly'." Is that the one he wants? We will wait and see.

Third. "On the instant that; as soon as; immediately when; a common but incorrect English usage." He gives an example from Dickens, "Directly he stopped, the coffin was removed by four men." Does he want that one?

Fourth. "Openly; expressly; without circumloctution or ambiguity; without a train of inferences." And the example from Hooker, "No man has been so impious, as directly to condemn prayer." Is that the meaning of the word in his proposition?

Fifth. "Exactly; precisely; just; as 'He is directly in the way'." Is that his definition?

Sixth. "Without the interposition or intercession of any person or thing; as, 'I conducted my business directly with the owner'." There's the only definition that can apply to the word as used in his proposition. The word directly, therefore, means "without the interposition of any person or thing;" and when he says the Holy Spirit operates directly upon the sinner, that's without the interposition of any person or thing. It's not through an agency—"without anything between;" "without anything intervening." That has to do with method or manner, and that's the issue. I am persuaded that Glenn V. Tingley knows that's the issue and is afraid to face it.

He said in the opening of his speech just made that he did not come here to win victories over an opponent, but that he was here that people might know the Lord. Well, friend Tingley, don't you know that you're wasting your energy. They can not know the Lord through your preaching. You argued last night that they can not know and no need to preach to them until the Spirit operates on their hearts and prepares them for it. And so if these people are to know the Lord, they'll not learn it from your preaching or mine, according to you. They'll have to know Him some other way. So the "how" is still there; and he must face the matter.

Then he came down to Cornelius. Was Cornelius an alien sinner when the Holy Spirit fell on him? He said, "Yes, he was a sinner." I want you to remember that it goes down on record that Glenn V. Tingley says that this man was a sinner; and he said he was converted or saved by the outpouring of the Holy Spirit and the preaching of the word—both of them. Why, Tingley, that outpouring of the Holy Spirit there was a miraculous outpouring. You said last night, in answer to a question which I gave you, (and I can read it here if you deny it), that the miraculous outpouring of the Holy Spirit is not the same operation as that that converts the sinner. Yet you gave the case here of Cornelius—one of whom the Holy Spirit fell miraculously—and said that saved him, after having said that the operation that saves a sinner is not the miraculous outpouring of the Spirit. Well, now, just which do you want? You can not have both of them. You are going to have to give up your miraculous operation and hold to the other; or you are going to have to give up the other if you hold to that, because you have said they are not the same operation. Let him deny it if he wants to. I will read it right here and the record will show it. We already have some transcriptions of the debate last night. You can go to his speech and see whether or not that is what he said. "It is not the same operation." So you have the wrong operation there to save the sinner. You are going to have to find a different one, friend Tingley.

Then he came to the question about the fish and the ham, and he said, "Yes sir. God feeds me directly." He said one time he ran out of rice, and they did not have anything to eat. He said he waited upon the Lord until a certain time, and he heard a noise at the door, and he went to the door, and there was a bushel basket full of food—enough that they could have their breakfast and a number of meals through a number of days. He said God chose a man and a woman. Well, that was not "directly" then—it was through means. You have the wrong thing. I asked, "Does God send you food directly from heaven?" That's the point. You say God sent it here in a bushel basket brought by a man and a woman. Well, that was using an agency; that was using means. That is not in harmony at all with your contention, for "directly" means "without the intervention or interposition of means," agencies or things of that kind. So you will have to try again. That's over on my side of this deal. It is not with you at all.

Then to the five thousand languages. He said the churches who believe in a direct operation of the Holy Spirit believe in carrying out the Lord's message to preach the gospel unto all the world and thus do missionary work. He had a number of things to say about the church of Christ's missionary activities. Well, we'll let that go for what it is worth and insist that he answer the question whether or not these four thousand out of five thousand who have not the translation of the Bible in their tongue are converted and saved by the direct operation of the Holy Spirit. I asked the question in writing, and I hope he will not forget it.

Then he said, "Porter pokes fun at miracles." No, I don't

poke fun at any miracles, Not at all. I believe there are miracles recorded in the Bible; and I'm certain of the fact that men performed miracles. I do not poke fun at miracles, but when men claim there are miracles which are not miracles, I don't accept them just because they say so.

Then he told about his daughter's being stricken with polio and God's healing her twisted limb when she was fifteen months old. May I ask here, Mr. Tingley, how long was that daughter in the hospital before God healed her? How long was that daughter in the hospital? We await your answer.

Then, just to show how the word operates—rather how the Spirit operates—he gave us a number of scriptures here. Luke 1:41-44. He said the Holy Spirit operated on a babe in the womb—on John the Baptist in the womb of his mother Elizabeth; that the Holy Spirit operated upon that babe. Well, Tingley, did the Holy Spirit operate upon that babe to convert it? We are talking about the conversion of sinners. I want you to tell me: Did the Holy Spirit operate upon that babe in the womb for the purpose of converting that babe? If not, then it does not have a thing to do with your proposition. Your proposition says, "The conversion of sinners." He does not like these questions. They force the issue. That's the point.

Now, 1 Sam. 10:10—The Holy Spirit brings inspiration. So it operates in that way. Well, I know the Holy Spirit operated to bring inspiration but to say that it still operates that way and inspires men today, as the apostles and prophets were inspired, is a different proposition. Now, let him prove it!

Genesis 28:11 to 17—it operated through a vision to Jacob. Was that for the purpose of converting Jacob, the alien sinner? Was that the idea of it? If not, then it is out of connection with your proposition. It even operated upon liars in Acts 5:3 when Anninas and Sapphira were struck dead because they had lied to God and the Holy Ghost. Well, what was the purpose of that operation? Now, there is a direct operation of the Spirit, he says, right along with his proposition. And it killed those upon whom it operated. The earthquake almost got the jailer last night, and now this operation has both these people killed; and that proves his proposition. That is a direct operation of the Spirit, friend Tingley, that did not bring salvation—it brought physical death. Is that what your proposition says? You had better read it again.

Acts 16:14. It prepares the heart for a gospel reception—the conversion of Lydia whose heart the Lord opened. Yes, I believe the Lord opened her heart. But I notice it did not read, "Whose heart the Lord opened with a direct operation of the Spirit." If he had just had that in, he would have had his proposition sustained; but he did not have that. Not whose heart the Lord opened with a direct operation. It does not say that. The fact was that Paul preached to her and her heart was opened. That is, the eyes of her understanding were enlightened, as we have in Ephesians 1:18. So being enlightened, her heart was opened, and she attended to the things there spoken by Paul. Let him find the direct operation in that.

Romans 5:5—"The love of God shed abroad in our hearts." I dealt with that on two occasions last night showing by 1 John 4:19 we love God because He first loved us. Our love for God is produced by God's love for us, and that love is revealed in the gospel. We learn of it only through the gospel as dictated and directed by the Holy Spirit; and therefore, the love is shed abroad in our hearts by the Holy Spirit through the preaching of the apostles of the Son of God. Let him find his direct operation.

Then to John 16:7-11, and he said, "Porter was as silent as the tomb about this." The record will show; and when you get a copy of this debate and read his first speech, on the second night where he said "Porter was as silent as the tomb about the one word in this passage," you take your copy, go back and read and see whether or not I was as silent as the tomb, or just what happened.

He said, "The Spirit will reprove the world of sin, of righteousness and of judgment." "Reprove the world"—there's the word he said Porter was as silent as the tomb about. I believe the Holy Spirit will reprove the world, that He will convict the world of sin, of righteousness and of judgment. Acts 2 is the fullfillment of this. In Acts 2 we find the Holy Spirit's coming and inspiring men to preach; and when Peter said, "Let all the house of Israel know assuredly, that God hath made this same Jesus, whom you have crucified, both Lord and Christ, they were pricked in their hearts." There's where the Holy Spirit convinced men of sin through the preaching of the apostle Peter. It does not say "directly" at all.

Then over in Titus 1:9 Paul speaks of certain ones holding

forth the faithful word or sound doctrine "that he may be able" by that sound doctrine "to exhort and to convince the gainsayers." The word "convince" in that passage is from exactly the same original word that "reprove" comes from in John 16. "Reprove the world" . . . "Convince the gainsayers." And Paul said you can do it by sound doctrine. Elder Tingley says, "You can not do it by preaching; it takes the Holy Spirit in a direct operation to do it." You can take your choice. I will stand with Paul.

Then on John 3, he said, "Here's another place he was as silent as the tomb." Turn back and read the record when you get the book and see whether I was silent as the tomb or not. "Born of the Spirit." I showed in connection with that from I Pet. 1:22-23 that you are born of the seed—the incorruptible seed—by the word of God, which liveth and abideth forever. As to the mother and things of that kind we shall say more presently.

He said it is the same word in John 3—"Born of the Spirit"—that we have in Genesis about Abraham, when it is said that Abraham begat Isaac; the same word as in Matthew 1:20 that Jesus was conceived of the Holy Ghost; the same word found in 1 John 5:18—"Born of God." Yes, all of them are from the same word. And, friend Tingley, did you not know that it is the same word exactly in 1 Pet. 1:23 that says, "Being born again, not of corruptible seed, but of incorruptible, by the word of God, which liveth and abideth forever?" Note, friend Tingley, that it is also the same word found in 1 Cor. 4:15 in which Paul said, " I have begotten you through the gospel"—the same word! Didn't you know that, Tingley? Didn't you know that I'd catch you when you tried a thing of that kind?

Well, it takes two, he said, "the father and the mother to bring about the birth." I am just wondering, then, in his application of it, who the mother is.

Now to some other matters. Regarding the bottle of ink, he said, regarding 2 Cor. 3:3, "Why I did not say the bottle of ink was spilled. I made no such statement as that." I know you didn't, but in order to sustain your theory that is what would have to be done. Not only "ministered by us," or written with the pen, but there must be a direct outpouring upon them if it fits your theory in your case. That's the thing you'd have to find. You did not find it. You did not say a word about it. I know that; but I called your attention to it, and I am insisting that you find it in order to make it fit your theory about it. Yes, Paul said, "ministered by us"—"written . . ." "How? How?" Well, you said, "Here's how." I thought you were not discussing how. I thought "how" had nothing to do with it. But he comes along and says, "How?" Well, the "how" is that "it is not with ink; that it is not the Bible; that it was not the letter; not the word; but with the Spirit." All right, then, Paul administered the Spirit, because he said, "Ministered by us." If that was not through his preaching or writing or anything of that kind, then tell me how Paul ministered the Spirit to those men and placed it upon their hearts. We await your answer. He does not like questions. I do not blame him.

He said Paul was saved by a miraculous operation of the Spirit. Well, what is a miracle? A miracle, respected friends, in the natural realm is when something occurs that is the result of a deviation from an established law. That is what it takes to make a miracle. Where a thing occurs in harmony with established law in nature, that is not a miracle. There must be a deviation from the established law. And in the spiritual realm the same thing is true; and if Paul was converted by a miracle, he was converted by a deviation from an established spiritual law. What does Paul say about it? Romans 8:2, Paul says, "The law of the Spirit of life in Christ Jesus hath made me free from the law of sin and death." Paul said he was made free by an established law. Friend Tingley says, "No, he was made free by a miraculous conversion." Take your choice.

Then he said, regarding Paul, "Why the Holy Spirit was operating (and they were all smitten); but all of them did not hear the word because the Spirit prepared the heart of Paul and did not prepare the others." Well, why didn't he prepare the others? Was God a respector of persons? Why were not the others prepared by a direct operation of the Spirit? It operated upon them. They were all smitten; they all fell to the ground, you say, but did not hear—because the Lord prepared Paul's heart but did not prepare the others. They were not to blame for it, then, were they? If the Lord did not make the preparation, then they were not to blame for it. But in Acts 26:14 we are told why they did not understand—because Paul said, "The voice spoke to me in the Hebrew tongue." That's why. Not because his heart had been prepared and theirs had not; but the Lord spoke in a language which he understood.

Then concerning the earthquake. He said, "I did not say that the earthquake led the man to attempt suicide." I know you did not say that, but that is the conclusion of your argument. He said the earthquake was a direct operation of the Spirit. So it led the man into an attempted suicide, for he started to take his own life and was hindered only by the voice of the preacher who spoke and said, "Do thyself no harm, for we are all here." And that stopped the suicide act. The direct operation almost caused that fellow to take his own life. The words of the preacher stopped him and then turned around and saved him when he obeyed the thing preached.

Now then he comes to the "how" again—Romans 15:9—"by signs."

Mr. Nichols: Three minutes.

Mr. Porter: Thank you. Yes, signs here were to make the Gentiles believe; but those signs were not worked upon the men to be saved. If so, prove it. Signs were for the purpose of confirming the word; and he preached a doctrine that had never been preached, and the words were confirmed by signs following. But the signs were not necessarily worked upon the man who was converted but upon somebody else—upon the afflicted.

Then in Acts 2, "by tongues." But that was a miraculous outpouring, and he said, "That's not the one I'm talking about." All those passages he gave along that line are right in the group with this one.

Then, one other scripture—Joel 2:28—here it is, he said, "All flesh." "Pour out my Spirit upon all flesh." Well, in Acts 2:16-17, regarding the miraculous outpouring of the Spirit on Pentecost, Peter said, "This is that of which Joel spoke." It was a miraculous outpouring. Tingley says, "That's not the operation in my proposition." Well, why did you use it then? What did you introduce that passage for when it had to do with miraculous operation and not the one in conversion? You said, "They are different."

1 Cor. 6:11—"washed and sanctified by the Spirit." Yes, but it does not say by a direct operation of the Spirit. Eph. 5:26 says we are cleansed and sanctified "through the washing of water by the word." Here we have it ascribed to the word, and the Spirit does it through the word.

Then he said that there is no passage saying the Holy Spirit operates only through the word. Well, will he find the passage that says the Holy Spirit operates directly? Let him produce that. He is in the affirmative.

Then to 1 Cor. 12:13—"Baptized by one Spirit." Yes, but does he mean that was a miraculous baptism? Let him tell us about that, and we will see his position on it.

He came to Romans 15:18, which was just mentioned, and Matt. 12:31—"Blaspheming the Holy Spirit." Is that the operation of the Spirit in conversion? He's getting entirely away from the proposition. To oppose the thing which my opponent is preaching is not blaspheming the Holy Spirit. To oppose speculations and human theories and traditions is not to blaspheme the Spirit. Let him produce the passage that has to do with the proposition.

That finishes everything he said; and if I have a moment or two, I will say some other things.

Mr. Nichols: About half a minute.

Mr. Porter. About a half minute. Just remember this. Paul said in Romans 1:16, "I am not ashamed of the gospel of Christ for it is the power of God unto salvation to everyone that believeth." And in James 1:21, "Receive with meekness the engrafted word which is able to save your souls." Now, friend Tingley says if it is able to do it, it does it. All right; so here is the word able to save your souls. If it is able to do it, tell me, friend Tingley, does the word save the souls of men?

I thank you very kindly.

SECOND NIGHT—TINGLEY'S SECOND SPEECH

Mr. Chairmen, Gentlemen Moderators and Worthy Opponent:

First, let me say I have not complained of legitimate, proper, and right questions. I was rather glad he asked the questions on the paper the other night, but it is the questions that are irrelevant, that have nothing to do with the proposition—or very little to do with it—but are simply wild goose chasing that I objected to.

In answering these questions that were handed me, the first one: "Was the outpouring of the Spirit upon Cornelius a miraculous outpouring?"

Anything that the Holy Spirit does, according to the natural man is miraculous. There are certain dispensational outpourings of the Holy Spirit but any operation of the Holy Spirit to any individual is miraculous.

"Since you say the miraculous outpouring of the Spirit is not the same operation as that used in the conversion of sinners, then is the case of Cornelius applicable to your proposition?"

And here is what I said: "Is the miraculous outpouring of the Spirit the same as the direct operation of the Spirit in conversion?" It is the same Spirit but not the same operation. The Cornelius instance was one for dispensational fullfillment. The Holy Spirit operates today directly upon any individual heart; in any miraculous despensational outpouring, the Holy Spirit can and does convert as part of its program. The Holy Spirit will convert whenever an individual receives the Spirit.

"If a direct operation means an operation through some means or agency, through what agency besides the word does the Holy Spirit operate directly?"

Through any matter, person or thing. My worthy opponent seems to forget that the Holy Spirit is a person, the third person of the Godhead—God present in our midst.

Again I started counting how many times he called the Holy Spirit "it." Whenever he forgets himself, he always—for my worthy opponent does not believe in the personal presence of the Holy Spirit in the world today. I challenge him to be honest with his heart and honest with the teaching of the church of Christ.

"As there are four thousand tongues into which the Holy

Bible has not been translated does the Holy Spirit operate upon these tongues to save people who are identified with those tongues?"

Yes, whenever any missionary or Christian bears witness and the Holy Spirit accompanies the witness of the word.

Now we have finally got down to the issue. I said in the first speech that I made and in the early part of it that my worthy opponent would try and dodge the issue entirely and cry out, "How? How? How? He said here, "How is the issue and it is the only issue." Ladies and Gentlemen, let me read the subject of debate especially for the benefit of my worthy opponent. "The scriptures teach that in the conversion of alien sinners the Holy Spirit operates directly upon them as well as through the Word of truth or Gospel of Christ." Where is the word "How?" Where is there a suggestion of "How?" My worthy opponent artfully dodges the issue.

Two or three more things:

"How long was daughter in the hospital?" She was only in the hospital for about ten days or two weeks and the doctors did their best to get us to consent to an operation. We refused and waited on God and after the congealing of the cartlige, three months after the infantile paralysis, a helpless cripple who could never have a straight leg—so the doctors said—God healed her. But what's that got to do with it? I am answering the questions that he insists on injecting.

My worthy opponent said I read 1 Corinthians 2, which had nothing to do with the sinners but only the disciples. Let me read to you the fourteenth verse: "But the natural man receiveth not the things of the Spirit of God for they are foolishness unto him; neither can he know them because they are spiritually discerned." Who is he talking about? The natural man. How can the Spirit get to the natural man? Not through natural avenues. It must be spiritual and spiritual preception.

Again I would call the attention of my worthy opponent—his definition is very good. It's not the latest one. I have what seems to be the latest one from Webster's New Dictionary of the English Language, Unabridged. I would call attnetion to this. This is one that he read: "In a direct way. Without anything intervening." My worthy opponent seems to dwell upon the matter and I suppose that will be acceptable. Look up the word "intervening." I have a dictionary before me and the word "intervening" says: "To enter as something extraneous. To come in between by way of hindrance or modification." To operate directly I may operate upon my child with a paddle, a kiss, with a gift. I may operate by word. That's operating directly. The Holy Spirit may operate in any way, with any matter, with any thing or any person. But if the Holy Spirit operates directly through matter, thing or person contacts and speaks to or deals with a person that is direct operation. I gave you eleven ways whereby the Holy Spirit in the scriptures operated directly.

My worthy opponent said Paul said he was converted by an established law. He said, "Tingley says he was converted by a miracle—not by an established law." He said that a miracle was something deviating from the known laws of nature. Did you get that? "Known laws of nature." "Known laws of nature." My worthy opponent may not know all the laws. The balance of the definition, "transcending our knowledge of these laws." A miracle is not something contrary to law as my worthy opponent suggested. A miracle is something subject to higher law than laws which we know. So says the dictionary.

In regard to two or three other matters: Ladies and gentlemen, I wish that we could be honest as we will wish we had been when we stand before our Lord, and read 2 Corinthians 3:3— "For as much as ye are manifestly declared to be the epistles of Christ ministered by us, written not with ink." The apostle Paul ministered to the people the word but it was not even the writing of the word that wrought change in their hearts, "but with the Spirit of the living God not in tables of stone but in fleshy tablets of your heart."

Ladies and gentlemen when you go home tonight get your Bible and kneel by your bed and open it and ask God to show you what the Word says, then read at least twenty times 2 Cor. 3:3.

They my worthy opponent found fault with what I said about John 3:1-8. He is exactly correct that 1 Pet. 1:23 and other scriptures which he gave the word "born" is exactly the same one used in "born of the Spirit." He says, "The way we are born in John 3 is by incorruptible seed." But John 3 doesn't say that. It says "Born of the Spirit." "Born of the Spirit." Show me any time where the Bible says that "born of the Spirit" means being born of incorruptible seed; that that is the way the Spirit causes individuals to be born.

Again, he said that John 16 was fullfilled on the day of Pentecost. "He will reprove the world of sin." He said that that happened on Pentecost. Was the world at Pentecost? This is the age of the Holy Ghost. The Holy Spirit, whether you believe it or not, is present in the world today—operating as a Person and will operate on any heart who will be sky blue and brutally

(Blackboard)
THE NEW BIRTH

WORD		HOLY SPIRIT
I Pet. 1:23	as well as	John 3:5, 6
Psalms 119:50	as well as	John 6:63
Luke 8:11	as well as	Rom. 5:5
Mark 4:14	as well as	II Cor. 3:3
John 17:17-20	as well as	I Pet. 1:2
II Cor. 4:4	as well as	Gal. 4:29
II Thess. 2:14	as well as	II Cor. 3:6
Rom. 1:16	as well as	John 15:26
Heb. 4:12	as well as	John 16:7-11
I Cor. 1:21	as well as	Rom. 8:9
John 15:3	as well as	I Cor. 12:13
John 8:32	as well as	Rom. 15:16
Rom. 10:17	as well as	I Cor. 12:3
Matt. 13:19	as well as	Acts 7:51
Luke 16:31	as well as	Acts 10:44
John 20:30, 31		Rom. 8:1-2
Acts 4:4		Acts 2:4
Acts 15:7		Acts 15:8
Rom. 10:13, 14		I Cor. 2:14
Psalms 19:7		John 4:24
James 1:18		Rom. 15:19

NOT ALONE True — Both Direct True GROUND — NOT ALONE True

Sinner is converted by Word AND the Holy Spirit

honest with his own heart. **The world was not at Pentecost!** This is the mission of the Holy Spirit throughout all this age. "He will reprove the world"—all men.

Then he asked, "Whose heart was opened by direct operation of the Holy Spirit?" I will ask him to read Acts 16:14, "Lydia's heart was opened." Lydia's heart! God works through the Spirit of God now. This is the age of the Holy Spirit.

I called your attention to the fact that it is the Spirit and the word. On the blackboard behind me—(I am sorry that you will be unable to see at the back but I will read the scriptures to you. I ask that my moderator point out the scriptures as I read them to you.)

I want you to see: (1) What the Word does in conversion, (2) what the Spirit does in conversion. The Word operates, the Spirit operates! My worthy opponent can not erase this part (pointing to the "Word" on blackboard) and say the Spirit does it all this way. There is not a word in any of these that says the Spirit does it this way (pointing to "Word"). It says the Spirit does it! That's operating directly! How He does it, I again repeat, is not the question. He operates directly, without anything coming in between, without anything pushing him aside, without anything intervening. That is from the dictionary that my worthy opponent read!

1 Peter 1:23—"Being born again not of corruptible seed but of incorruptible by the word of God." John 3:5—"Except a man be born of water and of the Spirit he can not enter into the kingdom of God." "That which is born of the flesh is flesh, that which is born of Spirit is spirit."

Psalms 119:50—"Thy word hath quickened me." John 6:63—as well as the Word—it is the Spirit that quickeneth.

Luke 8:11—now in the parable "the seed is the word," as well as, Rom. 5:5—"the love of God shed abroad in our hearts by the Holy Ghost."

Mark 4:14—"the sower soweth the Word," as well as that, 2 Cor. 3:3—"written not with ink but with the Spirit of the living God."

John 17:17-20—"Sanctify them through thy word, thy word is truth. Neither pray I for these alone but for them also which believe on me through their word." The Word as well as 1 Pet. 1:2 —"Elect according to the foreknowledge of God the Father through sanctification of the Spirit."

2 Cor. 4:4—"Lest the light of the glorious gospel of Christ who is the image of God should shine unto them," and as well as that the Holy Spirit, Gal. 4:29—"As he that was born after the flesh persecuted him that was born after the Spirit."

The Word: 2 Thess. 2:14—"called you by our gospel." The Spirit as well as the Word, 2 Cor. 3:6—"the letter killeth but the Spirit giveth life."

Rom. 1:16—The gospel of Christ is "the power of God unto salvation" as well as, John 15:26—"Even the Spirit of truth which proceedeth from the Father."

The Word: Heb. 4:12—For the "word of God is quick and powerful—sharper than any two-edged sword," as well as the Spirit, John 16—the Comforter: "I will send him unto you. When He is come He will reprove the world of sin and of righteousness and of judgement."

The Word: 1 Cor. 1:21—"By the foolishness of preaching to save them that believe." Rom. 8:9—Just as well as the Word dierctly the Spirit operates. "Now if any man have not the Spirit of Christ he is none of his."

John 15:3—"Now ye are clean through the word" and as well as the Word, 1 Cor. 12:13—"By one Spirit are we all baptized into one body."

John 8:32—"the truth shall make you free." Rom. 15:16—"being sanctified by the Holy Ghost."

Rom. 10:19—"the hearing of the Word of God" as well as 1 Cor. 12:3 that "no man can say Jesus is Lord but by the Holy Ghost."

Luke 16:31—"they hear not Moses and the Prophets" as well as Acts 10:44—"While Peter yet spake the word the Holy Ghost fell."

John 20:30-31—"Many other signs truly did Jesus, but these are written that you might believe that Jesus is the Christ, and that believing you might have life," as well as that, there is the direct operation of the Spirit. Rom. 8:1-2—"Walk not after the flesh but after the Spirit."

Acts 4:4—"Many of them which heard the word" coupled with that—as well as Acts 2:4—"They were filled with the Holy Ghost."

Acts 15:7—"Should hear the word of the gospel and believe" as well as the Word there is the Spirit, Acts 15:8—"Giving them the Holy Ghost even as He did unto us."

Rom. 10:13-14—"How shall they hear without a preacher," as well as the preaching there must be the Holy Spirit, 1 Cor. 2:14—"Receiveth not the things of the Spirit of God."

Psalms 19:7—"The law of the Lord is perfect, converting the soul." John 4:24—"God is a Spirit and they that worship him must worship him in Spirit and truth."

James 1:18—"Of his own will begat he us with the word of truth," as well as Rom. 15:19—"Through mighty signs and wonders by the power of the Spirit of God."

Both of these are necessary. Both are direct. Both are true. Neither of them is alone. Not once does it say the Word without the Spirit. Not once does it say the Spirit without the Word.

Ladies and Gentlemen, let's not be specious in our arguments. Let's not be prejudiced in our thinking; and let's not be so set that we can not honestly examine the truth. If it said, "The word—and the word operates only by the Spirit—the Spirit does not operate direct," or if it said, "The Word only operates by the person of the Holy Spirit" then we could do away with one or the other. He accepts the one. I accept the one. He refuses to accept this. (Pointing to the Spirit). I accept it. I believe the whole Bible is the Word of God.

If I say, "I am going to eat," you believe that I am going to eat without anything entering between it. You believe that I am determined to do this, and if I were God, nothing could intervene. God over and over says the Spirit converts. He says the Spirit sanctifies, the Spirit justifies, the Spirit washes, the Spirit cleanses—the Spirit is the one that operates. Likewise the Word but it takes the two—the positive and the negative. That is the ground for a sinner coming to Christ. He is converted by the Spirit and the Word.

Now I was speaking in our last speech about our nature

and the kind of individuals we are. In 2 Cor. 5:18 it says, "Therefore if any man be in Christ, he is a new creature; old things are passed away and behold all things are become new." Ladies and Gentlemen, if a complete regeneration, renewal has not taken place in your being by a power greater than you so that you are a changed creature—the old things passed away—you have no part nor lot in this matter. That change can be wrought by a person—"not with ink," "not written" but "by the Spirit written on fleshy tables of the heart."

Titus 3:5—"Not by works of righteousness but according to his mercy he saved us by the washing, of regeneration and the renewing of the Holy Ghost." Rom. 8:5—"For they that are after the flesh mind the things of the flesh." There is many a sin bound person in this place who is chained by sin, and you know you are tied and hamstrung and can not get free; and there are a thousand passions within that possess you; and you are a slave to the flesh and its desires and its passions. Men and women, you can be born of the Spirit. "They that are after the Spirit mind the things that are of the Spirit." Conversion means a complete, dramatic, drastic change whereby I accept the gospel of Jesus Christ and the Spirit of God makes me a new creature in Christ Jesus. That is conversion. Apart from the Word there is no conversion. Apart from the Spirit dealing directly with the sinful nature of the person there is no conversion.

After the sinner is convicted by the Holy Spirit, has faith in the gospel of Christ and Christ as his Savior, he receives an internal witness of personal salvation so that faith becomes a matter of knowledge with him. Rom. 8:16—"The Spirit beareth witness with our spirit that we are the children of God." I John 4:13—"Hereby know we that we dwell in him and he in us because he has given unto us his Spirit." Gal. 4:6—"Because ye are sons God hath sent forth the Spirit of his son into our hearts crying, Abba, Father." The word is Aramaic and is signifies our common word, "Papa." To the sinner God is the Creator, the great God before whom we must stand. The apostle Paul says that when an individual is born or converted by the Spirit of God an automatic change takes place and you know he is born again because he says not "great Creator," "great Judge," but "Papa, God."

2 Cor. 1:22—Who hath sealed us, given us the earnest of the Spirit in our hearts. 2 Cor. 5:5—"Now he that wrought us for the selfsame thing is God who hath also given us the earnest of his Spirit." In Rev. 22:7 we have, "And the Spirit and the bride say come. Let everyone that heareth say come."

In Luke 2:26 we have the Holy Spirit revealing to Simeon directly.

In 1 Thes. 1:5 we have "For our gospel did not come in words." It was not in the preached word only. It was not in the word of God that we declared. It was not in the written word only. Listen to the wording "But also"—I will let the debate stand or fall on this verse. If I say, "But—also," it means something additional or something operating directly. As I come here, this comes here. Listen, "For our gospel came not to you in word only but also in power and in the Holy Ghost and in much assurance." The word as well as the Holy Ghost both must operate or the sinner can not be saved.

In Acts 5:30 we read "The God of our fathers raised up Jesus whom you slew and hanged on a tree as we are witnesses as we are witnesses of these things and so is also the Holy Ghost." The disciples were witnesses of it so is also another voice—the voice of the Spirit of God was witnessing that Jesus was raised from the dead. He operates directly.

"It is the Spirit that quickeneth. The flesh profiteth nothing." There is no life imparted except by the positive and the negative—the word and the Spirit operating directly one as well as the other operating upon the sinner.

2 Thess. 2:7 tells us further that the mystery of iniquity doth already work only he who now letteth will let till he be taken out of the way." The Holy Spirit is still in the world. The Holy Spirit even restrained the development of evil until God's purpose is fullfilled.

My worthy opponent is still following the same program that the enemies of the apostle Paul followed. He speaks of them in Gal. 4:29—"For then he that is born after the flesh persecuteth him that is born after the Spirit." So now, two kinds: the flesh and the Spirit. If you have not been born of the Spirit you are hopelessly, irreparably, eternally lost without God and without hope.

Now, Ladies and Gentlemen, I have proven to you in the course of my debate "that the scriptures teach that in the conversion of alien sinners the Holy Spirit operates directly upon them as well as the word of truth or the gospel," because:

(1) The Holy Spirit was omnipresent in the Old Testament age.

(2) He has come from the Father in Christ's name.

(3) He is the third Person of the Trinity.

(4) He is deity and can not be limited.

(5) He is God and Lord and is worshipped.

(6) He is a person with personal names and a personal pronoun is used to describe Him. Therefore, if He is God He can operate directly.

(7) The Holy Spirit does the things a person can do. He does divine work, gives life, prophesies, has all the atributes of personal deity, therefore, He can operate directly upon the sinner.

(8) The Holy Spirit invites the sinner to Christ. Man's sinful nature can only be changed by a divine miracle of the Holy Spirit. Man only receives the Spirit, therefore, the Holy Spirit does operate directly upon the sinner.

(9) The Holy Spirit is the one who convicts the sinner and alone produces repentance. Anyone who has not the Spirit of Christ is none of His. The new birth is wrought by the Holy Spirit, therefore, the Holy Spirit operates directly upon the sinner because one can resist the pleading of the Spirit.

(10) Because you can accept and become epistles of Christ by the Spirit.

(11) Because the Love of God is shed abroad in our hearts by the Holy Spirit, therefore, the Holy Spirit does operate directly upon the sinner.

(12) Because the Holy Spirit operates directly upon Paul, because the Holy Spirit operated directly upon Cornelius, because the Holy Spirit operated directly upon the jailer, therefore, He can operate directly upon the sinner.

(13) The word is powerless unless it is accompanied by the Holy Spirit.

(14) No man can call Jesus Lord except by the Holy Spirit.

(15) We are baptized into the body of Christ by the Holy Spirit, therefore the Holy Spirit operates directly upon the sinner.

(16) The Holy Spirit is the lifegiver.

(17) The Holy Spirit is sent that we might know the Word.

(18) And the Gentiles were converted by the Spirit of God, therefore, the Holy Spirit operated directly upon the Gentiles.

(19) Because one is born either of flesh or of the Spirit.

(20) Because the Holy Spirit restrains evil until God's purpose was complete.

(21) The Holy Spirit is witness added to the Word proving its authenticity, therefore the Holy Spirit can operate directly upon the sinner.

(22) Finally, because the Holy Spirit operated directly upon Simeon.

(23) The Holy Spirit can be blasphemed.

(24) The Holy Spirit by direct miracle operated on three thousand on the day of Pentecost, therefore the Holy Spirit can operate directly upon the sinner.

I thank you my friends.

SECOND NIGHT—PORTER'S SECOND SPEECH

Mr. President, Gentlemen Moderators, Respected Opponent, Ladies and Gentlemen:

I am before you now for the closing speech on this particular proposition. After this, of course, other questions will be discussed for the remaining nights.

Just a few things regarding the closing remarks of my friend, and then I shall go back to the beginning. He ran a great number of scriptures in, showing the operation of the Spirit on this and that, among which he said that the Spirit operated directly upon Simeon; therefore, it operates directly upon the sinner. Now, then, I just wonder why my friend did not tell whether Simeon was an alien sinner. He fails to get to those things. He gives a lot of scriptures where the Spirit operated, or where there was a spiritual manifestation, or revelation of some kind, upon God's children and then assumes and concludes from all of that that the Holy Spirit operates directly upon the sinner. Well, there's just no connection between his passages and his proposition. The scriptures he gives have to do with the children of God and his conclusion has to do with the alien sinner. So there's no connection between them in that way.

He came back to the idea of "can." He said the Holy Spirit can operate. Well, I dealt with that last night. We are not talking about what the Holy Spirit can do but what he does. You know I said that God can feed a man with bread directly from heaven, as He fed Israel in the wilderness, but He is not doing that. "The Lord is able of these stones to raise up children to Abraham," I gave you from Matthew 3, but He did not do that. So just because God can do a thing, or the Holy Spirit is able to do a thing, does not prove that it does it! All of his efforts along that line is wasted energy.

Now to his chart just briefly and then I shall go back to the beginning of his speech.

(Blackboard)
THE NEW BIRTH

WORD		HOLY SPIRIT
I Pet. 1:23	as well as	John 3:5, 6
Psalms 119:50	as well as	John 6:63
Luke 8:11	as well as	Rom. 5:5
Mark 4:14	as well as	II Cor. 3:3
John 17:17-20	as well as	I Pet. 1:2
II Cor. 4:4	as well as	Gal. 4:29
II Thess. 2:15	as well as	II Cor. 3:6
Rom. 1:16	as well as	John 15:26
Heb. 4:12	as well as	John 16:7-11
I Cor. 1:21	as well as	Rom. 8:9
John 15:3	as well as	I Cor. 12:13
John 8:32	as well as	Rom. 15:16
Rom. 10:17	as well as	I Cor. 12:3
Matt. 13:19	as well as	Acts 7:51
Luke 16:31	as well as	Acts 10:44
John 20:30, 31		Rom. 8:1-2
Acts 4:4		Acts 2:4
Acts 15:7		Acts 15:8
Rom. 10:13, 14		I Cor. 2:14
Psalms 19:7		John 4:24
James 1:18		Rom. 15:18

NOT ALONE True / Both Direct / NOT ALONE True
GROUND
Sinner is converted by Word AND the Holy Spirit

He called our attention here to a number of things on this side (pointing to chart) dealing with the word and on this side (pointing to "Spirit" on blackboard) dealing with the Holy Spirit; and in between them "As well as." 1 Pet. 1:23—born of the word as well as born of the Spirit. All through the whole list on both sides he has distinguished between the word and the Spirit—the word on the one hand, and the Spirit on the other. In other words, the word does certain things, and the Spirit does certain things, both accomplishing the same result; but according to friend Tingley's argument, there is no word in the Spirit and no Spirit in the word. The Spirit is not operating through the word, and the word is not operating through the Spirit. Each one is distinct and separate from the other and carries on independent of the other. That's his argument. Yet his proposition says that the Holy Spirit operates through the word. It says, "The scriptures teach that the Holy Spirit in the conversion of the alien sinner operates upon him directly as well as through the word." The proposition says the Holy Spirit operates through the word. Then, when the word is said to do a certain thing, and the Holy Spirit is said to do the same thing, why the Spirit does it through the word! The proposition says that. Then in addition to that, he must have an independent, direct operation that isn't through the word—and so that does not come through the word. So there's no word in the Spirit and no Spirit in the word of his operation, according to his chart.

I believe all these passages given here (pointing to the blackboard). I believe that there are certain things ascribed to the Spirit, and that, as these passages show, the same things are ascribed to the word. Since friend Tingley's proposition says that the Holy Spirit does operate through the word, I insist that he should have shown that this was a direct operation and not that which goes through the word, because he admits that it does operate through the word. That takes care of the whole chart because it is all along the same line. Every passage deals with the same principle, and to answer one of them answers the whole chart. I am insisting the Holy Spirit does these things, and the word does these things, but the Spirit does them through the word; and thus the operation is carried on. But Tingley says, "Not so. He does them through the word, all right, but He does them again." So he has to have two effects and two operations. Sometimes the Spirit does all these things through the word, but then besides that, he must do them all independent of the word. Now, that's his contention; that's his theory; that's the issue.

Now, then, back to the beginning.

He said he had not complained at the written questions; it was those other questions that he complained about. Well, I don't insist that he answer them from his seat. I press these questions because I do not want him to forget them in his next speech, and whether they are written or given orally they're the same questions; and if he doesn't complain at them when they are in writing, why complain at them otherwise, because they're the same questions exactly?

He spoke concerning the questions—and I want to notice them here:

"Was the outpouring of the Spirit upon Cornelius a miraculous outpouring?" He says, "Every operation of the Spirit on men is a miraculous demonstration or outpouring." Is that right? I do not want to misrepresent you.

Mr. Tingley: Yes, that's right.

Mr. Porter continues:

I certainly do not want to misrepresent him. That's certainly what he said—that every operation of the Spirit upon man, as it connects with man or concerns man, is a miraculous outpouring. All right; then the operation here was a miraculous outpouring upon Cornelius, and every one upon any man, anywhere any time, is also miraculous. Last night I asked him this question: "Is the miraculous outpouring of the Holy Spirit the same as the direct operation of the Holy Spirit in conversion?" He said, "It's the same Spirit but not the same operation." All right, then it's not miraculous. If a miraculous outpouring is not the same operation as that that takes place on the sinner to convert him, then the operation on the sinner to convert him is not miraculous. Since he says now in answer to this question that every operation of the Spirit on man is miraculous, then there is no operation on man by the Spirit in his conversion, Tingley being witness. Every one is miraculous, he says, but the miraculous outpouring is not the one that converts him. So there is none that converts him then, because, he says, they all are miraculous! There's where he is and there's where he's going to stay!

Then on the next question he never gave any answer, but he talked around it. "Since you say that the miraculous outpouring of the Spirit is not the same operation as that used in the conversion of sinners, then is the case of Cornelius applicable to your proposition?" He talked all around that but never did say whether it applied.

All right. Next: "If a direct operation means an operation through some means or agency, through what agency besides the word does the Spirit operate directly?" He said, "Through any matter, person or thing." Well, we'll have more about that presently.

"As there are four thousand tongues into which the Bible has not been translated, does the Holy Spirit operate and save the people identified with those tongues?" He said, "Yes." Well God has changed his program since last night. Since last night God has changed his program, because last night I asked my friend this question: "Is it possible for the direct operation of the Holy Spirit to save a sinner without the preaching of the word?" He said, "Yes, it's possible for God to do that because all things are possible with God, but it is not His program." It is His program tonight, isn't is Tingley? Last night it was not. Last night he said, "That's not God's program. God does not do that. That's not the Holy Spirit's program. It could be done that way, but it is not." That's what Tingley said last night. Tonight he says the Holy Spirit operates upon those people in the four thousand tongues that have no written word and converts and saves them without the word. So, then, it's His program tonight to save men without the preaching of the word by a direct operation of the Spirit; it wasn't last night. I wonder when God changed His program. Whenever you get the book you'll just have to turn back and read and see if that isn't what he said. I stake my word of honor upon it that you'll find it in the record just that way. That it was not His program last night to save people independent of the preaching of the word, but tonight it is His program, and so He saves the people of the four thousand tongues without the preaching of the word. (Mr. Tingley held up the question with his written answer. Mr. Porter glanced at it and read):

"Yes, when any missionary or Christian bears witness." What do you mean by that? "Yes, he does it without the word when any missionary or Chrsitian bears witness." Does the Christian bear witness in words or how?

(Mr. Tingley nods: Yes.)

He bears witness in words? Well, that's through the word. I said "without words." You have got right back on my side of it. (Laughter). "Why yes, he does it when the Christian bears witness. When the Christian preaches the word, then God saves the sinner without the word." Friend Tingley, I would not be in a position like that at all. I would not want in a place like that. If I could not contend for a doctrine that would keep me out of a hole like that, I'd give up the doctrine, because I'd be sure it's false. Yes, sir, the Holy Spirit operates upon those men in the four thousand tongues who have no written word when Christians bear witness through the preaching of the word. God saves them without the word when the word is preached! Now if you can accept that, you can accept almost anything.

Then he came back to the matter about "it"—that I referred to the Holy Spirit as "it," and that I did not believe the Holy Spirit is a person. Well, I'll just read some of the passages he quoted awhile ago in some of those statements he made to explain that. He gave us last night Rom. 8:26 about the Holy Spirit's interceding. The record will show that he introduced the passage—that "the Spirit itself intercedes for us"! The Spirit itself"—the very passage you gave called the Spirit "it." Then you gave one awhile ago, just before you sat down, Rom. 8:16, "The Spirit itself beareth witness with our Spirits that we are the children of God." He left out the "itself." He did not put the "itself" in, but it's in there. "The Spirit itself beareth witness;" and so the very passage he gave calls the Holy Spirit "it." So I'm in pretty good company when I simply refer to it sometimes that way. The record will show that I have also referred to him as "he" and "him" and "his" and things of that kind. He is referred to in the scriptures both ways; so I am in perfectly good company when I use it that way.

Then he gave Gal. 4:6 just before he sat down. "Because ye are sons, God hath sent forth his spirit into your hearts, crying, Abba, Father"—or "Papa, papa." Why? Why, Tingley, you have the wrong passage; you ought to find the passage that says, "In order to make you sons, God sent forth his Spirit into your hearts, crying, Abba, Father." "In order to make you sons!" That passage says, "Because ye are sons." Does that refer to an alien sinner?

Then he said about the how and the where, "No, there's no how in it. Where does the proposition say anything about how?" Well, the word "how" dosen't occur there, but the words occur there that show method. "That the Holy Spirit operates through the word"—isn't that method? Why didn't you say something about it, Tingley? Were you afraid? "The Holy Spirit operates through the word." Isn't that method? Doesn't that tell how? If it operates through the word, isn't that method or manner? Certainly the how is there; and "in addition to that" or "as well as that" Tingley says it operates "directly," and there's your method too. There's the "how" again.

He said, regarding those definitions that I read from Webster, that they were all good but not the latest. Well, if they were good, why didn't you tell me which one applied to the term in your proposition? I asked you to do it. One of them says, "Without interposition of any means or agency," or anything of that kind. If that isn't the one that applies, why didn't you point out the definition that does apply? Oh, he said, this latest definition gives it "nothing intervening." And so it means the Holy Spirit operates "without anything hindering." Well, if nothing can hinder that operation of the Spirit—if that's the meaning of it, Tingley—how was it that it converted Paul and prepared his heart and did not convert the other fellows? Did something hinder? Did something hinder? You said it operated on all of them; it knocked them all down; but only Paul's heart was prepared. He didn't prepare the other fellows. Did something hinder?

Then he came to his daughter in the hospital and said she was in the hospital about two weeks—about ten days or two weeks—and then God healed her. He said, "What has that to do with the proposition?" Nothing. But you introduced it. Not a thing on earth! We are not discussing the working of miracles, the healing of the afflicted of broken and twisted limbs or things of that kind. We're talking about the conversion of sinners, and certainly it had nothing on earth to do with it; but you are the man who introduced it; and so I had to reply to it. I'm in the negative; I'm simply following Tingley, that's all.

Back to 1 Cor. 2:14. He said, "Now, Porter said I read a whole chapter here that applied to the disciples, and I just call your attention to 1 Cor. 2:14 that the natural man receiveth not the things of the Spirit; neither can he know them, because they are spirtiually discerned. Now, here's the unconverted man, and he can not receive the things of the Spirit." I ask Tingley, Is conversion one of the things of the Spirit? Is the power of the Spirit one of the things of the Spirit? Well, this says the natural man does not receive them, and you say the natural man does receive them in order that he might become a child of God. This passage says he does not receive them. So you have the wrong passage or the wrong position.

Now, he said regarding the "intervening matter" that when you "operate directly" you may still have an agency. He said he might operate upon his child in various ways, or through various means, by a kiss, by paddling and so on. Well, I suppose if he used a paddle on it, he would still have an agency. That would still be a means or a medium through which he administered his power; that would not be direct.

Then back to this statement: He said. "I have shown there are eleven ways in which the Holy Spirit operates directly." I thought "how" had nothing to do with it; and here he has found eleven ways, eleven methods, eleven manners, in which the Holy Spirit operates. And yet the "how," the manner, or the method has nothing to do with it.

Rom. 8:2 again. He said a miracle is not something contrary to law. I showed that a miracle is not a result of an established law. If a thing takes place in harmony with established law, and by the working of that established law, it's not a miracle. When a child is born as a result of the operation of established law, that's not a miracle. If a child is born like Jesus was, that's a miracle. That was a deviation from established law, and there's the difference. And so in the spiritual realm there must be a deviation from the established law to have a miraculous regeneration. Paul said in Rom. 8:2 that "the law of the Spirit of life in Christ Jesus hath made me free from the law of sin and death." Tingley says, "No. It was a miraculous regeneration and not an established law at all." Take your choice.

Back to 2 Cor. 3:3—"Ye are our epistles, ministered by us; written not with ink, but with the Spirit; not on tables of stone, but on fleshy tables of the heart." Now he said, "Paul ministered the word." Well, but this says the writing was done by the Spirit and Paul said, "It was ministered by us." I plead with my opponent to tell me how Paul ministered the Spirit to them in a direct way.

John 3:1-8—"the same word again." Yes, the same word as found in 1 Pet. 1:23—"begotten," and so his argument fell flat upon that proposition.

Back to John 16:7-11—where "when the Spirit is come he will reprove the world of sin" and "Porter said this was fulfilled at Pentecost." He said, "Was the world at Pentecost?" Well, a part of them was there. A part of the world was there, and that's when the Spirit came. Jesus said, "When he comes"—and that's when he came—on Pentecost. Right then and there he began to reprove the world of sin, of righteousness and judgment; and he is still doing it today in the same way that he did on Pentecost—through the preaching of those inspired men.

On that day of Pentecost when the Spirit came, Peter spoke as the Spirit directed him to speak and said, "Let all the house of Israel know assuredly, that God hath made that same Jesus, whom you have crucified, both Lord and Christ. When they heard this, they were pricked in their heart." "When they heard this, they were pricked in their heart." Why, Tingley's proposition says they have to be pricked in the heart first before they can hear. The Holy Spirit must quicken their heart first to enable them to hear, for they can not know a thing about it until the Spirit first operates; and, then they can understand and know! Peter said they were pricked when they heard this—not when the Spirit operated upon them to enable them to hear this —but "when they heard this, they were pricked in their heart." All right. The Spirit convinced those men of sin, of the fact that they had murdered the Son of God. How did he do it? Through the preaching of the apostle Peter; and through that same means the Holy Spirit is convincing the world today. That's not a direct operation.

And, by the way, did you notice how he dealt with Luke 8:12? Did you notice how he set that thing aside? Did somebody say something about somebody being as "silent at the tomb?" Seems like I heard that expression sometime—about somebody being "as silent as the tomb." I gave him Luke 8:12 and I do not think he was asleep when I gave it to him. In Luke 8:12 Jesus explains the parable of the sower. He tells about the seed that fell by the wayside and was picked up by the fowls of the air and explains that to mean a man who hears the word, but the devil comes and catches the word out of his heart, lest he should believe and be saved. Remember, Tingley said, "The word does not reach the heart; that reaches the head." I wonder why he forgot that? He has a marvelous forgettery. Oh, it's marvelous how he can forget those things! Yes, the word was in the heart. Jesus said so. Tingley said, "It is not so. The word doesn't reach the heart; the word reaches the head." You remember I asked Tingley to tell me what is the heart and somebody was as "silent as the tomb." I wonder who?

Now, what is the heart of man? Was the word in the heart? Did the word reach the heart? If the word did not reach the heart, how was it in the heart? How did it get there if it didn't reach it? Jesus said in order to keep that man from being saved the devil caught the word away. The devil comes and takes the word out of the heart, lest he should believe and be saved. This shows that the devil knew if the word remained in the heart, the man would believe and be saved. The word could not get to the heart, according to Tingley. It just reaches the head. Well, that will look all right in print. I will be glad for some of you to search that some time and find out just what the heart is—whether or not Tingley told you about it, or whether the Lord told the truth.

He came to his chart again, but I have dealt with that, showing that the Holy Spirit does operate—that it operates through the word—and the thing that is ascribed to the Holy Spirit is also ascribed to the word. Since Tingley admits that the Holy Spirit does operate through the word it is his responsibility to prove that these passages do not refer to that operation, but that they refer to another operation in a direct manner. That's what he failed to do. He merely assumed that. He made an assertion that it was so, but he gave no proof, for his proposition does admit that the Holy Spirit accomplishes them in connection with it by a direct operation; and so he assumed the thing and gave no proof of it whatsoever.

2 Cor. 5:17—"If any man be in Christ, he is a new creature; old things are passed away; behold, all things are become new." Then in connection with that—Titus 3:5—"By the washing of regeneration and the renewing of the Holy Spirit." Yes, I believe the Lord saves us by the washing of regeneration and renewing of the Holy Spirit; but it does not say by a renewing accomplished by a "direct operation of the Holy Spirit." Since you agree that the Holy Spirit does renew men through the word, then it is up to you to prove that this does not refer to that, but that it refers to the other operation (that you have not found anywhere in God's book) upon an alien sinner.

Then he said, "If I say, I am going to eat, then nothing intervenes," and that, therefore, he eats directly. In other words, he does not use a fork nor a knife nor a spoon—he does not use any kind of means or agency when he eats; he operates directly! Well, what does that have to do with the question? Nothing, but he introduced it. I am simply following Elder Tingley. He is in the lead, and where he leads I will follow.

Rom. 8:16—"The Spirit beareth witness with our spirits that we are the children of God." Yes, "that we are the children of God," but your proposition says, "alien sinners." You have the wrong passage. You want to find a passage that says the Spirit itself converts the alien sinner through a direct operation. That isn't what you found. It is not there. You found a passage that applies to God's children, and you make it apply to alien sinners.

2 Cor. 1:22—"He sealed us with his Spirit." And Eph. 1:14—He gave us the earnest of the Spirit. Well, who is the "us?" Do you tell this audience, Elder Tingley, that the "us" applies to alien sinners? Why, Paul said, "He hath given unto us . . ." "Us" who? Why, "us" children of God, "us" Christians! That's not an operation upon an alien sinner. That passage applies to God's people, not to alien sinners. Can't you beat that, Tingley? I believe I could beat that.

Rev. 22:17—'The Spirit and the the bride say, come," and since the Spirit says, "Come," that means the Spirit operates directly upon alien sinners. Well, since the bride says, "Come," that means the bride operates directly upon alien sinners. I wonder how the bride does it? The bride is the church, I presume. How does the church operate upon sinners without means? If it proves it in one case, it proves it in the other.

Then back to Luke 2:26—where he revealed to Simeon. But Simeon was not an alien sinner.

Then I Thes. 1:5—"Our gospel came not to you in word only, but also in power and in the Holy Ghost, and in much assurance." And so he said, "Here is the word; and here is the power; and here is the assurance; and here is the Holy Spirit." "Our gospel came not in word only." Well, I believe that. But Paul said it also came in power, and it came in the Holy Ghost; but that's not your position. Your position is the Holy Ghost comes first and prepares the way for the word. The word does not come in the Holy Ghost; the word does not come in power; the power comes first and prepares the way for the word to come. So that does not fit.

Acts 5:30—The Holy Ghost witnessing to certain things there. Well, again, that's aside from the proposition. What he wants to find is where the Holy Ghost operates upon an alien sinner to convert him—where it operates directly—not through the word. That's the thing he has not found.

John 6:63—"The words that I speak unto you, they are Spirit, and they are life;" and it's the spirit that quickens. Well, I believe that, but there is not a word said in it about any direct operation of the Spirit on sinners.

2 Thess. 2:7—He restrained evil—and still he has nothing there about a direct operation upon an alien sinner to convert him.

And Gal. 4:29—He said it is true, as it was then, that he that is born after the flesh persecutes him that is born after the Spirit. In other words, Porter is persecuting Tingley. That's the application. That's the thing that he indicated by the passage—that Porter is persecuting Tingley. Porter is born after the flesh and Tingley is born after the Spirit, you see, and so I am after him and I'm persecuting him. That's the application. If that's not the meaning of it, and if that's not the connection it has with this proposition in this debate, I wonder just what connection it does have.

He says I am persecuting him. Well, we'll let the audience decide that. I'm certainly "prosecuting" the false doctrine he's trying to put over to you—I'm "prosecuting" that. Maybe he thinks the "prosecution" of a false doctrine is a persecution of the man that teaches it. I don't know. He confuses prosecute and persecute; he confuses false teaching with the false teacher, I suppose. So I "prosecute" his false teaching, and he thinks I'm persecuting the false teacher. No, I'm not persecuting him; I'm just "prosecuting" the thing that he's teaching. That's all.

Now, then, that covers his speech and how much time do I have?

Mr. Nichols: About three minutes.

Mr. Porter continues.

About three minutes. All right; we will just make that three minutes long and just take a look at a few things.

I gave you last night, in my first speech, a number of negative arguments, showing what the word does and what it accomplishes. To only one of these did friend Tingley find time and disposition to refer. 1 Cor. 1:21 says that it pleased God by the foolishness of preaching to save them that believe. "It pleased God by the foolishness of preaching to save them that believe." The thing that pleased God did not please Tingley; and Tingley says, "No, preaching can not save anybody. It takes the Holy Spirit in a direct operation to accomplish that."

Then I showed how faith comes. John 17:20—Jesus prayed

for "them that believe on me through their word"—not through a direct operation of the Spirit.

Rom. 10:17 says "faith comes by hearing the word of God"—not "faith comes by a direct operation of the Spirit upon the heart."

John 20:30-31 says, "These are written that you might believe." "You can not believe as a result of what's written. You have to have the Spirit to first convince you in a direct way before you can even hear and understand," says Tingley. ,

And then Acts 4:4—"Many of them which heard believed." They believed as a result of hearing and not as a result of a direct operation.

Acts 15:7—"The Gentiles by my mouth should hear the word and believe." Their faith came as a result of preaching.

Rom. 10:13-14—"How shall they believe in him of whom they have not heard," showing that belief results from preaching.

Luke 8:12—the devil removed the word from the heart, lest the man should believe and be saved; and so if the word had remained in his heart (that it could not reach and could not be in because Tingley said it could not, but Jesus said it was), then that man would be saved. The devil knew that; so he simply removed the word of God.

I showed what the gospel does—that it is "the power of God unto salvation." Rom. 1:16. I showed that Paul said, " I have begotten you through the gospel."—I Cor. 4:15.

I have shown what the law of the Spirit does. "The law of the Spirit of life in Christ Jesus hath made me free from the law of sin and death." Rom. 8:2.

Psalms 19:7 says that "The law of the Lord is perfect. or complete, converting the soul." But Mr. Tingley says, "No, it's not complete; it's not perfect. You must have a direct operation to perceive it or it can not convert at all."

I also showed what the word does. It begets. Jas. 1:18. It quickens. Psalms 119:50. That is cleanses. Psalms 119:9. That it sanctifies. John 17:17.

My time is up, and I thank you very much.

PORTER-TINGLEY DEBATE

Third Session: 7:30 P. M., February 26, 1947
Central Church of Christ — Birmingham, Alabama
Chairman: Emerson J. Estes — Birmingham, Alabama
Introductory Announcements: A. E. Emmons, Jr.,—Birmingham, Alabama
Singing Directed by: H. A. Sikes — Birmingham, Alabama
Prayer: C. C. Burns—Huntsville, Alabama
Moderators: Gus Nichols, Jasper, Alabama for Mr. Porter; Lowell Leistner—Birmingham, Alabama, for Mr. Tingley

Proposition: The Scriptures Teach that Water Baptism to a Penitent Believer of the Gospel is Essential to Salvation From Alien Sins.

W. Curtis Porter, Affirms
Glenn V. Tingley, Denies

(Affirmative Address by W. Curtis Porter)

Mr. President, Gentlemen Moderators, Respected Opponent, Ladies and Gentlemen:

I am glad indeed for this privilege of affirming the proposition that has just been read in your hearing.

I have engaged, through the years, in a number of just such religious discussions as this; but as far as I now recall, I have had an experience today that I have not had before—that of having such a discussion on my birthday anniversary. I do not know a better way to celebrate that than to engage in this discussion. I am glad indeed to be here.

As many of you know, some five years ago, it was discovered by medical science that I was a victim of one of the rarest blood maladies known, called Polycythemia vera. If you have difficulty in remembering that name, then just call it Erythrocytosis. But the malady consisted in the production of too much blood. The malady was inevitably fatal. No remedy was had and the only thing I could do was to give my blood away. During the first two months I gave away fourteen pints of blood. For nearly two years I gave, on an average, a pint of blood every three weeks. The doctors gave me only two years to live. When the two years were nearly up, there was developed in California an experimental treatment with atomic energy. I went and took the treatment and my life was spared. Because of that I have been able to reach this milestone in life today. Since I received the treatment of atomic energy, however, my brethren have had to treat me gently, lest I explode. (Laughter).

At the present time my malady is out of control, and for the past year I have been giving away blood once every three weeks; but I have promise of another treatment soon of the atomic energy. So I am glad that through the development of medical science and the providence of God, I have been able to reach this milestone in life and that I can engage in this discussion tonight in defense of what I am fully convinced is the truth of God Almighty.

The proposition is: "The scriptures teach that water baptism to the penitent believer of the gospel is essential to salvation from alien sins." The rules require, of course, that we define the terms of the proposition. By "the scriptures" I simply mean the word of God, the book that we often times call the Bible. By "teach" I mean that it says so in so many words or that words are used to convey that idea or make necessary that conclusion. By a "penitent believer of the gospel," I mean, of course, by the term "gospel" that which we recognize as the word of truth revealed to us in the New Testament scriptures. The "penitent believer" is the believer who has repented of his sins. To that man "water baptism"—and by water baptism I mean immersion in water by the authority of Jesus Christ in the name of the Father, the Son and the Holy Spirit—is "essential" or is necessary to his justification. "Essential to salvation from alien sins." By "alien sins" we mean sins that have been committed while an alien sinner; that is, prior to obedience to the gospel of Jesus Christ. By "salvation" I simply mean the forgiveness of sins, pardon or remission of sins.

I believe that defines sufficiently the terms of the proposition, and the issue is simply this: Is baptism a condition of salvation from sin? I affirm that it is and my opponent denies. That is the issue between us tonight. Of course, what the scriptures teach here makes room for faith and repentance; and we believe that faith and repentance are necessary and without them a man could not be baptized according to the requirements of the New Testament. All the statements made in God's book relative to faith and repentance as conditions of salvation we whole heartedly believe and accept. But along with that there is also a condition that is called baptism; and that, too, is essential to the salvation of men.

I call your attention to a number of arguments which I wish to introduce at this time to sustain the proposition.

My first argument will be based upon the statement made by the apostle Paul in I Cor. 1:12-13. Here Paul says, "Now everyone of you saith, I am Paul; and I of Apollos; and I of Cephas; and I of Christ. Is Christ divided? Was Paul crucified for you? or were ye baptized in the name of Paul?" Now this statement made by the apostle Paul lays down an eternal principle, and to that principle I certainly invite your attention. Here were men in the church at Corinth calling themselves after men; some saying, "I am of Paul;" others, "I am of Apollos;" "I am of Cephas;" and some saying, "I am of Christ." Or as some translations of the scripture give it, 'I belong to Christ; I belong to Paul;" "I belong to Cephas." Of course, to be "of Paul" would mean to belong to Paul; to be "of Apollos" would be to belong to Apollos; to be "of Cephas," to belong to Cephas; and to be "of Christ" would be to belong to Christ. The apostle Paul shows that in order for one to be of Paul there are two things that must be necessary. There may be other things, but these things are absolutely essential. Here were men saying, "I am of Paul" and Paul showing that they could not be of him because these two things were not true. He says, "Was Paul crucified for you? or were you baptized in the name of Paul?"—thus showing that in order for a man to be of Paul, or to belong to Paul, he must first, have Paul crucified for him; and in the second place, he must be baptized in the name of Paul. If Paul had been crucified for him, that would not be sufficient to make him of Paul unless he had been baptized in the name of Paul. Since Paul had not been crucified for him, and he had not been baptized in the name of Paul, then he had no right to say, "I belong to Paul."

The same principle holds true with respect to Apollos. In order for men to belong to Apollos, Apollos must be crucified for them, and they must be baptized in the name of Apollos. Without those two things being true, according to the principle laid down by the apostle Paul, men could not belong to Apollos.

Then the same with respect to those who said, "I am of Cephas." Cephas must be crucified for you, and you must be baptized in the name of Cephas. If that had not been true, then they were not "of Cephas" and they did not belong to him.

That same principle comes on down to those who said, "I am of Christ," or "I belong to Christ." The same two things must be necessary. In the first place, in order to belong to Christ, or to be of Christ, Christ must be crucified for you. In the second place, you must be baptized in the name of Christ. If the principle does not mean that, it does not mean a thing beneath the stars tonight. These two things are necessary that men belong to Christ, or that they be of Christ. Christ must be crucified for them; they must be baptized in his name. It is true that Christ has been crucified for us. That we can take as a fact. But it is also true that we must be baptized in his name or we do not belong to him. I, therefore, insist that this passage shows beyond any doubt that baptism is an essential condition in the plan of salvation—that men who have not been saved from their sins do not belong to Christ; but if men belong to Christ, if they are of Christ, then they have been saved from their sins. And that applies to those for whom Christ has been crucified and those who have been baptized into his name. I shall insist that my opponent pay attention to this and attempt to set it aside or make a very strong effort to do so.

The second argument to which your attention is called is this. All the verses of the New Testament which mention baptism and salvation together put the salvation after baptism. Now remember that. All the verses in the New Testament which mention salvation and baptism together put the salvation after the baptism. They never put the salvation before! I have not time just here to call attention to all of them but here are some samples: Mk. 16:16 says, "He that believeth and is baptized shall be saved." Where's the salvation placed? After baptism. "He that believeth and is baptized shall be saved." Baptism first; salvation follows. Acts 2:38—Peter said, "Repent, and be Baptiz everyone of you in the name of Jesus Christ for the remission of sins." Baptism placed first, followed by the remission of sins. Acts 22:16—Ananias told Saul, "Why tarriest thou? Arise, and be baptized, and wash away thy sins." First baptism; then the washing away of sins. Gal. 3:27—"For as many of you as have been baptized into Christ have put on Christ." First baptism; and then "into Christ." 1 Peter 3:21—"The like figure whereunto even baptism doth also now save us." First the baptism and then the salvation. I give these simply as examples of the principle stated in the argument introduced. Others could be added but that will suffice. Some of these passages will come up for individual investigation as I give them in additional arguments.

My third argument in substantiation of the proposition that baptism is a necessary or essential condition of salvation from sin is found in the language of Jesus Christ in Mark 16:16. I quoted it briefly a moment ago. Now, I wish to elaborate upon it to some extent. Here we have Mark's record of the great commission the Lord gave to his apostles. I begin reading with verse fifteen. We hear the language, "Go ye into all the world, and preach the gospel to every creature. He that believeth and is baptized shall be saved; but he that believeth not shall be damned." Note the fact that it does not say, "He that believeth and is saved can then be baptized if he wants to." It is not, first believe; second, salvation; and third, baptism. It is first, believe; second, baptism; and third, salvation. "He that believeth and is baptized shall be saved; he that believeth not shall be damned." The Lord placed belief first, baptism second and salvation third. If that passage makes belief necessary to salvation, it also makes baptism necessary to salvation. The salvation is conditioned, in the language of Jesus, upon those conditions. Remember that no amount of reasoning can make that read, "He that believeth and is saved can then be baptized," because that is not what the Lord said. People will quibble about it, and will try to reason around it, and get it out of the way; but if the thing were expressed in material value, there would be no quibble about it. Suppose, for example, that when you go home from this discussion you turn on your radio and hear the President of the Ford Motor Company broadcasting this statement: "He that believeth and is baptized shall receive a new Ford." Do you suppose there'd be any quibbling about it? Would people try to reason the thing away and claim that it is not essential—"you do not have to do that, just believe in Ford and that is all that's necessary." No, you would not hear any quibbling about it. If you should hear that broadcast tonight from the Ford Motor Company, there'd be the biggest baptizing in Birmingham before daylight that you ever heard of. You would not be able to keep people knocked out of the river or the creeks with a club; and among the first to get wet would be my friend, Elder Tingley. (Laughter).

(Mr. Tingley laughingly nods, and says "I expect that's right.")

He says he expects that's right! If a Ford were involved, Elder Tingley would not try to reason it away! But if salvation is involved, he tries to get around it. Is salvation worth as much as a new Ford, Tingley? Do you think more of a new Ford than you do salvation? You said you'd do it if it were a Ford involved. You would not try to reason it away; you'd accept it; you'd do it. You'd be one of the first men to get wet; but where the salvation of the soul is involved he tries to reason the thing out and get it entirely out of the way. He knows if he tried to do that with a new Ford, somebody else would get the new Ford, and he'd be left out, you see. I am saying if it were expressed in material values, there'd be little quibbing about it. Why quibble, then, when salvation is the thing involved, and the Lord said, "He that believeth and is baptized shall be saved"?

We pass from that to my fourth argument, which is based upon the statement made by the apostle Peter in Acts 2:38. Men had just inquired, "Men and brethren, what shall we do?" Peter had stood there in the presence of the multitude of people who had been guilty of crucifying the Lord of glory. He told them of the fact that they had crucified him—that their hands were dripping, as it were, with the innocent blood of the Son of God. They were pricked to their hearts. They cried out and said, "Men and brethren, what shall we do?" What were they wanting to know? Why, they realized they stood condemned in sin; the guilt of sin was upon them. They had crucified Jesus Christ. They desired to be free from that condemnation. So they inquired, "Men and brethren, what shall we do?" Peter said in Acts 2:38, "Repent, and be baptized everyone of you in the name of Jesus Christ for the remission of sins, and ye shall receive the gift of the Holy Ghost." Now notice that. He laid down two conditions as essential to remission of sins. He did not merely say, "Repent," but he said, "Repent and do something else." He said, "Repent, and be baptized for the remission of sins." He made both the conditions of repentance and baptism necessary to the promise offered—the remission of sins. Both of them were for the remission of sins or in order that the remission of sins might be obtained.

That expression is used on other occasions. For example, in Matthew 26:28, Jesus, referring to his blood, said it was shed "for the remission of sins." I wonder if that meant the Lord shed his blood because sins were already remitted. You have the same expression there, both in the Greek and in the English, that we have in Acts 2:38—"for the remission of sins." Jesus shed His blood "for the remission of sins." But we are told to be baptized "for the remission of sins." If, when Jesus shed his blood for the remission of sins, that does not mean that remission was already obtained but that remission of sins might be obtained, then when Peter said be baptized for the remission of sins, it means the same thing. And so he told men to be baptized that remission of sins might be obtained. That's what we mean by salvation from alien sins for the penitent believer. Peter shows it here to be a condition of salvation with which men must comply in order to get the remission of their sins.

In Mark 1:4 we have even the same thing with reference to John's baptism. "John did baptize in the wilderness, and preach the baptism of repentance for the remission of sins." Now you have the expression three times: Mark 1:4 says, "For the remission of sins;" Acts 2:38 says he baptized for the the remission of sins." Matt. 2:38 says he baptized "for the re-the remission of sins." You have this same expression in all three of the passages. If Jesus did not shed his blood because sins had been remitted already, then John did not baptize because their sins were remitted. If it means in order to obtain in one case, it means the same in the others. We have the same identical expression. I insist the language of the apostle Peter proves beyond doubt the truthfulness of my proposition.

Then we find, too, a number of translations may be referred to to give us that expression. I want to read just a few of them briefly on the statement in Acts 2:38—"For the remission of sins."

The King James Version reads, "For the remission of sins."

The Catholic Revised Version reads, "For the forgiveness of your sins."

John Wesley's translation, "For the remission of sins."

Moffatt's translation, "For the remission of sins."

Wilson's Emphatic Diaglott, "For the forgiveness of your sins."

Weymouth's translation, "For the remission of your sins."

20th Century translation, "For the forgiveness of your sins."

The Revised Standard Version, a production that appeared

in 1946, "For the forgiveness of your sins."

The American Bible Union, "Unto remission of sins."

American Revised Version, "Unto the remission of sins."

Charles Foster Kent's translation, "That your sins may be forgiven."

Goodspeed's translation, "In order to have your sins forgiven."

Charles B. Williams' translation, "That you may have your sins forgiven."

Thayer, the great Greek-English Lexicographer, renders this passage, "To obtain the forgiveness of sins."

That's the language of the apostle Peter in Acts 2:38, "Repent, and be baptized for the remission of sins"—in order to have your sins forgiven, to obtain remission of sins; unto the remissions of sins.

Just here I want to say a little about the word "unto" in that connection. Let me read from the Revised Version. "Baptized unto the remission of sins." We find that word "unto" used a number of times. Romans 10:10—Paul informs us, "With the heart man believeth unto righteousness." First the belief and the righteousness follows—"unto righteousness." In Acts 11:18, God hath unto the Gentiles granted "repentance unto life." First the repentance, and that followed by life. Romans 10:10 "With the mouth confession is made unto salvation." That shows the confession first, and then the salvation. 1 Peter 1:3—the Lord "hath begotten us again unto a lively hope by the resurrection of Jesus Christ from the dead." "Begotten unto a lively hope." First the begetting, and then the lively hope. We have the same thing in Acts 2:38 in the Revised Version, "Baptized unto the remission of sins." First the baptism, and then the remission of sins to follow.

Then I pass on to my next argument which is based upon the statement made by the apostle Peter in 1 Peter 3:21, "The like figure whereunto even baptism doth also now save us (not the putting away of the filth of the flesh, but the answer of a good conscience toward God), by the resurrection of Jesus Christ." Now I want you to note this language in 1 Pet. 3.21, "The like figure whereunto even baptism doth also now save us." I have written on the board here, but I know you cannot see it from all parts of the audience:

Baptism doth now save us.

Baptism doth not save us.

"Baptism doth now save us." That's what Peter said in 1 Pet. 3:21. "The like figure whereunto even baptism doth also now save us." Peter says baptism now saves us! He did not say it is the only thing—certainly not. But he did say that "Baptism doth now save us." You would not have to change that much to make it read like my opponent would like for it to read. Not a very great change would be necessary; just one letter, that's all. Just erase that "w" from the little word "now" and put a "t" there. You have exactly what friend Tingley is preaching. "Baptism doth not save us." That's all the change you would have to make. Just change the "w" to the "t" and you would have it. Peter said, "Baptism doth now save us."

I heard one time of a preacher discussing this matter with a certain lady, and she said, "My Bible does not read that way." He said, "Oh yes, it does." She said, "No, it doesn't." He said, "I know it does." She said, "I know it doesn't." She went and got her book and brought it, opened it to the passage, and sure enough it didn't. She had taken the scissors and cut it out. If you have not taken your scissors and cut it out, it reads that way in your Bible. 1 Pet. 3:21—"Baptism doth also now save us." I am going to ask my opponent, friend Tingley, to erase from the board the statement that he does not believe. They are not the same. One says, "Baptism doth now save us." The other says, "Baptism doth not save us." I challenge him to erase from the board the statement that he does not believe. Will you do it, Tingley? (Mr. Tingley: "Yes.") He says he will do it. All right. Tingley says he will do it. We are going to see how he lives up to his promise now. We want him to erase from the board the statement that he does not believe. We will await further developments and the activity along that line.

I come now to Galatians 3:26-27. Here we are told that you "are all the children of God by faith in Christ Jesus. For as many of you as have been baptized into Christ have put on Christ." Now notice that. "As many of you as have been baptized into Christ have put on Christ." Let's get the twenty-sixth verse which I just quoted in connection with it. "Ye are all the children of God by faith in Christ Jesus . . . for." That little word "for" comes from an original word "gar" which means "the cause" or to "introduce the reason." That's the way lexicographers define this term. "You are all the children of God by faith in Christ Jesus, for"—the reason is, "as many of you as have been baptized into Christ have put on Christ." This shows that the man who has not been baptized into Christ is not a child of God by faith. Only those who have been baptized into Christ have the reason assigned. The reason introduced by the apostle Paul is that you are God's children "because you have been baptized into Christ." You are God's children by faith because you have thus been baptized. If you have not been baptized into Christ, then this statement certainly shows beyond doubt that you are not the children of God by faith.

You know too, that every affirmative has a negative. I want to read verses 26 to 29 and let you see the negative of that idea there. Gal. 3, beginning with verse 26, and it reads this way, "For ye are all the children of God by faith in Christ Jesus. For as many of you as have been baptized into Christ have put on Christ. There is neither Jew nor Greek, there is neither bond nor free, there is neither male nor female: for ye are all one in Christ Jesus. And if ye be Christ's, then are ye Abraham's seed, and heirs according to the promise." Now let's see what the negative of that would be. "Ye are not all the children of God by faith in Christ Jesus. For as many of you as have not been baptized into Christ have not put on Christ. There is Jew and Greek, there is bond and free, there is male and female: for ye are not all one in Christ Jesus. And if ye be not Christ's, then ye are not Abraham's seed, nor heirs according to the promise." That shows the man who has not been baptized into Christ is not Abraham's seed; and he is not an heir according to the promise. He has not put on Christ; and he is not a child of God. I am willing to fight it out upon those passages tonight. But we have others.

Next I call your attention to the statement made in the conversion of Saul.

(Mr. Nichols: You have two minutes.)

Mr. Porter: Well, I'll get this much of it. In Acts 9:6, when Saul had cried, "Lord what wilt thou have me do?"—the Lord said, "You go into the city and there it shall be told thee what thou must do." It was not what he might do if he wanted to, but "you shall be told what you must do." I am going to ask my friend Tingley, since my time is just about up now, to tell me when he comes to the stand what Jesus told Saul to do. What was Saul told that he must do when he got to the city of Damascus? He would there be told something that he must do. I want friend Tingley to tell me what it was that was told him over there that he must do. I shall wait for him to tell that; and if he does not tell it, then I will tell you myself when the proper time comes. I am insisting that he tell us just what it was that Saul was told when he was told something that he must do. The Lord said, "Thou shalt be told what thou must do." I am certain that there was something told him over there that was essential; something that was necessary; something that he needed to know; something the Lord wanted him to do. Thank you, ladies and gentlemen.

THIRD NIGHT—TINGLEY'S FIRST SPEECH

Mr. Chairman, Gentlemen Moderators, Worthy Opponent, Ladies and Gentlemen:

I am very happy to stand in the defense of the truth. The statement has been made very clearly and I accept the definition of my worthy opponent in regard to the subject we are debating. "The Scriptures Teach that Water Baptism to a Penitent Believer of the Gospel is Essential to Salvation from Alien Sins."

I have some questions tonight that I want to ask my worthy opponent that are not sidestepping but are definitely questions in regard to the issue. They are:

(1) Do you believe that if a man believes, repents and is baptized, he shall be saved?

(2) Can such a believer who is saved so sin as to be lost?

(3) Can he be restored?

(4) Does he have to be baptized again?

(5) Are Methodists, Presbyterians and all pedo-Baptists lost and will they go to hell?

(6) Are Moody, Finney, Sankey, Billy Sunday, Wesley, Whitfield, Luther and all have not been baptized by immersion lost and in hell?

(7) What baptism saves—church of Christ baptism, Missionary Baptist baptism or Christian and Missionary Alliance Baptism?

(8) Will you accept one whom I have baptized without re-baptizing them?

(9) If baptism is essential to salvation then are babies lost?

(10) Are those baptized by the Missionary Baptist and Christian and Missionary Alliance save or doomed?

(11) Show me one scripture which states that a man is lost if he is not baptized.

(12) Give me a scripture which states that a man who re-

pents and believes on his deathbed and can not be baptized is lost.

(13) A most imortant question: I want my opponent to tell this crowd whether or not it is true that he believes that a person has no chance to be saved who is not baptized in his particular church of Christ.

(14) I challenge my opponent to tell this audience why Paul did not baptize a new convert every time he believed.

These questions as you can see are very pertinent for we are dealing not with the teaching of the Word, but with an ancient controversy which has made Roman Catholicism what Roman Catholicism is. It builds bigotry, prejudice; religious organizations that separate themselves from every other religious organization; set up states and institutions of their own; separate from every other one; demand that they and they alone have the only perogative of seeing men brought to God by their organization.

We will deal first with the first Scripture that he dealt with. I shall not follow him up blind alleys nor will I try to lead him in blind alleys; but I will meet him head on in the face of every single scripture in the Bible that any intelligent man can read or study that teaches the doctrine that my worthy opponent is advocating.

The scripture which he first read was Mark 16:16. He compared an automobile to salvation. I would answer my worthy opponent, for he asked me to answer you, I have been baptized by immersion—by immersion! I believe in it with all my heart. I probably baptize as many, perhaps more, than any other minister in the city not excepting the church of Christ ministers. That I have done consistently for eighteen years. I believe in it. I was was baptized by one who himself had been baptized by immersion. It may seem funny to compare the destiny of a man's soul and salvation with a Ford. Salvation has no comparison to a new Ford. We dare not quibble about these things.

"He that believeth and is baptized shall be saved." Why is it he insists on only reading part of the verse? Why is it he does not read all this portion of Scripture. He rang the changes on that several times but did he ring the changes on "BUT he that believeth not shall be damned?" It does not say, "He that believeth not and is not baptized shall be damned." Does it not look reasonable that if baptism were essential to salvation that it would have been made plain that damnation is conditioned on unbelief and disobedience to the ordinances of baptism? My worthy opponent may fail to quote all the passage but it's there, "BUT" . . . why will a man be damned? By not being baptized? Lest some would twist and wrest the Scriptures, God said, the thing that damns a man is not believing! Never once, does He suggest that lack of baptism mean damnation.

The first point to settle is: What does "shall be saved" mean? Does it mean that a baptized believer shall be saved in heaven? It does not say a baptized believer shall be saved if he does not backslide, but it does say, he "Shall be saved." Does my friend accept that? I will.

Who is to be baptized? The believer. What is the condition of the believer?

(1) "He shall not perish," according to John 3:14-15-16. "As Moses lifted up the serpent in the wilderness, even so shall the Son of man be lifted up; that whosoever believeth in him should not perish, but have eternal life. For God so loved the world, that He gave his only begotten Son, that whosoever believeth in him should not perish, but have everlasting life."

(2) The believer is not condemned; but he that believeth not is condemned already, because he hath not believed on the name of the only begotten Son of God."

(3) The believer hath everlasting life. John 3:36, "He that believeth on the Son hath everlasting life; he that believeth not the Son shall not see life; but the wrath of God abideth on him."

(4) What is the condition of the believer? "He has passed from death unto life." John 5:24, "Verily, verily, I say unto you he that heareth my word, and believeth on him that sent me, hath everlasting life, and shall not come into condemnation; but is passed from death unto life."

(5) He is justified. Romans 5:1—"Therefore being justified by faith, ye have peace with God through our Lord Jesus Christ."

(6) His soul is saved. The believer who is to be baptized— his soul is saved. 1 Peter 1:9, "Receiving the end of your faith, even the salvation of your soul."

(7) He is born of God. 1 John 5:1, "Whosoever believeth that Jesus is the Christ is born of God." Now is that man to be baptized? Yes. Why of course he "shall be saved." Does my opponent accept that position? Jesus Christ taught it, and the believer is saved! He is saved by faith!

Now if you add baptism to his religious life, he is still saved. Being saved by faith, baptism does not undo what faith has already done so "He that believeth and is baptized shall be saved." We believe that only believers should be baptized. All believers should be baptized. By it they enjoy the rights and privileges of the Christian life; by it they are manifested as children of God. By it they show forth the symbol of the death, burial and resurrection of our Lord. Baptism is a picture of their salvation—a likeness of it and the atoning work of Christ whereby it is accomplished—but baptism itself does not give salvation and Jesus never once intimated such a thing. The man who is saved by faith proceeds at once to lovingly obey his Lord and to be baptized. Such a man will be saved, not because baptism helps to perfect salvation; but because he has faith that saves him and that leads him to do all that His Lord commands him to do.

"He that entereth a train and is seated shall reach Atlanta." "He that believeth and is baptized shall be saved." Now suppose a man enters a train but does not take a seat. Will he not go to Atlanta anyhow if that train goes there? The taking of the seat involves his comfort but does not involve his going to Atlanta. So baptism relates to the privileges of the Christian life and does not secure such a life. The believer has entered the gospel train and whether he takes a seat or not, he will reach heaven if the train does.

Again, note the language, "He that believeth and is baptized shall be saved but he that believeth not shall be damned." The contrast is between salvation and damnation. To what point of time does that damnation look? Eventually to the future. Then to what period does its word of contrast look? Also to the future. Then salvation means salvation in heaven. Does my worthy opponent believe that "He that believeth and is baptized shall be saved" in heaven? Of course my opponent does not believe that.

All the absolute essentials to salvation are stated in God's

Word both negatively and affirmatively. For instance, (1) repentance unto life—the positive; negative, "Except ye repent ye shall all likewise perish." (2) "Believe on the Lord Jesus Christ and thou shalt be saved," positive; negative, "he that believeth not shall not see life." (3) Positive, "the blood of Christ cleanses from all sin"; negative, "without the shedding of blood there is no remission." (4) Positive, "He that loveth is born of God"; negative, "he that loveth not, let him be accursed." He that (believeth) is baptized shall be saved—but in all the sixty-six books of the Bible there is not one word that says that he that isn't baptized shall be damned. I defy my opponent to trot out one Scripture that says "He that is not baptized shall be damned."

Now watch my worthy opponent. He will come back and harp on Mark 16:16 and Acts 2:38 and will not answer these questions I have advanced and will not touch a large number of the Scriptures that I am going to quote. I was down to see Governor Graves one time and he had some pet squirrels in a cage. In that squirrel cage was a little squirrel and four or five steps. That little squirrel started around in that squirrel cage. He made that thing jiggle and jiggle. I never saw so much effort and so much wind and so much work and no body getting anywhere in my life. When the squirrel stopped, he was exactly where he started. My worthy opponent will get on these steps that you have heard him outline in his first speech—(which was a very good speech. He outlined his points well. I appreciate him giving me this material)—From now on—tonight and tomorrow night—he will run, hop, skip and jump and sweat and steam and work himself into a lather and all it will be will be on the same thing. And we will be exactly no place—if we follow my worthy opponent in his final speech tomorrow night—any farther than we are after his first speech tonight.

Now, J. W. McGarvey, one of the greatest preachers and authorities in the church of Christ in the past generation, he and every scholar on earth will tell you that Mark 16 from the ninth verse to the end of the chapter—the authorities in the church of Christ and every other scholar and your own Bible will have brackets around it—will tell you that that portion is not in the oldest and most reliable manuscripts.

Now since my worthy opponent takes this scripture in showing that you must be baptized to be saved he must take the following. Let me read: "He that believeth and is baptized shall be saved and he that believeth not shall be damned." If this applies in this age of the Holy Ghost which began according to my opponent at Pentecost this other is also for this whole age and "these signs shall follow them that believe. In my name shall they cast out devils. They shall speak with new tongues." I am going to ask my worthy opponent (1) whether he believes in speaking tongues. If he wants to take just part of the scripture let him cut out the part he does not want. Let him do it honestly. My friends, my worthy opponent rejects the balance of Mark. He will argue around it in every possible way. I want my worthy opponent to tell you whether he believes in speaking in tongues. If one is true, the other is true.

The next verse says, "They shall take up serpents and if they drink any deadly thing it will not hurt them. They shall lay hands on the sick and they shall recover." I want to ask my worthy opponent (2) to tell this crowd whether or not he will accept fully the scriptures and handles snakes. I want to ask him (3) if he believes in drinking poison. Now you can not take part of the scripture and not take all of it. I want him to explain that. Why does my worthy opponent wrest this verse from its context—only quoting part of the verse? Why is it that the churches of Christ so conveniently forget the verse that immediately precedes Mark 16:16, "Go ye into all the world and preach the gospel to every creature." And the church of Christ has the fewest missionaries and do the least missionary work; and it professes to believe that only by the preaching of the Word can men be saved; and yet it is the most lax in teaching the word around the world of any and all denominations in America! Let me ask my worthy opponent (4) to explain why he does not follow the fifteenth verse as well.. He places such great emphasis on the sixteenth and forgets to remember the fifteenth, seventeenth and eighteenth.

Listen my friends, are you going into all the world? My worthy opponent cuts out part of the scripture. He does not quote the whole verse. Is that fair? By this method I could prove by the Bible that there is no God. The Bible says so in plain unmistakable terms according to the logical procedure of my worthy opponent. But the portion in front of it, part of the same verse, says "The fool hath said in his heart, there is no God." And all the fools are not dead yet.

Keep this in mind. Here's one Scripture which says, "He that believeth and is baptized shall be saved, he that believeth not shall be damned." This is not in the oldest manuscripts and it is the only Scripture where baptism is thus placed with belief and the next word says, "He that believeth not shall be damned" and does not mention baptism; therefore my worthy opponent tells you salvation depends on baptism, and he bases it on doubtful authority.

Mark 16:16 does not show that baptism is essential to salvation. It does not read, "He that believeth and is not baptized shall be damned." This plainly tells the believer this is the condition of salvation—believing. He might as well add to believing other things such as "He that believeth and is baptized" takes the Lord's supper, attends church, brings his tithe shall be saved. That would still be true. Add all you want. It would not take a solitary thing away from the truth but lest people misunderstand, God said, "Wait a minute. It's a failure to believe that damns the man." Yes sir, I will make you that statement. It does not say the things that come after faith are necessary to salvation. The very fact that it says, "He that believeth not shall be damned," shows the one, prime essential.

Listen, if baptism is necessary to the soul's salvation do you think a great God would have left it out and have made the mistake of not saying, "He that believeth not and it not baptized shall be damned"? Our God loves men too much for that. Now my opponent said very plainly that a man—a believer—has to be baptized to be saved or that baptism is necessary to salvation. That's what he said. Now let's stop right there a moment. My opponent says that the penitent believer before he can be saved has to be baptized. The Roman Catholic Cathecisms of Christian Doctrine, No. 1, says—they give it to their children, compel them to study it—in this Cathecism you can find identically the same phrases and words that my worthy opponent uses when he says that a man has to be baptized in order to be saved. I want to get that clearly before us so that we will not have any dispute about what baptism means. Quoting now. (1) "Subject: Baptism. What is baptism? Baptism is a sacrament which cleanses us from original sin and makes us children of God and the church." (2) Roman Catholics) "Is baptism necessary to salvation? Baptism is absolutely necessary to salvation."

I want to ask my opponent a question. He makes the church and the kingdom synonomous and says they began at Pentecost and will end at the coming of Christ. My worthy opponent tells you that unless you are baptised into the church of Christ you are not going to be saved. Dismissing that phrase there are, my friends, some forty million people who believe in other modes than immersion—and I think every one of them ought to be baptized as an act of obedience by immersion; not in order to be saved but because they are saved! My worthy opponent declares that faith saves when it obeys the command of Jesus. That settles it. Even granting that my worthy opponent it right when he makes that statement, let's concede for arguments sake the following now: Faith obeys before baptism, because to confess Jesus is obedience. My opponent will concede that when one obeys, he confesses Jesus Christ. My opponent may say we must obey all the commands of faith to save. Well then what will follow? It follows—that if one must obey all the commands—that one is not saved even when he is baptized because there are many commands beside baptism. That's not all. If one must lead a perfect life before baptism saves him, my opponent's position— mark my word: my worthy opponent will probably not refer to this again (I know a multitude of good Methodists and Presbyterians. Their word would be accepted in any court and they have never been baptized by immersion. So would millions of others. According to the statement of my opponent and the Roman Catholics these forty million good Methodists and Presbyterians are bound for hell because my opponent has not baptized them)—baptism is necessary to salvation, he says. That's what the word essential means and I'm sure my worthy opponent will stand by his word. Now the burden is upon him.

It means, my friends, that Dwight L. Moody who was never immersed and was one of the world's greatest evangelists and soul winners—it means that Dwight L. Moody is in hell if my opponent is right in this debate. It means that John Wesley, the founder of Methodism, is in hell if my opponent is right. It means that John G. Paton, that great Presbyterian missionary to the New Hebrides where they ate men for breakfast, dinner and supper—he changed the whole country from cannabalism to

Christianity—it means he is in hell if my opponent is right. It means that Dr. James M. Gray, head of the Moody Bible Institute for so many years, is now in hell. He was never immersed. If baptism is essential to salvation, then babies are lost for they go astray speaking lies as soon as they are born, says Psalms 58:3. It means every soul who repents and turns to God on his death bed is lost if my opponent is right. It means that uncounted millions of saints of God who have been saved by the grace of God and have gone their way home to heaven from dying beds— that just because they have not been baptized according to my friend's plan—they're in hell now! Ladies and Gentlemen, God is not a God of vindictive and horrible judgement. Our God is a God who makes the way so plain that a wayfaring man though a fool need not err therein.

Now the second scripture my opponent introduced was Acts 2:38. Will my opponent take Acts 2:38? Again he deliberately did not read the rest of Acts 2:38. He only read part of it. I will show you time after time that his entire argument is always built on little phrases lifted out of their setting. You put it into its place and it falls to pieces. The rest of the verse reads, "And ye shall receive the gift of the Holy Ghost for the promise is unto you and to your children"—all Jews following you —"and to all afar off"—a scriptural term describing the Gentiles. For two nights my worthy opponent has been arguing that there is no direct influence of the Holy Spirit and now he accepts the first half of Acts 2:38 and does not even read the last half of it. I want him to read all the scripture in its context.

Now coming to this: I am going to be perfectly frank and tell you that this is one scripture where it may mean either way. Years ago I said, "God I want to be brutally honest so I can meet you without shame." Now I hope my worthy opponent will concede that. Let me read. "Then Peter said unto them, Repent and be baptized every one of you in the name of Jesus Christ for the remission of sins and ye shall receive the gift of the Holy Ghost." Now the whole thing hangs on a little preposition. The preposition is "eis"—e-i-s. "For" "Into" "Unto" With reference to. Every Greek scholar knows that it means two ways—one of two ways—and a possibility of a third way. First, in order to— that is necessary, essential for a definite purpose; or with reference to, the basis of, the ground of. It can mean two things:

(1) in order to; (2) or, with reference to, or on the basis of. I am going to be fair and say that it might mean either way. But this is not the only scripture on baptism. Peter tells us that no scripture is of any private interpretation, that is, it must be interpreted in the light of all the rest of the scripture. I will show you what I mean by saying the preposition "eis" may mean and does mean here "on account of" taking for example Matthew 26:28—"For this is my blood of the New Testament which is shed for many for the remission of sins." Therefore "eis" means in the first case "in order to," for Christ did not shed His blood on account of remission of sins but remission of sins comes because His blood was shed therefore this is the first meaning of the preposition. You take this next statement. I will read this. I want you to make it very plain—Matthew 10:41, "He that receiveth a prophet in the name of a prophet shall receive a prophet's reward. He that receiveth a righteousness man in the name of a righteous man shall receive a righteous man's reward." Now here is the second meaning: "In the name of a prophet" can not mean in order to a prophet but the reward comes on account of or because of the prophet.

I thank you.

THIRD NIGHT — PORTER'S SECOND SPEECH

Mr. President, Gentlemen Moderators, Respected Opponent, Ladies and Gentlemen:

I never felt better nor had less to do in my life than I have now facing me with respect to the speech which my opponent has just made. That was certainly a very fine appeal for prejudice and sympathy. Whenever a man finds himself cornered on a proposition and finds he can not meet the issue, then he begins to plead for sympathy and to stir up prejudice against his opponent by claiming he's going to send somebody to hell.

Well, the fact is there is only one theory that might be proclaimed that would not send somebody to hell and cause somebody to have prejudice against the advocate of it, and that's the theory of Universalism—that everybody is going to be saved. If that is what he wants in order to please everybody and keep everybody in a good humor, why, then, that's the thing that he should preach. Suppose that what I am preaching does send somebody to hell—that is, if it is true, somebody goes to hell who has not obeyed it. Would that make it not true because somebody goes to hell? How about that which my opponent preaches? Are we going to determine the truthfulness of a thing by whether it sends somebody to hell or by what the Bible says? What's the criterion? What's the standard, anyway, by which we are to judge this thing—whether somebody goes to hell as a result of it or whether the Bible teaches it?

According to the position of my friend Tingley tonight, there are millions going to hell who do not accept his doctrine, because, he says, "You must believe or you will go to hell." There are millions of people living now who do not believe, and they are good people, and their word would be accepted in courts, too. He has referred to Methodists having their word accepted in court, and all of that, and said, "According to what you preach, you send them to hell". There are men who do not believe in Christ whose word would be accepted in court, and whose word is a word of honor, and could be depended upon; but they do not believe in Christ. His theory sends them to hell. Well, if that means anything against me, it means just as much against him. If he wants to create prejudice instead of meeting the argument, that's his privilege; but I'm here to tell you what the Bible says.

I was amused at how my opponent met those arguments "head on". You know he said, concerning scriptures I introduced, he was going to meet them "head on"—he was not going to side-step any of them or go around them. He said, "I'll just meet every one of them head on." And when he made his lunge at them he missed the locomotive entirely and hit the coal tender, for he missed completely the very first argument I made—did not even refer to it.

My friend said the first argument was Mark 16:16. Everybody in this audience knows that my first argument was 1 Cor. 1:12-13, in which men said, "I am of Paul; and I of Apollos; and I of Cephas; and I of Christ." I challenge my opponent to come up and explain it and face it and tell us something about it. He did just like all the rest of them I have ever met have done. He saw the handwriting on the wall and passed it by. Men must be baptized in the name of Paul, and Paul must be crucified for them, in order to belong to Paul. Apollos must be crucified for men, and they must be baptized in his name, in order to belong to Apollos. Cephas must be crucified for men, and they must be baptized in the name of Cephas, in order to belong to Cephas. And Christ must be crucified for men, and they must be baptized in His name, in order to belong to Christ. Elder Tingley, didn't you hear that argument when I made it? Were you asleep when I made that? You said you were going to meet this thing "head on", and that was the very "head," and you missed it completely. He did not get within eleven hundred miles of it—didn't even mention it. Yet he was going to meet them "head on!" He was afraid of a head on collision, it looks like; so he side-stepped that one. And out of all the arguments I introduced, my opponent mentioned two of them. That's all! Mark 16:16 and Acts 2:38 are the only two that he even referred to during his thirty minute speech.

He was talking about a man running around in a squirrel cage. I wonder where he's going. Why, he said, "In that squirrel cage there were little steps, and the squirrel goes around and around and around." And these scriptures I have introduced on baptism are the steps in the squirrel cage. Well, bless your life, the last two nights of this debate he will not even have any steps to go in his squirrel cage, because he is going to affirm that salvation is by faith alone, and he can't even find one scripture that says anything that even resembles it. He will not have any steps for his squirrel cage. In fact, he will not even have any cage except that one he is in as a result of the arguments he has made, and he is going to stay in that one.

Now, then, he resolved a good long while ago that he was going to be brutally honest. I suppose he thinks I'm honestly brutal. (Laughter.) But I'm going to attend to him just the same and let him think what he pleases about it.

Now, we come to his questions. I was amused at my friend. Last night and night before he complained about my asking questions; and he said that when men ask question that shows that they are in desperation. Wonder where he is tonight! (Laughter.) "They are in desperation when they begin to ask a lot of questions." He asked more on this one paper than I asked on both of mine in two nights. Yet, when I asked them I was in desperation! I wonder where he is. What prompted him to ask them? Well, we are going to answer them.

"Do you believe that if a man believes, repents and is baptized, he shall be saved?" Yes—the salvation mentioned in my proposition.

Second. "Can such a believer who is saved so sin as to be lost?" Yes. Will you say he can not? Let my friend tell you tonight if he believes that a man can not so sin as to be lost. If a child of God dies drunk, will he go to heaven or hell? Now, you come up here and tell us. We will put him on the spot on that since he has introduced it.

"How can he be restored?" By meeting the requirements of the gospel. Acts 8:22.

Next: "Does he have to be baptized again?" No.

Next: "Are Methodists, Presbyterians and Pedo-Baptists lost and will they go to hell?" Another appeal for prejudice. Everybody who fails to obey the gospel of Jesus Christ will be lost, whether that is his Methodists, Baptists, Glenn V. Tingley, W. Curtis Porter or anybody else! We are depending upon the word of God for our proof. We are not resorting to the idea of how many will go to hell in order to see whether a proposition is true or not, but what the Bible says about it. That's our standard. When men can not meet the argument they resort to these things.

"Are Moody, Finney, Sankey, Billy Sunday, Wesley, Whitfield, Luther and all who have not been baptized by immersion lost and in hell?" The same answer as the preceding one. You could have put them both in one question.

"What baptism saves, the Church of Christ, Baptist or Christian and Missionary Alliance?" The baptism of the New Testament.

"Will you accept one whom I have baptized without rebaptizing him?" Not if you baptize him according to what you preach.

Next: "If baptism is essential to salvation, then are babies lost?" No! You remember, my friends, just before my opponent sat down he said, "Babies are lost if baptism is necessary to salvation." We are going to hand it back to him and just let him take the other end of it. My opponent says that faith is necessary to salvation. Then babies are lost, because they can not believe; and Tingley is in the same hole where he thought he had me. (Laughter.) Tingley says, "Babies are lost." Now, all you mothers who are thinking about the theory of Porter sending somebody to hell, just think about the theory of Tingley sending babies to hell because they can not believe. I do not believe they need any faith, baptism or anything else to go to heaven, because I do not believe they are lost to start with. But Tingley does. He sends babies to hell, by his theory, because they are in sin; they are little depraved devils and can not be saved because they can not believe. Now, that's the doctrine of Glenn V. Tingley. If you want to swallow it—line, hook, sinker and all—it's your privilege. My appetite does not run that way.

"Are those baptized by a Missionary Baptist or Christian and Missionary Alliance saved or doomed?" The administrator is not the thing that determines whether the baptism is scriptural, but if they are baptized according to what you preach, that is not New Testament baptism. That's all.

Again: "Show me one scripture which states that a man is lost if he is not baptized?" Luke 7:30 says those who rejected

John's baptism rejected the counsel of God; and 2 Thess. 1:7-9 says those who obey not the gospel will be punished with everlasting destruction. All right.

"Give me a scripture which states that a man who repents and believes on his death-bed and can not be baptized is lost." Well, I don't know of any passage that mentions any man on his death bed, but the scriptures show that a man must obey or be lost, whether he is on his death bed or wherever he is.

"A most important question I want my opponent to answer is to tell this crowd whether or not it is true that he believes that a person has no chance to be saved who is not baptized into his particular 'Church of Christ?" I have no particular church of Christ nor one that isn't particular. I have no church at all. But men must obey the gospel of Jesus Christ, as given by the Lord Himself in Mark 16:16, or they can not be saved.

"I challenge my worthy opponent to tell this audience why Paul did not baptize a new convert every time he believed." Well in Acts 18:8 we are told that "many of the Corinthians hearing, believed, and were baptized." Paul baptized only a few of them. Somebody else baptized the rest. The record says many of them were. How do you know that none of them were baptized?

Now, then, back to his speech. He came to what he called the first scripture, Mark 16:16, but that was not the first. Mark 16:16: "He that believeth and is baptized shall be saved." He said, "Porter read only a part of it." I deny the allegation and charge the "alligator." (Laughter.) The record will show—and it's on these records right here—that I quoted the entire verse. "He that believeth and is baptized shall be saved; but he that believeth not shall be damned." That can be played back to anybody that may want to hear it; and you will find out that it is so—that I quoted the entire verse.

He said, "I have been baptized, and I believe in baptism with all my heart." Well, we'll see how much of his heart is involved as we go along. Baptism, after all, you remember, is revealed in the word. Of course, the word can not reach his heart anyway, he said last night. I wonder how he believes in baptism with all his heart if the word can not reach his heart. It's through the word that he finds out about baptism; it's the word that commands baptism; and faith comes by hearing the word; but the word can not reach his heart. So how's he going to believe it with his heart if the word never reaches his heart? Would you tell us about that, Mr. Tingley, in your next speech? "I'm dying to know!"

"But salvation here has no comparison with a Ford," he said. Well, I guess not. He put the Ford above salvation, because he would do what Henry Ford would say about being baptized to get a Ford; but he will not do what the Lord said to get salvation. If Ford would say, "He that believeth and is baptized shall get a new Ford," he says, "I would do that. Yes, sir." He said, "I would be one of the first men to get wet because I'm concerned about a new Ford." But when the Lord said, "He that believeth and is baptized shall be saved," he said, "Oh well, that's all right; I'll get the salvation in spite of whether I'm baptized or not. If I am baptized, it will not keep me from getting the salvation, but I'll get it anyway." But, of course, he would know that Ford would not give the Ford to him unless he met all of the requirements. He would not take a chance on missing the Ford, you see; but he would take a chance on missing salvation. So there's no comparison between the Ford and salvation. I believe that salvation is greater and worth a greater effort than a Ford. Elder Tingley would do more to get the Ford than he would salvation! So it's just a matter of which you put on the upper plane. That's all.

But the rest of the verse says, "He that believeth not shall be damned." It did not say, "He that believeth not and is not baptized shall be damned." No. I know it did not. If it had, it would have been silly. Suppose that some of you teachers who have a class in school, would give your class this statement tomorrow: "He that eats food and digests it shall have health." You require the class to bring the negative of that on the following day. The next day Johnnie comes back with this: "He that eats food and digests it shall have health; but he that eats no food and does not digest it shall starve." I wonder what kind of grade little Johnnie would get on that? What kind of grade would you give him, Elder Tingley, if you were his teacher? "He that eats food and digests it shall have health; he that eats no food and does not digest it shall starve!" What's the person going to get, Elder Tingley? Would you give him 100% on that? What kind of grade would you give him? Why, that's silly—

the very idea of digesting food that you haven't eaten. Let me tell you, my friends, the man who has not believed can no more be scripturally baptized than a man can digest food that he has not eaten. Not any more. They are parallel. It takes both eating the food and the digesting the food to bring health; but eating no food alone will bring starvation; and you do not have to say, "And does not digest it." It takes both belief and baptism to bring the salvation; but unbelief alone will bring the damnation; and you do not have to say, "And is not baptized". It would be silly if you did. That's the way he hits it "head on," and when he hit it "head on," he hit it in a hard spot, didn't he?

But the scripture says, "He that believeth and is baptized shall be saved." "Now," he says, that does not say that he shall be saved if he does not backslide, but it says he shall be saved. Friend Tingley, why didn't you read the rest of the verse? "He that believeth not shall be damned." The "shall be damned" is just as forceful and just as emphatic as the "shall be saved." If the statement, "He that believeth and is baptized shall be saved," means the man who does that will go to heaven in spite of everything—that he can not ever become an unbeliever and be lost, then, when the rest of the verse says, "He that believeth not shall be damned," that means he never can become a believer and be saved. One is just as emphatic, one is just as strong, as the other. "Shall be saved"—"Shall de damned." Do you believe the rest of it? The unbeliever shall be damned? And that means he never can be saved, that he is doomed forever? No chance of his becoming a believer, because it says, "He shall be damned." If "shall be saved" means saved in heaven, "shall be damned" means lost in hell!

Then he introduced a few scriptures on faith. John 3:16—Believe on the Lord that you may everlasting life. "No baptisim there." Yes, and no prayer there either, Elder Tingley.

John 3:36—"He that believeth not shall not see life." And the American Revised Version reads, "He that obeyeth not shall not see life."

John 5:24 and Rom. 5:1—"Hath life and is justified." That's the believer, you see. And 1 Peter 1:9—the end of faith is salvation. All of these ascribe salvation to faith. Not a one of them says anything about faith only. That's the thing he will have to try to find the last two nights; and all those will come up for investigation again.

1 John 5:1—the believer is born of God. Yes, and 1 John 4:7 says, "He that loveth is born of God," and that is not faith alone. 1 John 2:29 says, "He that doeth righteousness is born of God." Are there three births—one by faith, another by love, and another by doing righteousness? Or does it take all of these to bring about the one birth? Wonder if he will tell us?

He said, "All believers should be baptized to enjoy the privileges of the Christian life." Now, if you have not been baptized, you can not enjoy the privileges of the Christian life. Saved all right, a child of God, but you can not enjoy the privileges of a Christian life unless you are baptized! You should be baptized that you might enjoy those privileges. You can't do it unless you are baptized, according to my friend Tingley. Well, that's slipping some. He's scooting a little bit. He may get to the truth after awhile.

Then to his train proposition. "He that enters a train and sits down shall go to Atlanta." I want to put that on the board just here if I can in a minute. Here we have it: "Enters the train (marking "E" on board) and sits down (marking "SD" on board) and goes to Atlanta (marking "A" on board)." He that believeth (marking B on board) and is baptized (marking another B on board) shall be saved (marking S on board)."

(Blackboard)
Enters train—Sits down—Reaches Atlanta
Believeth—Is Baptized—Shall be Saved

He makes belief equal to entering the train; and being baptized equivalent to sitting down; reaching salvation equivalent to reaching Atlanta. Since the man who "enters the train" can "reach Atlanta" without "sitting down," so the man who "believes" can "reach salvation" without "being baptized." "Sitting down" is not necessary in "reaching Atlanta"; "being baptized," therefore, is not necessary in "reaching salvation." So we cross them out. (Marking "Sits down" and "Is baptized" off the board). Entering the train is the thing necessary to reach Atlanta. My friend, did you know that I could go to Atlanta without "entering the train?" Didn't you know that

I could go to Atlanta without entering a train?" Why I could walk or go in an automobile. There are a dozen ways I could go to Atlanta without "entering a train." So "entering the train" is not essential to going to Atlanta. We'll cross that out (Marking off "Enters train"). And since faith is equivalent to it, we cross that out too (Crossing out "Believeth"). So we do not have to believe or be baptized either to get salvation, according to his illustration.

Then, we look at it from another angle. "He that enters the train and sits down shall reach Atlanta." The "sitting down" is not necessary. "He that believeth and is baptized shall be saved." The "baptism" is not necessary. But in order for it to fit my opponent's theory, since he says "He that believeth is already saved," it should say, "He that enters the train reaches Atlanta before he has time to sit down." (Laughter). "He that believeth is saved before he has time to be baptized." Is that so, Tingley? That's your position, isn't it? "He that believeth is saved before he has time to be baptized." So "He that enters the train is already in Atlanta before he has time to sit down." (Laughter). Now, I know anybody can see that. You may not accept it, but you can see it. I'm just certain of that.

He comes, then, to the matter of verses 9 to 20—that all the scholars say that this is not in some of the oldest manuscripts. (Verses 9 to 20 of Mark 16). Friend Tingley, I want to ask you this question—I wish you would tell me in your next speech: Do you accept Mark 16:9-20 as the word of God? Put it down and tell me about it. Do you accept Mark 16:9-20 as the word of God? He said that's not in some of the old manuscripts, but the very same manuscript that leaves it out leaves out the entire book of Revelation, where he goes to get his thousand year reign. It leaves out a lot of other parts, too, if that's the way he is going to deal with it. So we wait to see what he will say about it. He's a Fundamentalist, but here he is rejecting the scriptures; setting aside all of these closing verses of Mark 16: because he can not meet the issue. That's the easiest way out of it—turn infidel and get rid of it.

Then, he was speaking about missionary work and talking about the Church of Christ being the most lax of all people in missionary work, which is required in Mark 16:15. Well, the fact is we do not advertise our missionary work, and friend Tingley knows nothing about it. We have one church today—the Broadway church in Lubbock, Texas—that is sponsoring forty missionaries to Europe! And $160,000 is being spent in the effort. What do you know about what the Church of Christ is doing? Nothing! Just as you know nothing about what the Bible teaches on the plan of salvation.

Then, he said this theory that I am preaching is Roman Catholicism—"you must be baptized to be saved." He said, "The Roman Catholics believe that." Well, suppose they do. The Roman Catholics also believe that little babies are born depraved, just like you said awhile ago. And Roman Catholics also believe in a direct revelation, just like you have been preaching the past two nights. And Roman Catholics believe in working signs and miracles, just like you are claiming. And so I have three to your one. What difference does that make?

Then to Acts 2:38. Here he said again, "Porter did not read all of the verse." If some of you want to go tomorrow and hear the record played, you can see whether I read all of the verse. "Repent, and be baptized everyone of you in the name of Jesus Christ for the remission of sins, and ye shall receive the gift of the Holy Ghost." He said, "You did not read the rest of it—"And ye shall receive the gift of the Holy Ghost." Yes, I did. The record will show it. And furthermore, Tingley is the man who rejects it because he says, "The man who repents and is baptized has already received the gift of the Holy Ghost." That's what he has been contending for the past two nights, but this says "ye shall receive it as a result of it." So he's the man who rejects the rest of the verse.

Then to the Greek word "eis." He said, "Used to mean in order to and with reference to." In Matt. 26:28 he says they would receive remission because of the sacrifice that Christ made. Yes, that's true. And in Acts 2:38 they would receive the remission of sins because of the compliance with the condition of repentance and baptism. Now, my friend indicated that the little Greek word "eis" means "because of". I want to ask you, Friend Tingley, is there a translation on earth that translates Acts 2:38 "because of" for the little Greek word "eis"? If so, I want to read it. I gave you some awhile ago that translate it "in order to obtain," "that you may have," and things of that kind.

I want to read the translation that says "because of." If he has it, let him produce it. I want to see it.

And then again, "With reference to." Yes, it sometimes means "with reference to," but does "with reference to" mean you already have it? Why, my brethren wrote me "with reference to" this debate. That did not mean the debate was already over. Not at all. Some of you will go down tomorrow to talk to your employer "with reference to" your salary. That does not mean that he has paid you everything that you are ever going to get, because you talk to him with reference to it. "With reference to" does not mean "because of," that you already have it; so that's simply his assertion along that line.

That covers his speech, and if I have just a few more minutes I want to get back and call attention to some things . . .

Mr. Nichols: About four minutes.

Mr. Porter: About four minutes. All right; that will be just fine. Back now to some of these arguments which I gave.

Remember 1 Cor. 1:12-13. Friend Tingley, that was the first on the list. Please do not forget it as you make the head on collision in your final speech. Let's have something about it. Give your self a tangle with that. Butt right into it. A man must be baptized in the name of Paul to belong to Paul. He must be baptized in the name of Christ to belong to Christ. Let him meet it if he can—head on, or any other way.

Then, I gave you also the statement made in 1 Peter 3:21—"Baptism doth now save us." And my friend says, "Baptism doth not save us." I asked him: Will you erase from the board, when you come to your speech, the statement that you do not believe? He promised definitely and faithfully and "brutally honestly" that he would erase from the board the statement that he did not believe. It's still on there. I'm waiting for him to erase it.

> (Blackboard)
> Baptism doth now save us.
> Baptism doth not save us.

Friend Tingley, Peter said, "Baptism doth now save us." 1 Peter 3:21. You do not have to take my word for it. Go home tonight and get your Bibles. Turn to 1 Peter 3:21 and read it for yourself. "Baptism doth now save us." My opponent says, "Baptism doth not save us." I'm still calling upon him to erase from the board the statement that he does not believe. He has made us a promise that he will do it. It's up to him to fulfill his promise.

I also gave Galatians 3:26-27 about being baptized into Christ, and about men being the sons of God by faith, because they had been baptized into Christ. Not a word did my opponent say about it.

I gave Acts 9:6 where Saul was told, "You go to Damascus and there it shall be told you what you must do." I pleaded with my opponent to tell me what was told Saul that he must do. He has not told us yet. If he does not tell us in the next speech, I will tell you tomorrow night. I am waiting for him to tell us. What was told Saul that he must do? It was something, the Lord said. "When you get to the city, it will be told thee what thou must do." I am wondering what it is. You tell this audience what it was that was told him when he got to Damascus. Something that he must do. The Lord said it would be something; so we want to find out about it—just what it was that he must do.

And, thus, we see these passages stand. My friend has not disturbed them in the least. They are right here just as well as when we began and when I introduced them awhile ago in my first speech. "Baptism is for the remission of sins," Peter says. Jesus said, "He that believeth and is baptized shall be saved." Peter said, "The like figure whereunto even baptism doth also now save us." And Paul said, "As many of you as have been baptized into Christ have put on Christ." And furthermore, that Christ must be crucified for you, and you must be baptized in His name, in order to belong to Christ. Can a man belong to Christ and not be a Christian? Can he be a Christtian and not belong to Christ? We want to know about it. Does a man get salvation and still not belong to Christ? He can not get salvation until he is baptized in the name of Christ because he can not belong to Christ, he can not be of Christ, until he has been baptized in the name of Christ.

My friend predicted awhile ago that I would not answer his questions; that I would pass all his arguments by. I thought he had learned Porter better than that by this time. I am certainly not here to dodge anything that he introduces. In fact, there is not a sectarian preacher on earth that can give an argument in favor of his doctrine that I'm afraid to meet. And I'm here to meet everything that he introduces. And we're waiting for that "head on" collision with 1 Cor. 1:12-13.

Thank you.

THIRD NIGHT—TINGLEY'S SECOND SPEECH

Mr. Chairman, Gentlemen Moderators, Worthy Opponent, Ladies and Gentlemen:

I have my Bible open at I Corinthians the first chapter. Again my worthy opponent does not read all of the scripture; he takes it completely out of its setting and does not read the balance of the scriptures in First Corinthians. Let me read it, all of it, the part he read and the part he didn't read. "For it hath been declared unto me of you, my brethren by them which are of the house of Chloe, that there are contentions among you. Now this I say, that every one of you saith, I am Paul; and I of Apollos; and I of Cephas; and I of Christ. Is Christ divided? was Paul crucified for you? or were ye baptized in the name of Paul? I thank God that I baptized none of you, but Crispus and Gaius; Lest any should say that I had baptized in mine own name. And I baptized also the household of Stephanas: besides, I know not whether I baptized any other. For Christ sent me not to baptize, but to preach the gospel not with wisdom of words, lest the cross of Christ should be made of none effect." That is the portion he omitted—the last of it—"the preaching of the cross is to them that perish foolishness but unto us which are saved it is thhe power of God."

This is the first time that I have ever had an opponent try to prepare the way for that which my worthy opponent does not want to answer at all. Why did Paul positively say God sent him not to baptize but to preach? Note please, in this division that was in the church of Corinth various ones were saying: we belong to the school of Peter, we follow Paul, we follow Apollos and others saying, "Well we are just following Christ." Then the Apostle Paul says, "Is Christ divided? Is there any division in Christ. All ought to belong to Christ. Was Paul crucified for you? were you baptized in the name of Paul? I thank God I baptized none of you."

Now, ladies and gentlemen, why was it the Apostle Paul did not baptize but very few? You say well perhaps Paul was not the one that led them to Christ, but in I Corinthians 4:15 he says for "in Christ Jesus I have begotten you through the gospel." The word translated "begotten" is the same word translated "born" in John 3:5 and in other places. It's the word that means the new birth! Paul said, "I have begotten you through the gospel" and then he says of these he had begotten, "I thank God I baptized none of you but a few, for my mission is not to baptize, my mission is to preach the gospel."

"My worthy opponent said last night he was a preacher following in the footstep of Paul, preaching the gospel of Christ. Then my worthy opponent is sent not to baptize but to preach the gospel and he ought to thank God he doesn't baptize but a very few—if he is going to follow this method of reason. Now how is it that he begot all of them, caused all of them to be born again when he did not baptize them. If baptism is necessary to the new birth, and Paul begot them or caused all of them to be born again, then he would be under necessity of baptizing all of them, but he did not baptize any of them except a few mentioned. Therefore, it follows that baptism has no part with the new birth. It won't do any good to say that others baptized them. Paul said he begot all of them but he did not baptize all of them. He did not say that he helped others to beget them, he said he did it himself—all of them were born again by him—a very few were baptized by him and he thanked God that he didn't baptize the rest of them. Yet all of them were born again. My worthy opponent says, "You can't be born again unless you are baptized." Then Paul and my worthy opponent differ. Paul begot them, my worthy opponent says that to beget them they would have to be baptized. Paul says that he htanks God that he didn't baptize them.

What is the mission of the church? Paul says, "He sent me not to baptize but to preach the gospel not with wisdom of words lest the cross of Christ should be made of none effect." The Apostle Paul was not sent to baptize, no minister is sent to baptize. He is sent to preach the gospel. We are preachers of grace. The Apostle Paul was sent not to baptize but to preach not with words of wisdom lest the cross of Christ should be made of none effect. The Apostle Paul was sent to preach the gospel of Christ. They would not accept him in the Church of Christ as a minister of that church today because he was not sent to baptize. You see, Paul was saved after Pentecost. Paul was saved before he was baptized. Paul was the Apostle of grace. Paul was the minister to the Gentiles. Yet the Apostle Paul says that Christ sent him not to baptize but to preach the gospel. Here's the outstanding New Testament preacher who thanks

God that he doesn't baptize many people. "Not with wisdom of words lest the cross of Christ should be made of none effect." It is belief in the Christ of Calvary and not in baptism that saves, it is belief not in the wisdom of words, not in baptism but in the atoning work of Jesus Christ that saves. That answers his first argument.

Back to Acts 2:38—"Then Peter says unto them, Repent, and be baptized every one of you in the name of Jesus Christ for the remission of sins, and ye shall receive the gift of the Holy Ghost." I said it all hinged on a little preposition in Greek, "eis." It could be translated "in reference to," or "because of," or "in order to." Now, listen to this. Notice Matt. 12:41—"The men of Nineveh shall rise in judgment with this generation, and shall condemn it: because they repented at the preaching of Jonas and, behold a greater than Jonas is here." They repented "eis"—in order to Jonas preaching? No. But because of the preaching of Jonas. Not "in order to" Jonas preaching, but "because of" Jonas preaching. There it is translated "because of." Here it is impossible to take "eis" other than on the basis of or occasion of the repenting. Notice again, Acts 2:38—two verbs. My worthy opponent knows grammar, so he knows the two verbs "repent and be baptized" are tied together by the conjunction. The word "repent" is in the second person, plural number, therefore it is a direct, unequivocal command—repent is a command in the Greek and the Greek "be baptized" is in the third person, singular number. Now get this further: the command to repent is in the second person, plural number—everybody should repent. And here when we come to be baptized it changes completely in the original, though the King James does not show the translation clearly in the change, it is changed to the third person, singular number. My worthy opponent knows grammar, he knows the verb must agree with the subject in number and person. Therefore the two verbs repent and be baptized can not be joined to the same predicate, therefore I am going to read you just exactly as the original language gives it to us. I want you to get this and keep it in your mind. The word repent is second person plural, be baptized is third person singular. Therefore it means this, the correct rendering "ye"—plural; "all of you"—plural; "repent and let everyone of you"—individually, singular, "be baptized for the remission of sins." Repentance is unto life and when we repent and we receive life then everyone who by repenting receives life, on the basis of life he receives by repentance is to be baptized. We will interpret it in the light of all the balance of scriptures on baptism. We can not take one scripture out of its setting and make it mean a certain thing contradictory to all the rest of the scriptures.

The Greek preposition eis—"into" or "unto" according to Thayer's Greeek Lexicon—the highest authority in the world—says that it means "into" when the idea of place is meant, but when the idea of relation is meant it means "with reference to." Most certainly in salvation the idea of relation is expressed. Take an illustration, Congress gives a man a medal for his bravery on the field of battle which has been the custom for a long time. Does Congress give him the medal in order for him to be brave in the future? No, because he has already been brave, so in the case of baptism. Repent for the remission of sin, a person is baptized because he is already saved. Now, for instance, simple labor, common ordinary day trade. A day laborer works for $50 a week. He is paid for the work he has done, not in order to work in the future. He is paid because he has already worked. Therefore, a man is baptized because he has been saved not in order to be saved. A man is electrocuted for murder, not in order to commit murder, but because he has already committed murder. Same word—we are baptized "for remission sins." Not "in order to be remitted or forgiven" but because they are remitted and forgiven.

Now in I Peter 3:21, he wants me to do some erasing. I will. I certainly will. I will be very happy to erase. (Erases bottom line from blackboard.

(Blackboard)
Baptism doth now save us
Baptism doth not save us
(Line remaining on blackboard:)
Baptism doth now save us not

But again my worthy opponent leaves out the scriptures and the next word here is "Not". (Adding word "Not" to line remaining on blackboard). Look in your Bible and see if it isn't (Laughter). And on that hinges it all. He deliberately leaves it out. On purpose he leaves it out to confuse men and women who are hungry to know the way of God. "Baptism doth also save us not"—does what? I will read it to you, "The like figure whereunto even baptism doth also now save us (not the putting away of the filth of the flesh, but the answer of a good conscience toward God) by the resurrection of Jesus Christ." (Laughter). Now I would suggest to you that here's one preacher you can't back down. Alexander Campbell, the founder of the Church of Christ on the design of baptism, declares that baptism is emblematic. Here's Campbell's exact language, page 262 in Campbell on Baptism, and "Peter after having said," quoting now, "that baptism doth save us immediately adds that it is not the putting away of the filth of the flesh but the answer of a good conscience toward Good which proceeds from faith. But on the contrary Baptism promises us no other purification than that by the sprinkling of the blood of Christ." Alexander Campbell said, "Baptism promises us no other purification than that by the sprinkling of the blood of Christ. Which is emblematically represented by water on account of its resemblance to washing and cleansing." On page 273 of the same address, Campbell said, "The like figure corresponding where unto baptism doth also save us not indeed that there is anything in the mere element of water or in the form of placing the subject in it or in the formula used upon the occasion though both good taste and piety have come to do with the particulars but all its virtue and efficacy is in the faith and intelligence of him that receives it." "The like figure whereunto even baptism doth also save us not the putting away the filth of the flesh—the washing of the outside by baptism." Not that. "But the answer of a good conscience toward God by the resurrection of Jesus Christ."

Now there my friend says is a baptism that saves based on Noah. Noah was saved a long time before the flood by the grace of God. Noah found favor—grace—in the eyes of the Lord. He didn't have to be saved by anybody's baptism. It states specifically "not the putting away of the filth of the flesh." It's not an outside washing, it's not any external matter that saves a man. The Holy Spirit put in the explanation lest people have ground for false doctrine that sends souls into hell. And the Holy Spirit makes it plain what he says. There is no cleansing, no separation, no forgiveness of sin in putting away the filth of the flesh by outward washing. That is what that phrase means

—emblematic, ceremonial. Let the scriptures speak. Rom. 3:20 —"Therefore by the deeds of the law shall no flesh be justified in his sight."

In II Corinthians 7:1—"Having therefore these promises, dearly beloved, let us cleanse ourselves from all filthiness of the flesh and spirit, perfecting holiness in the fear of God." "Let us cleanse ourselves from all filth and sin of the flesh." Therefore, baptism means not the putting away of sin, baptism is not the remission of sin it is not essential to salvation—"the like figure whereunto even the baptism does also doth save us" but how? Not in the forgiveness of your sins. How? He tells us what it is. He gives us the answer. Listen to this. What is the purpose of baptism? He says what it is not and, second, he gives the affirmative he tells what it is. What baptism is not and what it is. The very scripture my opponent tells us means that baptism is essential to salvation tells us these two things: (1) what baptism is not (2) and what it is. First it tells us negatively, and, second, affirmatively. Why does the Lord thus say it negatively and then affirmatively? Because he knew that beginning with the Roman Catholic Church and coming on down to the days of my opponent men would try to deny the blood atonement of Christ by adding baptism as necessary to salvation. Now we are getting down to the foundation of matters.

Coming back to first Peter my opponent wants me to answer first, baptism is not the putting away the filth of the flesh; that is, not the forgiveness of sin. Second, he gives the affirmative answer, "What does save us"? "But the answer of a good conscience toward God" to do what? "By the resurrection" "with reference to the resurrection"—that is what it means in the original Greek "with reference to the resurrection of Jesus Christ." Now when I believed in Christ, walked down into the watery grave, was buried in the likeness of his death, raised in the likeness of His resurrection, my conscience tells me that I am satisfied. I've seen the Lord on the cross, I declared him to the world in the act of baptism—that's what it means—a figure of salvation and it is not salvation but it is wrought by the resurrection of Jesus Christ.

Let me again—notice please, again, "the like figure." Baptism is a figure "whereunto"—what figure? "Baptism." What is it a figure of? A figure of salvation unless some thus misinterpret it. It is not putting away filth of the flesh in the act of baptism that saves, it is the fact that there is the answer of a good conscience and the power of salvation is the resurrection of Jesus Christ the living Lord. If "confess with the mouth and believe in my heart that God hath raised him from the dead I shall be saved." And I confess that faith in Christ by entering the waters of baptism. I am baptized, that is the outward washing, it is the figure of what has already transpired within me. "Baptism doth also now save us not the putting away." I beg this audience, when you go home, read that carefully with your Bible opened over and over reading it asking God to show you the meaning of His word.

He asked me for Galatians 3:27. He said, "If you are not baptized you are not Christ." Well, my worthy opponent again does not read the verses around it. He only reads in the direction that he can seem to make a point out of. I read before and after. Again he leaves out before. What does the verse just before say? "For ye are all the children of God by faith in Christ Jesus." Now Jamison, Faucett and Brown says, "Ye did in that very act being baptized into Christ put on or cloth yourselves with Christ." That's what the Greek says.

When I was a lad in knee pants I wanted to get on long pants. There has always been a certain age—approximately at the age of 12—according to Roman custom it was at the age of 12. The ceremony went on in the Roman home and the boy put on a Toga Virilis—exactly the word here. He put on a man's clothes when he was a man. And the whole scriptures says, "For ye are all the children of God by faith in Christ Jesus." That's the way to become a child of God—by faith. After you become a child of God, what ought you to do? You ought to follow him in baptism and you ought to grow up and put on, grow up into Christ putting on Christ—the Toga Virilis. That Roman garment was a garment of a full grown man. Listen, Verse 24 and 25, "Wherefore the law was our school master to bring us to Christ that we might be justified by faith. But after that faith is come we are no longer under the law." The law brings us up to Christ, the law leaves us in the presence of Christ. We have faith in Him and we become children of God by faith, and then we are baptized and grow up to know Jesus Christ, is exactly what it says. Now you have the responsibility—you who have been baptized—the responsibility of manhood in Christ. Labor for Him, rightly represent Him—that is a common phrase used in scripture. I Thessalonians 5:8—"But let us, who are of the day, be sober, putting on the breastplate of faith and love; and for an helmet, the hope of salvation." Epesians 6:11—"Put on the whole armour of God, that ye may be able to stand against the wiles of the devil."

My worthy opponent is very excited about Paul. I am very thankful that I have time to get to Paul. Acts 22:6-10—the Apostle Paul was born again when he had faith in Jesus as Lord. That was 3 days before he was baptized. I will prove it beyond the shadow of a doubt. "And it came to pass, that, as I made my journey, and was come nigh unto Damascus about noon, suddenly there shone from heaven a great light round about me. And I fell unto the ground, and I heard a voice saying unto me, Saul, Saul, why persecutest thou me? And I answered, Who art thou, Lord? And he said unto me, I am Jesus of Nazareth, whom thou persecutest. And they that were with me saw indeed the light, and were afraid; but they heard not the voice of him that spake to me. And I said, What shall I do, Lord? And the Lord said unto me, Arise, and go into Damascus; and there it shall be told thee of all things which are appointed for thee to do." When was the Apostle Paul born again? When he saw the Lord and accepted Jesus as his Savior, believed on him as Lord or when he was baptized? Which? Now listen, that is the entire question of the debate. I hinge the debate on this one instance, as well as any of the others that we have dealt with. If Paul was saved when he saw the Lord then my worthy opponent's position is untenable and the millions of unimmersed believers in Christ are saved and all who believed in Christ, but who have not been baptized by the Church of Christ ministers are saved as well. (Incidentally, Ladies and Gentlemen, some of you Baptists try to join the Church of Christ and see if they will accept your baptism. My worthy opponent begs the question and will not face the facts and everyone of you know that's so.) But if the Apostle Paul was not saved until he was baptized then I am wrong. And everyone of the millions who believed in Christ but who have not been immersed are damned, and the only hope for any of us is to get into the Church of Christ and be baptized and have our sins washed away. Listen, the most competent person in the world to answer this question is the Apostle Paul and he answers that question completely and entirely in I Corinthians 15:8—"And last of all he was seen of me also, as of one born out of due time." Listen, when was Paul saved? Was he lost or saved between the seeing of the Lord and baptism? He believed and three days after he was baptized. I want my opponent to tell this audience during these three days time between the time be believed and the time he was baptized was he saved or lost? My opponent said Paul heard and believed. Now listen, let him tell this audience, between the time he saw the Lord and believed and the time he was baptized was three days, let my opponent tell you what Paul was in those three days—saved or lost. Listen, what does this mean I Corinthians 15:8—"And last of all he was seen of me also, as of one born out of due time." It means the following wonderful facts, first the fact of his new birth, second that he was born again when he saw the Lord. "Last of all he was seen of me as of one born out of due time." It was the one person seeing another person the person—Saul of Tarsus seeing the person of the Son of God. He saw the Lord when he said, "Who art thou, Lord?" He saw the Lord three days before he was baptized. He was born again three days before he was baptized for he says that he was born again when he saw the Lord. Therefore, Paul's baptism was not essential to his new birth or to his salvation. Listen, my friends, when Paul said, "Lord, Lord, who art thou, Lord?" Jesus said, "I am Jesus." That moment he believed. A believer is saved.

Let me pause just a moment and take the balance of this time for my worthy opponent's interest tomorrow night. I draw a line straight down the blackboard and I put believers in God, unbelievers in God; Lovers of God, Haters of God; Followers of God, Disobedient to God.

(Blackboard

Unbelievers	Believers
Haters	Lovers
Disobedient	Followers

What crowd is to be baptized? This crowd right here (Pointing to first column on board). And yet the Bible says believers in God are saved, the Bible says lovers of God are saved, the Bible says followers of God are saved—everyone of these are saved. And this is the crowd he believes and I believe ought to be baptized—only he says believing, obeying if you cannot get to the baptismal pool right away——loving, following, believing does no good—a man is lost if he is not baptized. One further word. If any individual here tonight can see any of these ministers of the Church of Christ and says, "I believe in Jesus Christ and I want to be baptized," there will be some time elapse before you are baptized. Suppose you die before then. Will that minister of the Church of Christ consign you to hell? Ladies and gentlemen, these are most serious issues. Believers, lovers of God, followers of Christ the Bible says are saved. May God bless you and I thank you.

PORTER-TINGLEY DEBATE

Fourth Session: 7:30 P. M., February 27, 1947

Birmingham Gospel Tabernacle — Birmingham, Alabama

Chairman: Emerson J. Estes — Birmingham, Alabama

Introductory Announcements and Welcome to Visitors: Dr. Glenn V. Tingley, pastor of the Tabernacle.

Singing Directed by: Lowell Leistner — Birmingham, Alabama

Prayer: R. W. Conner — Birmingham, Alabama

Moderators: Gus Nichols, Jasper, Alabama, for Mr. Porter; Walter Hemingway, Bessemer, Alabama, for Mr. Tingley.

Proposition: The Scriptures Teach that Water Baptism to a Penitent Believer of the Gospel is Essential to Salvation From Alien Sins.

W. Curtis Porter, Affirms

Glenn V. Tingley, Denies

(Affirmative Address by W. Curtis Porter)

Mr. President, Gentlemen Moderators, Respected Opponent, Ladies and Gentlemen:

I come before you again to affirm the proposition which was under discussion last evening, and which has just been read in your hearing, that the scriptures teach that water baptism to a penitent believer of the gospel is essential to salvation from alien sins. Of course, the proposition just simply resolves itself into this: Is water baptism a condition of salvation from sin? I affirm that it is, and Mr. Tingley denies. And so that's the issue that's between us on this proposition tonight.

I introduced a number of affirmatives on my proposition last evening. I have just a few more that I want to introduce now, and then I shall go back to the things that have been introduced before, and reply to the things which my opponent said in his closing speech last night, and notice again some of those arguments introduced in support of the proposition, that we might keep before you just the things that are revealed in God's eternal word.

My next argument in proof of the proposition is found in the statement made by the apostle Paul in the sixth chapter of Romans, verses 3 and 4. Here the apostle said, "Know ye not that so many of us as were baptized into Jesus Christ were baptized into his death? Therefore we are buried with him by baptism into death: that like as Christ was raised up from the dead by the glory of the Father, even so we also should walk in newness of life." Now, note that the statement made here by the inspired apostle is to the effect that men are baptized into Jesus Christ and that they also are baptized into His death. I submit to you tonight the fact that if men can be saved without baptism, they can be saved out of Christ, because in this passage, as well as in another given last evening, Paul declares that men are baptized into Christ. I would like for my friend to tell me tonight whether men can be saved out of Christ. If men cannot be saved out of Christ, then they can not be saved without baptism, because Paul says baptism puts men into Christ. Not only so, but we also note that it was in the death of Jesus Christ that His blood was shed and that the blood of Jesus Christ cleanses us from all sins. We must, therefore, contact that blood to receive the benefits of the blood. Since the blood was shed in His death, we must reach the death of Jesus to share its benefits. The third verse of the passage introduced says we are "baptized into His death." We reach the death of Jesus Christ when we are baptized, not before we are baptized, and thus reach His blood and the benefits of His blood. Since we are baptized into the death of Christ, and thus into the blood of Christ, then I insist that baptism is essential to the forgiveness of sins which is made possible by the blood of the Son of God.

Then, too, this passage shows that we walk in the newness of life, or that the new life comes, after the baptism. Note that it says in verse 4, "Therefore we are buried with him by baptism into death: that like as Christ was raised up from the dead by the glory of the Father, even so we also should walk in newness of life." Here is a burial and a resurrection, Paul says. As Christ was raised from the dead, so we are raised to walk in newness of life. The newness of life, of course, is the spiritual life or condition in which there is forgiveness of sins; and we walk that newness of life after we are baptized—not before. According to the position of my friend Tingley, we walk the new life before baptism, but Paul says, "We are raised to walk in newness of life."

The next argument will be based upon a statement made by the apostle Paul in Col. 2:11-13. I desire to turn and read this passage from the pen of the inspired writer in which he tells us something more about what is accomplished in baptism. The apostle Paul is the writer upon this occasion, and he says, "In whom," referring to Christ, "also ye are circumcised with the circumcision made without hands, in putting off the body of the sins of the flesh by the circumcision of Christ." Now, here is something referred to as "the circumcision of Christ"—an operation which God performs; therefore, an operation made without hands. And this operation is the cutting loose of the sins of the flesh, or the putting off the body of the sins of the flesh. I ask how and when and where is that accomplished? When does God cut loose the body of the sins of the flesh? When does that circumcision take place? Going right on, the next verse says, "Buried with him in baptism, wherein also ye are risen with him through the faith of the operation of God, who hath raised him from the dead." All right, then, in being buried and raised through the faith of the operation of God, who hath raised Jesus from the dead, we comply with that condition upon which God cuts loose the body of the sins of the flesh. And, then, the next verse declares, "And you, being dead in your sins and the uncircumcision of your flesh, hath he quickened together with him, having forgiven you all trespasses." Thus God forgives all trespasses when He cuts loose the body of the sins of the flesh. He does that when the circumcision of Christ occurs. And that occurs when men are buried and raised in baptism.

Then I pass to another argument based upon a matter of type and anti-type in respect to the baptism of the Israelites. In I Cor. 10:1-2, Paul said, "I would not have you ignorant, how that all our fathers were under the cloud, and all passed through the sea; and were all baptised unto Moses, in the cloud and in the sea." Thus he refers to the crossing of the Red Sea by Israel as their baptism, which is typical of ours, and we turn back to the Old Testament we find out where their salvation from Egyptian bondage occurred—just when it took place. In Exodus 14:30, when they crossed the sea, Moses said, "God saved Israel that day out of the hand of the Egyptians." Thus they were saved from

Egyptian bondage, from Egyptian dominion, when they crossed the Red Sea, which Paul refers to as their baptism, typical of ours. "And God saved Israel that day"—not the day before, not three days before, but "God saved Israel that day"—the day they crossed the sea. Then, beginning with the first verse of the next chapter, the 15th chapter of Exodus, we are told that after they crossed the sea they sang the song of deliverance. According to my friend Tingley, they were saved before they crossed the sea, in the type, and the song of deliverance was sung before they crossed; but in the type given by God Almighty they sang the song of deliverance after they had crossed the sea, which was their baptism.

Now, I turn back to some things mentioned last night to refer to them, and the second argument I introduced last evening, which was not noticed by my friend, Mr. Tingley, was the fact that every passage contained in God's book that mentions both salvation and baptism always puts the salvation after the baptism. To this there is not a single exception. He did refer to some of the passages when I introduced them as individual arguments, but to this particular argument he paid no attention whatsoever. Every passage mentioning both salvation and baptism in the book of God puts salvation after the baptism, as Mark 16:16—"He that believeth and is baptized shall be saved." I am giving these briefly because we will have more on them presently. And Acts 2:38—"Repent, and be baptized for the remission of sins." I Peter 3:21—"The like figure whereunto even baptism doth also now save us." Acts 22:16—"Arise, and be baptized, and wash away thy sins." In every one of those passages you find remission of sins, or salvation, or washing away of sins, placed after baptism and not before.

Now, then, to the speech which my opponent made and to a reaffirmation of the arguments which I introduced last evening. I want to call your attention to these things very carefully that you might see just the predicament my friend is in.

There were three passages introduced last night—Mk. 16:16; Acts 2:38; Gal. 3:38—concerning which my opponent said I did not quote all the verse. In Acts 2:38 he said I failed to quote all of the verse; and in Mk. 16:16 he said I failed to give all of the verse. In Gal. 3:27 he said I failed to read the verse before it.

I insist that I gave every one of these passages. He claimed that I did not give them. I am insisting tonight that the same is true even now. In fact, last night after the debate was over, I had played back that speech of mine to see whether I had given all of those passages—whether I had given the entire verses which friend Tingley said I did not give. When the record was played back it was there easily heard and easily seen that the entire verses were quoted, and in some instances they were quoted more than one time in their entirety. My friend was entirely wrong about it. If he desires to have the record played back to him, I am sure he will find that I am stating the truth tonight.

But, now, to I Cor. 1:12-13. This was the first argument introduced last night in which Paul said, "Every one of you saith, I am of Paul; and I of Apollos; and I of Cephas; and I of Christ Is Christ divided? was Paul crucified for you? or were you baptized in the name of Paul?" I showed that in order for men to belong to Paul, Paul must be crucified for them, and they must be baptized in the name of Paul. In order to belong to Apollos, Apollos must be crucified for them, and they must be baptized in the name of Apollos. In order to belong to Cephas, Cephas must be crucufied for them, and they must be baptized in his name. And just so, in order to belong to Christ, Christ must be crucified for us, and we must be baptized in His name, thus showing that men are not of Christ, they do not belong to Christ, unless and until they have been baptized. My friend has not touched that argument until this good hour. Oh, he said something about it, but he made no effort to reply to the argument made. He just read on a little through the chapter and endeavored to array one verse against another and thus try to offset what Paul said in this verse by what he said in another verse, which does not offset it at all. I am going to turn and read that. He said I did not read it all. Well, I read all the verses I quoted and introduced—I did not read the entire chapter. I left a few verses for him to make his quibble, and now I come to attend to his quibble.

In the next verse, Paul said, "I baptized none of you but Crispus and Gaius; lest any should say that I had believed baptism was essential to salvation." Now, that's the position that my opponent must sustain in regard to this—that Paul thanked God that he did not baptize but a few of them for fear somebody might think that he thought baptism was essential. That isn't what Paul said. He didn't say, "Lest any man should think that I believed baptism necessary to salvation." He said, "Lest any man should say that I had baptized in my own name." Certainly under the same circumstances today, I would make the same statement of the Apostle Paul. If men were calling themselves after me, I would thank God that I had baptized but few, lest any should say I had baptized in my own name. Paul didn't say, "Lest somebody would think baptism was necessary to salvation."

Then, he goes on into the seventeeth verse where Paul said, "For Christ sent me not to baptize, but to preach the gospel." And that proves baptism is not essential. Well, my friend, Mr. Tingley, if Paul had said, "Christ sent me to baptize," would that have proved it was essential? That, my friends, is certainly the meaning of the argument. He promises to answer, and so I am going to expect him to answer when he comes up. He just as well to begin to answer some of these things, because tomorrow night and the next night we are on the same subject, jûst reversing positions—that's all. And the same subject of baptism will run throughout the rest of this debate. If he does not begin to answer some of these things, then tomorrow night I will be on his heels, and I shall see that he answers, because I will put them in writing. So I want him to tell me: If Paul had been sent to baptize, would that have proved that baptism is essential to salvation? He said the fact that Paul was not sent to baptize proves that it is not essential. Well, if it does, then if Paul had been sent to baptize, that would prove that it is essential. If that's not the meaning of it, then there is no argument beneath the stars in the thing tonight. I await further developments along that line.

Does Tingley mean to say that Paul baptized without authority? That he had no authority to baptize? Why, I can make the very same statement: "I came to Birmingham not to baptize. I came to preach the gospel." That doesn't mean that I don't believe baptism is necessary, but my mission here is to preach the gospel, and not to baptize. Yet I insist that baptism is a condition of salvation; and so the argument falls flat, and my friend will have to try it over.

But he came to verse 15 of I Cor. 4 and claimed this set the whole thing aside, because Paul said, "I have begotten you through the gospel." And he said, "Paul baptized only a few of them; therefore, baptism was not necessary to their new birth, because Paul had 'born' them, so to speak, or had begotten them through the gospel." Certainly, Paul had begotten them through the gospel; and I wonder if my friend does not know that a begetting precedes a birth. I wonder if he does not know that.

All right; we come next, then, to Acts 2:38 and to the things my friend said about that. He said, "Scholars say that the Greek word 'eis' means 'in order to', 'with reference to' and 'because of'." Well, I know the scholars say the word means "in order to" and "with reference to," but I am demanding him to produce the standard lexicon today that says it means "because of". I am demanding that he produce a translation today, made by competent scholars, that translates it "because of". He says it means that, and we want him to produce the translation or the standard Green lexicon that gives it that definition—"because of". I shall expect him to do it, and we are waiting to see what he does about it.

Well, he said in Matt. 12:21 "they repented at the preaching of Jonah"—"at" is from the same word, and it does not mean they repented in order to get Jonah to preach. No, it certainly does not mean that; and it does not mean what my friend says it means. It still has the prospective meaning there. They repented at or unto or into the preaching of Jonah. It looks forward just the same as it does in all the other cases.

Then, he gave Acts 11:18 about "with reference to"—that it means "with reference to". Well, Acts 11:18 uses the same word—"repentence unto life." If baptism unto remission in Acts 2:38 means remission is already obtained, then repentance unto life means the life is already obtained. Therefore, men are saved before they repent, and they repent because they have the life already.

Then he said, "In this passage Porter knows that 'repent' is second person plural and 'be baptized' is third person singular in the Greek." And, furthermore, he said, "They can not be joined together with the same predicate." Yes, I know in the Greek that 'repent' is second person plural, and I know that 'be baptized' is third person singular. But he did not have to go to the Greek to get that. That's true in English. That's true in the English right here; so he did not have to go to the Greek to find that. But here's the statement my friend made about it. He said, "Repent—(plural)—all of you. Be baptized—(singular)—everyone of you." Now, I wonder how many more are embraced in "all of you" than are embraced in "every one of you". How many more does "all of you" mean than "everyone of you"? Now, the fact is, my friend is all wrong about this—that is, his application of it. Let me give you another example. The teacher says to a class in school, "Come ye, and be examined everyone of you in the name of the state for your certificate of promotion." Now, "come ye" is second person plural; "be examined everyone of you" is third person singular. Yet, they are joined to the same predicate to secure the same result. "Come ye and be examined everyone of you for your certificate of promotion." Now, does that mean some of them were to come and others were to be examined or does it include all of them?

Well, the expression, "everyone of you," comes from the Greek word "ekastos," and we are going to see what it means. Liddell and Scott's Greek-English Lexicon says concerning it, "The singular from its collective sense is frequently joined with a plural verb". 'Ye know each one of you' is the example he gives —almost the identical expression of Acts 2:38. So Liddell and Scott's Greek-English Lexicon says that this is often connected or joined to a plural verb. My friend says, "It can not be." And, then, Thayer's Greek-English Lexicon, which is recognized as the greatest in the world today, says concerning this word "ekastos": "When it denotes individually, every one of many, is often added appositively to nouns and pronouns and verbs in the plural number." (Page 192 of Thayer's Greek-English Lexicon). These Greek scholars say they can be joined together, and my opponent says they can not. Now, you can take him or you can take what the scholars say about it. I prefer to stand with them.

Then, he says, "Thayer says the word means 'into' when it refers to place and 'with reference to' when it refers to relation." And he says it is "relation" when the matter of salvation is concerned. All right. Then he says, "Be baptized for the remission of sins" means "be baptized with reference to the remission of sins"; and that means you have the remission of sins already. All right; try another passage. Rom. 10:10 says "Believe unto righteousness." The very same word, and my friend says that means "relation". Then, it means "with reference to righteousness". And that means you have the righteousness already, and then believe because you have it. There's his relation. And he gave some examples. He said, "Why a man works for fifty dollars." He said that does not mean in order that he might work but because he worked. Yes, but it does mean in order that he might have the fifty dollars. He "works for fifty dollars." That does not mean he has the fifty dollars already, but he works to obtain the fifty dollars. Then he gives two other statements as examples: A man being given a medal for bravery—not in order to have bravery, but because of bravery. And a man electrocuted for murder—not in order to murder but because of murder. I know the English word "for" sometimes means "because of"; and certainly it does in those two examples. But I am asking my friend this: Friend Tingley, will you tell me if those two examples, or those two statements, were translated into the Greek, would that little preposition "for" be translated into the Greek word "eis" that you find in Acts 2:38? Now, you tell me. If you do not, you will have to tomorrow night. Come on and tell me about this. Would you translate the word "for" in those two statements into the Greek "eis" that we have in Acts 2:38 from which the preposition "for" comes? If you can not, then it is not a parallel case. And if you do translate it that way, then let us know about it. We want to know.

Then, I come to I Peter 3:21. We want to get to that hurriedly here. On the board I have written the two statements I had last night.

(Blackboard)
Baptism doth now save us
Baptism doth not save us

"Baptism doth now save us." And then "Baptism doth not save us." I Pet. 3:21 makes the statement above, and my friend contends for the one below, as he signed the proposition to the contrary of that. All right; "baptism does not save us." I asked him to erase the one that he did not believe, and he erased the one below! "Baptism doth not save us." He said, "I do not believe that". All right; shake hands with me and let's stop the debate. (Laughter.) When he erased that he just as well to have taken his name from the proposition. (At this point the blackboard fell, and there was a full minute of good natured laughter while it was replaced.)

I will try not to touch the board any more.

Mr. Nichols: About seven minutes left.

Mr. Porter: Now, when Friend Tingley erased that bottom statement he just the same as took his name from the proposition, for he said, "I do not believe that 'baptism doth not save'." All right, if he does not believe that "baptism doth not save us," then he believes that "baptism does save us". If he believes that "baptism does save us," that's what I'm affirming; so we just as well stop the debate, because he has surrendered the whole thing. But he came along and read some and he said, "Baptism doth now save us not". He wrote the little word "not" up there.

"Baptism doth now save us not."

He quoted it that way a number of times, and then finally quoted the whole passage, but came back and quoted it that way again, that "baptism doth now save us not." Now, I have seen men twist and wrest the scriptures, but that caps the climax, because, listen friend, that word "not" is on the inside of a parenthesis. "Not the putting away of the filth of the flesh, but the answer of a good conscience toward God" is all with parentheses. He takes it from the inside of them and puts it on the outside and connects it with the word "save" and reads it, "Baptism doth also now save us not." Well, let me try a similar passage and just see how that will wind up. I am going to prove by that method of dealing with the scriptures that it's a sin for a woman to do her hair up in a little knot on the top of her head. In Matt. 24:17, Jesus said, "Let him which is on the housetop not come down." Now, then, let me read it and pause like he did with that, "Let him which is on the house (pause) top-not, come down." (Laughter). So that would prove it would be a sin to wear your hair in a topknot. That's just as sensible as that (pointing to the board) and is dealing with it just like he dealt with I Pet. 3:21.

Now, then, my opponent said that it should be this way, according to his application of it: "Baptism doth also now save us, but it does not save us—it is only a figure of our salvation." In other words, Peter crossed himself. He said, "Baptism does save us" but "it does not save us.' Well! "Not the putting away of the filth of the flesh"—he said that meant not the putting away of sin. All right, then, if it does not save us from sin, from what does it save us? Peter said it saves us from something. The word "filth" in that case comes from a word that means "dirt,' and a number of translations translate it, "not the removing of dirt from the body." In fact, my opponent went right on along that line and made the statement that it is not the washing of the outside. That's exactly what I contend for. It is not the mere washing of the outside. So it is not the washing of dirt from the body, or the filth of the flesh, but it is the answer of a good conscience toward God; and yet Peter says, "It saves us!' Tingley says, "It does not."

He said, "Noah was saved before the flood." He was not saved with the salvation mentioned here before the flood. In I Pet. 3:20 we are told "wherein few, that is, eight souls were saved by water"—referring to the ark. Eight souls were saved in the ark. My friend says he was saved before he ever got to the ark, before the flood ever came, or anything of that kind. He was not saved from the danger here—with the salvation mentioned here. In Heb. 11:7 it is said, "By faith Noah, being warned of God of things not seen as yet, moved with fear, and prepared an ark to the saving of his house." So he was not saved with the salvation there before the flood.

Then to Gal. 3:26-27, "Ye are all the children of God by faith in Christ Jesus. For as many of you as have been baptized into Christ have put on Christ." I made an argument last night upon the little word "for"—"to introduce the reason"—the little Greek word "gar." "Ye are God's children by faith" ... Why? What's the reason of it? "Because as many of you as have been baptized into Christ have put on Christ." If you have not been baptized into Christ, then, of course, you are not the children of God by faith. My opponent paid no attention to the argument on that little word "for," or "gar," meaning "to introduce the reason." Why doesn't he come up and deal with it?

Oh, he said, "this means to put on clothes like we put on the breastplate or put on the armor." Well, Friend Tingley, you are not in your clothes until you put them on, are you? He is not in his clothes until he puts them on. So we are not in Christ until we put Him on. We are said to put Him on in baptism. So we are not in Christ until we are baptized. If we are saved before that, we are saved out of Christ.

I must get to Paul's case briefly. Acts 22. He read that and

I thought he was going to tell us what Paul was told he must do.

Mr. Nichols: Two minutes.

Mr. Porter: Thank you. He said, "You will be told what thou must do." So we want him to tell us what the Lord told him to do. He read on down through a portion of it and stopped before he got to verse sixteen. Verse sixteen says Ananias said to him, "And now why tarriest thou? Arise, and be baptized and wash away thy sins, calling on the name of the Lord." And that's the thing that was told him to do. The Lord said he would be told what he must do. And so that's what he must do to be saved. Friend Tingley said Saul was born at faith—born out of due time. Now, Friend Tingley, I want you to tell me this: If Saul was born again at the point of faith, or by faith only, and that was out of due time, then what would have been the due time for him to be born again? Now be sure and tell us that. If Paul was born out of due time, what would the due time have been? Furthermore, he said, "Paul said that he was born again when he saw the Lord." I challenge my opponent, every inch of him from head to foot, to give me the passage that says that. It's not in the Book; and he knows it's not in the Book; and if it's in the Book, let him produce it. Paul did not say any such thing. Then he said, "Was Paul lost those three days?" Well, his sins had not been washed away—verse 16 said they had not. He was not in Christ, because in Rom. 6:3, he said he was baptized into Christ. And if he was saved, he was the most miserable saved man you ever read of, for in Acts 9:9, he did neither eat nor drink for those three days. As soon as he was baptized he received food and was strengthened. If he was saved, he was a very miserable man to be saved. And that's that.

Then he came with this statement. "Suppose a man is going to be baptized and he dies before he can get baptized?" What about it? Well, he is in the very same condition as that man who is seeking salvation at the mourner's bench and smothers to death before he gets through—in exactly the same position as a man who smothers to death at the mourner's bench before he gets through. Now, then, just let him tell us something about that.

And so that covers his speech, and I thank you.

FOURTH NIGHT — TINGLEY'S FIRST SPEECH

Mr. Chairman, Gentlemen Moderators, Worthy Opponent, Ladies and Gentlemen:

"The Scriptures Teach that Water Baptism to a Penitent Believer of the Gospel is Essential to Salvation from Alien Sins."

Evidently I did not hear one word my worthy opponent used last night. It has been called to my attention and I want to call it to your attention. If he made this statement I can not go with him. It is that teach may mean imply. I can not go with him on that but otherwise I can go with him all the way on his definition.

My worthy opponent has found some fault with my finding fault with his method of quoting scriptures. I said last night he did not quote Mark 16:16 and Acts 2:38—all of it—when he presented the scriptures in the argument. Now I, too, have consulted the record. Here is a shining example of the tactics of my worthy opponent. When my worthy opponent—according to the record—when my worthy opponent first quoted—and remember first impressions are lasting impressions—I challenge my worthy opponent to have that record produced from the start of his first speech, the first word, and let you hear he did not quote all of Mark 16:16 nor did he quote all of Acts 2:38. I leave that to my worthy opponent and the record. Later in his speech he did quote all of both verses but in the presenting of the verses, the introducing of them to you—knowing full well that first impressions are lasting impressions—he did not quote all of them. I defy him to produce that record. I objected. That is so. Later in his argument he did quote them all. I am sorry my worthy opponent did not state the facts clearly as they were. He left the wrong implication. I wanted to apologize for not having noticed that he quoted all of them later on. My worthy opponent made so much out of it there is nothing for me to do except stand for truth. His error seems to be deliberate.

Let me give you a sample of his failure to consider the context. My worthy opponent is familiar with this fact: The verses were not put into the Bible until recent times—five hundred years ago. There is nothing inspired about verses. I therefore say this in referring to single verses people get the idea that that is the complete meaning. But when my worthy opponent quoted

Galatians 3:37 he purposely, deliberately ignored the preceding very short verse and that preceding verse says, "For ye are all the children of God by faith in Christ Jesus." "You are!" As many of you as have been baptized have put on "the togo virilis," the clothes of manhood, the badge of Roman citizenship. You put that on. The "Togo virilis" of Christ."

Another sample. It is awfully easy for my worthy opponent to prove his point lifting scripture out of its setting. Then resorting to all kinds of sarcasm. I have tried not to resort to it. I can produce stage play too. These matters are too serious for me to resort to stage play. I want something to stick in your mind and heart. And my worthy opponent in putting up this statement "Baptism doth not save us" did it in connection with 1 Peter 3:21 and several times he kept turning around and pointing to the board in his argument. "That's what 1 Peter 3:21 says." And he did not write down all of it. When I wrote down that word I said, "I'm not writing down all of it. I'm just going to write down the next word that is in the Bible." "Baptism doth also now save us not." That's the next word! There are other words that follow it. Did you note that tonight not once did he refer to what preceded it. Of course not. It proves my point. "The like figure whereunto even baptism." Peter says, "Baptism is a figure." And he declares it positively and unequivocally. Is that up there on the board? No! My worthy opponent wishes it were not in the Bible!

Ladies and Gentlemen, I can prove "top not come down" by using my worthy opponent's method. I have not consciously ever used that method. I do not want it. He was talking the other night about one of my "cans". He said it exploded. Well he has hanged himself on his "not" which cannot be untied. Let him hang there.

He challenged me to show you one scripture where Paul says he was born when he saw the Lord. 1 Cor. 15:8, "Last of all he was seen of me also as one born out of due time." I challenge my worthy opponent to consult any Greek authority if he desires to prove it from the original, if this is not exactly what Paul is saying, "When I saw the Lord, that's when I was born again." There's the scripture.

I gave him some questions last night. My worthy opponent

followed the usual program of evasion. He refused to answer. There are certain questions there he is afraid to answer! He cries that I appeal to prejudice! There are forty million people who do not believe in immersion. I think all of them ought to. They go home to the Lord shouting the praises of God and with His name upon their lips. If the proposition is true, my worthy opponent is saying then they go to hell! He has not said that. He dare not say that. He is afraid to say that! I ask him if Methodists, Presbyterians and all pedo-baptists are lost and will they go to Hell?—Moody, Finney, Sankey, Billy Sunday, Wesley, Whitfield, Luther and all of those—are they in hell? I demand that he tell this audience. If they are in hell then my worthy opponent is right and only the church of Christ are to be saved. I dare him to say that to this audience.

I ask him what baptism saved? He will give another evasive answer. He will not come and meet it fairly and squarely. I have answered his questions fairly and squarely that he asked me. I have not knowingly ignored or side-stepped one. I plead with him to be as fair. What baptism does he accept? Will he accept one whom I baptize without re-baptizing them? He got again facetious and refused to answer fairly and squarely. He knows and every member of the church of Christ knows, every one that has ever been connected with the church of Christ knows that ministers of the church of Christ will not accept the baptism of Missionary Baptist, Christian and Missionary Alliance and my worthy opponent (your honored representative that you have brought here from Arkansas to debate with me) he refuses to stand up and say, "That's so." You young ministers of the church ought to make him say that's so because you have been preaching it all over the country. I challenge him to answer those questions fairly and squarely.

My opponent asked me whether or not I would accept Mark 16:9-20 as the word of God. I do! Moffat, whom my worthy opponent used as an authority, denies the passage and leaves it out, puts it in special brackets with a special note. Westcott and Hort, two of the best authorities, call the passage in question. The American Standard Version, the Revised Version, all call it into question. The passage is in question as to authenticity probably more than any other portion of the scripture but I do accept it—the entire passage—as the word of God. Now, my worthy opponent accepts only one verse of it. He will not accept healing, he will not accept handling snakes, he will not accept speaking in tongues, he will not accept laying on of hands. My worthy opponent lifts a verse right out and said, "Do you accept it?" I do! I accept it all! And if verse 16 is true today then all the portion is true today.

My worthy opponent asked me to deal further with Acts 22:16. I am happy to do so. I have not time to go back and retrace the steps like my worthy opponent. He gets in a squirrel cage and goes round on the same rungs continually. I answered Mark 16:16 last night. I answered Acts 2:38 last night. I answered every other scripture he gave including this one. But I will just suggest two or three things about this one to refresh your memory. Acts 22:16—"And now why tarriest thou? Arise and be baptized and wash away thy sins calling on the name of the Lord." (1) Paul says in 1 Cor. 15:8 that he was born when he saw the Lord. Now, (2) in John 3:5 Jesus says you must be born again. (3) The word born used in 1 Cor. 15:8 is "beget" or "bring forth"—it's the same word. (4) John 1:13—"Which were born not of blood nor of the flesh nor of the will of man but of God." (5) John 2:29—If ye know that he is righteous ye know that everyone that doeth righteousness is born of him. I John 3:9, I John 5:1, (6) I Pet. 1:23—"being born again." Paul says that word (the same thing) happened to him when he saw the Lord. (7) Now listen, "Last of all he was seen of me also"—he was born ahead of time. He was born just like the Jewish nation will be born when Jesus comes—as assuredly they will be. Listen: If a man is born when he sees the Lord—is he? Paul plainly says he was seen and "I was born when I saw him." What happened when he saw Him? He fell on his face. What else. He cried, "Lord, Lord what wilt thou have me to do?" What else? He had cried previously, "Who are thou, Lord?" He said, "I am Jesus whom thou persecutest?" Now here he says, "I was born out of due time." He is not talking about his first birth—Paul was a man up in years, thirty-five years old probably. He was not talking about being born of the flesh. My worthy opponent left that alone. Tries to ridicule me and asks me to give the scripture and last night I quoted it over and over and over. Paul says he was born when he saw the Lord and that can mean nothing but salvation.

Listen, I can take any great sinner when they see the Lord in His glory, see His face, see how wicked they have been, if they have been touched by the Spirit of God like the apostle Paul—there is great sorrow. Now, I will deal further in a few moments in this speech or in the next if I do not get time to, with the picture as in the sixteenth verse.

My worthy opponent last night—this slipped my attention so I bring it in—quoted Luke 7:30 to prove that baptism is essential to salvation. "But the Pharisee and lawyers rejected the counsel of God against themselves being not baptized of him." Now my worthy opponent introduced that passage. Once again if he had read the verse before, my worthy opponent would have been far wiser. This refers to John's baptism. Evidently my opponent believes that baptism was necessary to salvation before Pentecost for he is quoting before Pentecost dealing with John's baptism to prove baptism is essential to salvation in this day—after Pentecost. I'm not doing that. My opponent introduced that last night and I want him to face that.

I will show you one. Listen, if the terms of salvation are such now, they were that before Pentecost. The program and plan of God in its great underlying principles does not change. If these things produced salvation before Pentecost, before Christ, the same things will produce salvation after. The same things in this day will produce salvation. My worthy opponent did this introducing. I did not. I am simply going in, looking around seeing where he gets himself. Now if a man was saved before Pentecost as my worthy opponent quotes as proof for this debate—if he was—remember I am answering him and every scripture he gives. Not one have I left out or will I leave out. My worthy opponent quotes this if baptism is necessary for salvation in this age, my worthy opponent believes it was necessary in the age before and yet, I will show you one who was saved without baptism—John's baptism or any other baptism. Luke 23:42-32 "And he said unto Jesus"—now this is in the age that my worthy opponent quoted last night to prove his proposition—"Lord remember me when thou comest into thy kingdom. Then said Jesus unto him verily I say unto thee, Today thou shalt be with me in Paradise." My worthy opponent says baptism is essential to salvation. He quotes scripture referring to John's baptism to prove his point that baptism is essential to salvation. If baptism is essential to salvation I will agree with him that it must be before Pentecost as well as after Pentecost. God's way of salvation does not change. The way men were saved before is the way they are saved afterward. The Old and the New Testament agree on that matter. The scripture:"By faith Abraham believed God and it was counted unto him for righteousness." If we are saved that way before, I believe we are saved that way afterward. Upon the cross the dying thief had faith in Jesus as Christ and Jesus said he was saved. My opponent says he is damned because he has gone over there on that side the fence and quoted that scripture. It's my worthy opponent or my Lord and I will accept my Lord. Remember my opponent quoted Luke 7:30 to prove his point and I am only using his scripture.

Now, my worthy opponent also dealt with Acts 10:43 and I want to deal with it a little further. Now if baptism is essential to salvation it denies and contradicts Peter who says in I Peter 1:23 "Being born again not of corruptible seed but of incorruptible by the word of God which liveth and abideth forever." And again this same Peter says in Acts 10:43, "To him gave all the prophets witness through his name that whosoever believeth in him shall receive remission of sins." It does not say, "Whosoever believeth in him and is baptized shall receive remission of sins." And then at the close of that sermon on salvation—not a a word said about baptism in any form much less being essential to salvation—there follows Acts 10:44, "While Peter yet spake these words the Holy Ghost fell on them which heard the word." This is after Pentecost, Ladies and Gentlemen. Here are people after Pentecost, here are people that I believe beyond the shadow of doubt to any reasonable mind, any reasonable doubt at all to any thinking or unprejudiced person that these were saved before they were baptized—saved without baptism—and baptism was very reluctantly administered to them.

Listen to this: It does not say the Holy Ghost fell on them which heard the word and were baptized." But it shows that Cornelius was saved before he was baptized for here is what it says, Acts 10:46, "Can any man forbid water that these should not be baptized which have received the Holy Ghost as well as we." "What was I to withstand God," says Peter. These people were saved, the third person of the trinity had come upon them. Every last one of them in that room that believed on Christ received the Holy Ghost—God from heaven witnessing—and then Peter said, "What in the world was I to argue against God." He saved them without baptism.

Acts 8:37 Phillip said, "If thou believest with all thine heart thou mayst. And he answered and said, I believe that Jesus is the Son of God." Now Philip said to this eunuch that if he believed he would be saved and there was water. Listen to this record of Luke. There Philip baptized the eunuch after he confessed his faith in Christ and he was baptized not in order to be saved but because he had been saved.

If baptism is essential to salvation it denies and contradicts the plain words of John—"These are written that you might believe that Jesus is the Christ the Son of God and believing you might have life through his name." Then, that's written also before Pentecost.

Listen to I John 1:9. I would like to have my opponent deal with this. "Behold what manner of love the Father hath bestowed upon us that we should be called the children of God therefore the world knoweth us not because it knew Him not now are we the sons of God it doth not yet appear what we shall be but we know that when he shall appear we shall be like him for we shall see him as he is. Little children let no man deceive you, he that doeth rightousness is righteous even as he is righteous. He that committeth sin is of the devil for the devil sinneth from the beginning For this purpose the son of God was manifested that he might destroy the works of the devil." When the love of God is poured upon an individual God says their nature is changed, their being is changed and the devil is destroyed out of their heart and life and they are children of God. Not a mention of baptism at all. "Whosoever is born of God doth not commit sin because his seed remaineth in him"—because he is born of God. Paul said he was born of God when he saw the Lord. These others said they were born of God before they were baptized.

Listen. I John 5:1, "Whosoever believeth that Jesus is the Christ is born of God." Doesn't say a word about baptism. Now, my worthy opponent, quoted four verses that refer to baptism and salvation or have salvation in them and said that the only instance—but my worthy opponent ignores the fact of these scriptures that I have already given you. For instance in Galatians, "Ye are children of God by faith" and then you put on grown clothes of manhood, baptism, the "togo virilis." You put on the "togo virilis" of Christ. For instance in the scripture which I have just given—Cornelius' household. They were saved; the Holy Ghost fell on them; and then Peter very reluctantly baptized them. Salvation came before baptism.

Then he called my attention to Romans 6:3-4. "Know ye not that so many of us as were baptized into Jesus Christ were baptized into his death. Therefore, we are buried with him by baptism into death that like as Christ was raised up from the dead by the glory of the Father even so we ought also to walk in newness of life." Now there's that preposition into again, meaning, with reference to. The original Greek translation reads "so many of us as were baptized with reference to Jesus Christ were baptized with reference to his death. Therefore we are buried with him by baptism." Now that's exactly what it means when we come to the tenth chapter of I Corinthians. What do we find? Here's exactly the setting forth of relationship, Paul tells us: "Moreover brethren I would not that ye should be ignorant how that all our fathers were under the cloud and all passed through the sea and were all baptized unto Moses." Did that save their souls? That was physical salvation from Egyptian bondage. I want you to get this further. There is the same preposition "eis"—unto Moses. What does it mean? They were already saved, they were delivered by the passover, then God took charge of them and had the pillar of cloud by day and the pillar of fire by night. Then the "baptized unto Moses" came after their deliverance from the Egyptians. Get it, Ladies and Gentlemen, they were immersed and the cloud covered them and there was a wall of water on either side and there they gave the world a symbolic picture that they had accepted the leadership of Moses. His scripture proves my point! They were saved by God miraculously before they went into the sea. And God by His mighty deliverance came between them and the Egyptians. Now was there any change of leadership after baptism into Moses? Were they not under the leadership of Moses on the Passover night? They were baptized into Moses not in order to accept his leadership for he had already been appointed their leader and they had accepted his leadership and the baptism in the sea did not add to nor take from the relationship they had to Moses. The baptism declared the relationship.

My worthy opponent dared me to produce a scholar. I'll trot one out. I want to make this clear: H. T. Anderson, perhaps the greatest scholar and preacher that the disciples of Christ —the church of Christ—ever had, said, "The real translation of 'for' in Acts 2:38 occurs 119 times in the New Testament" and Anderson translated—probably my worthy opponent's greatest scholar—translated the Bible two times (the whole New Testament rather) and he tried to make the word mean "in order to" and he was honest enough to admit that he found it "in order to" only eight times out of 119. That's the church of Christ's greatest scholar that said that. Now that's an authority from the church to which he belongs. If he wants authorities, we'll trot them out.

Listen my friends. I wish my opponent would deal, for instance, with John 1:11-12, "He came unto his own and his own received him not but as many as received him to them gave he power to become the sons of God even to them which believe on his name." I'd like to have him tell this audience what is meant in John 3:5, "Except a man be born of water and of the Spirit." His preachers are going all over the country saying that's water baptism. I want him to stand up here and say so. And then we will operate on him like we did on I Peter.

Sin is the problem that men have. How in the world can an individual have a new heart—heaven or hell is the destiny and it's the most important question that faces man. If my opponent is right, every believer in Christ that has not been immersed is damned. This debate deals with a great fundamental issue. Is a man saved by faith or is he saved by baptism. If a man believes in Christ is a man saved before he is baptized? Certainly God would leave us in no doubt about this important question. He tells us the awfulness of sin in Rom. 3:23, then he said "We are justified freely by His grace through faith in His blood." Not one word of baptism. Salvation is not anything outward but it is inward. It's not of the body but it's of the inner being. I John 5:1—"He that believeth on the Son hath the witness in himself." Col. 1:27—"In whom God would make known what is the riches of the glory of this mystery among the Gentiles which is Christ in you the hope of glory."

My opponent asked me can a man be in Christ without being baptized. Well, how does Christ get into a man or how does a man get into Christ? Here's the answer. Eph. 3:17, "That Christ may dwell in your hearts by faith." Rom. 10:9-10, "If thou shalt confess with thy mouth the Lord Jesus." My worthy opponent says, "This isn't so. You've got to confess with your mouth, believe in your heart and you still aren't saved. If before you get to the creek you die and are damned and go to hell." That's what his proposition says. He has not the courage to face that matter and say that is so. But that's what his proposition says. The Bible plainly teaches that any who do not have this complete, dramatic regeneration within them, irrespective of forms and ceremonies, is lost, is damned, is eternally lost. Salvation is by faith in Jesus Christ and by this alone before baptism.

John 3:36—"He that believeth on the Son hath everlasting life. He that believeth not the Son shall not see life." Baptism is a declaration of a fact. I have already called your attention to Gal. 3:27. That tells us what it is. A policeman wears a uniform not to be a policeman but because he is a policeman. A Christian who is a child of God by faith is baptized not in order to be a Christian but because he is a Christian.

I thank you, Ladies and Gentlemen.

FOURTH NIGHT — PORTER'S SECOND SPEECH

Mr. Chairman, Gentlemen Moderators, Respected Opponent, Ladies and Gentlemen:

I am before you now for my closing affirmation on this particular proposition and, of course, my closing affirmation for the debate. I desire to take up and notice the things which my opponent has just said, and re-affirm the arguments that have been introduced, and let you see them stand forth in all of their clearness and simplicity as revealed in God's word.

On thing that he said he had overlooked; and that was that I said in my defining the proposition last night that "teach" mean "to imply". I think if he will search the record—have the record played back to him—he will find the word "imply" was not used.

Then he came to that matter of my failing to quote certain verses in their entirety. He said, "Porter said he had the record played back and found that he had quoted all of the verses." He said, "Yes. I had them played, too, and that was so; he did quote the entire verses before he got through with them, but he did not quote the entire verse when it was first introduced." That is not what my opponent said last night. When he came to reply to me he did not say, "Porter failed to quote the entire verse when he first introduced it." He just said, "Porter did not quote the entire verse." And he made a great play upon it—that not during that speech did I quote the entire verse; that I deliberately ignored the thing—that I stepped aside and missed it. Now, why didn't he say, "Porter did not quote the entire verse when he first introduced it?" If he had said that, I would have said, "Certainly, I did not quote the entire verse when I first introduced it." If you will have the record played again, you'll find that when I introduced those verses I said, "I am going to give them but briefly now, and then I will elaborate upon them as I introduce them as individual arguments." I wonder if he heard that when he had the record played back. And so the thing that Tingley should have said, instead of making that play last night upon the idea that I had not quoted the entire verse (you know he says, "First impressions are lasting ones") was that "Porter did not quote the entire verse 'as I knows of'." "He didn't quote the entire verse 'as I knows of'." That's what he should have said.

He said he wanted to apologize, but since I had come along and said I had quoted the entire verse, and since he found out it was so that I had, he was not going to apologize. That's up to him. He can just use his pleasure about that. It doesn't matter to me. The fact remains that what I said was true—that the verses were quoted in their entirety. And he found that it was so, but since they were not quoted in their entirety when they were first introduced, he says, "I would apologize, but since Porter said the thing was so that was so, I'm not apologizing."

Then to Gal. 3:27, and he said, "When Porter introduced this he deliberately ignored verse 26." "When he first introduced it." Well, if I deliberately ignored it when I first introduced it, why didn't I just deliberately ignore it all the rest of the way? If I were afraid to quote the whole thing when I first introduced it, why would I not have been afraid to quote it at any time during the speech? Now, I quoted the verse before and two verses following—in fact I read them and showed what the negative of the whole situation would be. "Ye are all the children of God by faith in Christ Jesus." That's verse 26. "For"—and that "for" is from an original word that means "the cause" or "to introduce the reason". It's not the same "for" that's found in Acts 2:38. It's from an entirely different word—a word that means "to introduce the reason". Now, Paul said, "Ye are God's children by faith." Why? What's the reason? "Because as many of you as have been baptized into Christ have put on Christ." So Paul said, "Ye are God's children by faith because you have been baptized into Christ." And as many as had not been baptized into Christ were not God's children by faith. My friend hasn't even touched it—top, edge, side nor bottom. He's afraid to get hold of it. If he's not afraid of it, let him come up and grapple with it and tell me about this little word "for". You know that word "for" is in there. Tell me what it means, Tingley. Show the connection there; let me know about what that word "for" means. (At this point Mr. Porter's glasses fell of and he said, "Well if I lose these, I can get some more where they came from. It might be that Elder Tingley can heal my eyesight and I wouldn't need them. (Laughter). You know he says he takes all of Mark 16 all the way through—tongues, miracles and every bit of it—drinking the deadly poison, too, I suppose. Friend Tingley, do you take 'drinking the deadly poison' and 'it will not hurt you?

Now, let us know about it.")

But he said, "This simply means to 'put on' like you put on your clothes—put on Christ like you put on your clothes." All right; I still say you are not in your clothes until you put them on! And, if to put on Christ is parallel with that, then you are not in Christ until you have put Him on. And if you are not in Christ until you have put Him on, and you put Him on in baptism, you're not in Christ until you are baptized. And if you are saved before you are baptized, you are saved before you put Christ on and be fore you get into Christ. Well, in I Cor. 1:30 Paul said Christ is sanctification and redemption. If you put on Christ in baptism, then you put on sanctification and redemption in baptism.

Then to I Pet. 3:21 again. This we have on the board. He said, "Yes, I read that, and I did read the next word." Yes, and he stopped.

(Reading from the blackboard):

"The like figure whereunto even baptism doth also now save us not." That changes the entire meaning of the passage. The case which I gave was entirely parallel: "Top not, come down." Just as much as that which he gave is that true. For he broke the sentence entirely in two and removed the "not" from one side of the parenthesis and put it on the other side. Peter said, "Baptism doth also now save us." He didn't say, "Save us not." Tingley puts the pause in the wrong place and changes the meaning of it entirely. "Baptism doth also now save us. (Not the putting away of the filth of the flesh"—not the removing of dirt from the body. In other words, it is not a mere bodily act, cleansing the old outside body, "but the answer of a good conscience toward God) by the resurrection of Jesus Christ." Peter says it does now save us, and Tingley says it saves us not. Well, if it saves us not, why didn't you erase that bottom statement from the board last night? He said he did not believe that. Tell me the difference between the statements, "Baptism doth not save us," and "Baptism doth save us not?" I'd like to know the difference between those two expressions. Tingley, will you please distinguish between them when you come up here in your next speech? What's the difference between "Baptism doth not save us" and "Baptism saves us not"? He said, "Oh, but he would not read the verse in front of it." Well, I will just accommodate him and read the verse in front of it. I Pet. 3:20—that's the one in front of it, and I'll just read it for his accommodation and see how it fixes it. "Which sometime were disobedient, when once the longsuffering of God waited in the days of Noah, while the ark was a preparing, wherein few, that is, eight souls were saved by water." That's the verse in front of it. Does he want that? "Wherein eight souls were saved by water. The like figure whereunto even baptism doth also now save us." Another translation gives, "After a true likeness, or in the antitype, baptism also now saves us." Now, watch the figure. My opponent says it says baptism is a figure of our salvation. It says no such thing. It absolutely is not there. But where's the figure? Why it's the type and the antitype. In the type Noah was saved in the ark by water. There's the ark, floating upon the bosom of the water, and it was transported from the old world to the new world. And, in the same way, baptism translates us from a condition of condemnation to justification. There's where your "like figure" is; there's where your "true likeness" is; and it does not say a word about its being a figure of our salvation.

Then, he came to I Cor. 15:8 and said, "Here is where Paul said that he was born again out of due time." I want to turn and read that. He went on about that and said Paul said he was born again when he saw the Lord. Let us read, "And last of all I was born again also, as one born out of due time, when I saw the Lord." No, No, it doesn't say that. "And last of all he was seen of me also, as one born out of due time." He did not say, "I was born again." The word "again" is not in there. He did not say, "I was born of God." The expression is not found there. He didn't even say, "I was born." He says "As of one born." He did not say, "I was born again, or any other time," but he said, "I saw Christ as one born out of due time." The next verse says, "For I am the least of the apostles, and am not meet to be called an apostle, because I persecuted the church of God." In other words, Paul says, "I saw the Lord"—it was necessary for him to see the Lord to be an apostle. (I Cor. 9:1). "Am I not an apostle? have I not seen the Lord?" But he was seen of Paul last of all—he didn't see Him when the others did. So when he saw the Lord and thus became qualified for an apostle, he was "as one prematurely born." Just like one "prematurely born," or "born out of due time," is inferior to one that reaches maturity, or comes to the mature time to be born, so Paul says, "I am the least of all the apostles, because I persecuted the church of God." So he tells here that he was inferior to the other apostles, because of what he had done, and, therefore, referred to himself as being like one that was prematurely born. Not a word about being born again; yet, my friend will come right up here and say over and over, "Paul said, 'I was born again when I saw the Lord'." Paul didn't say any such thing. I challenge him, every inch of him, to bring the passage that says it is so. It is not there. You read it for yourself when you go home and see that Paul didn't say a word about when he was born again.

I asked my friend if Paul was born again at faith, or faith alone, and that was out of due time, what would have been the due time? Well, he said the due time was—that is, he was born ahead of time—and the due time would be when the Lord returns and Israel is restored. That was the due time for Paul to be born. In other words, Paul lived about 1,900 years ago and was not due to be born again until Jesus comes again. I guess it was due Paul to remain alive all of that time to be born again. If not, why, then, it was Paul's due time to be born again after he was raised from the dead, and that would be a second chance of salvation. I wonder if that is what he wants?

Then, he said Porter refused to answer his questions. There is not a question in the list that I did not answer last night. There is not one of them that I am the least bit afraid of. Every one knows, and the record will show, that not one single, solitary scripture or question was skipped. Every one of them was dealt with—one by one. The purpose of them was to make a plea for sympathy and try to stir up prejudice and so on—at least many of them. And that is what my friend is still trying to do. So he comes along and wants to know about rebaptizing. Why he said, "You Baptists can't get into the church that Porter is with without being rebaptized." And, Tingley, you can't get into the Baptist church without being rebaptized. (Laughter.) Just because I don't take a Baptist on his baptism, if that means anything—why, then, will they take Tingley on some other baptism? Why, certainly they will not. There might be some kinds of Baptists that will, but there are many kinds of them that will not have him at all.

"Ah, the great number who are going to hell because of Porter's doctrine—forty million who are not immersed." Well, what about the Jews who have not believed in Christ? There are a lot of good, honest Jews—there are good people among them; and they believe they are going to heaven. They believe that they will be saved, and yet they do not believe in Christ. The doctrine of Elder Tingley sends everyone of them to hell that doesn't believe in Christ. Well, if that means anything against me, it means the same thing against him. If that proves I'm wrong when I say that baptism is necessary to salvation, it proves that he is wrong when he says that faith is necessary to salvation. Now, we are not determining what is true and what's untrue by what the results are about who goes to heaven or hell. That's not the standard by which we determine the truth. We determine that by what's revealed in the Bible.

He comes to Mark 16:9-20. He says, "Yes, I accept Mark 16:9-20 as the word of God." Then, why did you try to cast reflections on it last night? Why did you try to set it aside and claim that it isn't the word of God—at least, leave that implication in the argument you made in trying to get rid of it? Why did you do that if you believe it's the word of God? Why didn't you just say, "Yes, that's the word of God and I'll meet it," instead of twisting around about it like you did?

And he referred to some scholars and translations and so on. It's genuineness has sometimes been questioned; it's authenticity has not. He wants to know if I'll accept Mark 16:17 about the tongues. Well, I'll accept the tongues if he will accept the drinking of poison; and we will demonstrate it in your presence tonight.

Back to his squirrel cage—and that squirrel cage will give him trouble tomorrow night, and the next night, when he has no steps to put in it.

Acts 22:16. He said, "I'll come to that and if I don't reply to it now, I will in my next speech." Well, I'm sorry that he saved it until his last speech, but I can get to it tomorrow night, because we are still on the same question. Acts 22:16—Ananias said to Paul, "Arise, and be baptized, and wash away thy sins, calling on the name of the Lord." I did not put it in there. It's there. "Arise, and be baptized, and wash away thy sins, calling on the name of the Lord."

Back again to I Cor. 15:8. "Paul said he was born again when he saw the Lord." I demand the scripture. I Cor. 15:8 says nothing about it.

John 3:5 and John 1:13; I John 2:29; I John 4:7; I John 5:1—regarding the believer being born. All of this he said Paul had when he saw the Lord. Well, if he was born again when he saw the Lord, he was born again without being in Christ. In Rom. 6:3 he said he was "baptized into Christ." If he was born again when he saw the Lord, he was born again without remission of sins, for his sins were not washed away until he was baptized—Acts 22:16.

Luke 7:30—John's baptism. Now, he said, "If that's essential to salvation in John's day, Porter went back to that." And he said, "It's the same before that time as now—there's been no change whatsoever." Well, if there has been no change whatsoever, then, if Luke 7:30 proves that those who rejected John's baptism rejected God's counsel then, if men reject baptism now, they reject God's counsel now. If there's been no change, the same thing still holds true, Elder Tingley. That is not the only passage I gave. I gave also 2 Thess. 1:7-8-9, where Paul says those who obey not the gospel will be punished with everlasting destruction from the presence of God and the glory of His power.

As yet he hasn't touched I Cor. 1:12-13. "I am of Paul; and I am of Apollos; and I of Cephas; and I of Christ. Was Paul crucified for you? or were you baptized in the name of Paul?" Paul shows that for a man to be of Paul, or to belong to Paul, Paul must be crucified for him, and he must be baptized in Paul's name. Just so, in order for a man to be of Christ, or belong to Christ, Christ must be crucified for him, and he must be baptized in the name of Christ. Until both those things are true, he is not of Christ. My friend has not touched it, and there is not a man that lives today who can touch it. I don't care where he is. It has not been done, and it will never be done, by men who contend for a false doctrine as my opponent is doing tonight.

Then to Luke 23:42-43—the thief on the cross. Yes, Heb. 9:16-17 tells us that a will is not of force while men live, but after they die it becomes effective. If the Lord wanted to save the thief without baptism, without faith, without repentance—without anything—that was His privilege as a testator. When He died on the cross His will was ratified, and we are living this side of the ratification of that will.

I Pet. 1:23—born again by the word of God. Acts 10:43— Peter said also that "through his name whosoever believeth on him should have remission of sins." The same Peter said we receive remission of sins through His name. He said, "Peter did not say that through His name whosoever believeth and is baptized shall receive the remission of sins." No. He didn't say a word about repentance either. Not a word said about repentance. I wonder if my friend is going to get him saved without repentance? It does say, "through His name". Matt. 28:19 says we are baptized "into the name of the Father, Son and Holy Spirit." Besides, the same Peter who made those two statements also said in Acts 2:38, "Repent, and be baptized for the remission of sins." I'll take them all. My friend takes two of them and rejects the other. I'll take all three.

Then to Cornelius. He said, "Now Cornelius was saved. He received the Holy Ghost." Well, you said on the first proposition that Cornelius was a sinner when he received the Holy Ghost— that the Holy Ghost fell on the old alien sinner. Now, he comes along and tries to prove that because the Holy Ghost fell on him he was saved, and a child of God, before he was baptized. Now, just which one does he want? He can not have both of them. We will wait and see how he works out.

"The eunuch believed—Acts 8." Yes, and after he was baptized, the record says he went on his way rejoicing. My opponent would have him rejoicing before he was baptized.

I John 3:9—the man born of God can not sin. I am wondering if my opponent is going to take the position, that he indicated last night, that a child of God can not be lost, regardless of what he does. I wish he would tell us about that.

I John 5:1—that he gave said the believer is born of God, and he said, "Not a word is said about baptism." No, and not a word is said about repentance, nor prayer—not a word. Cut them all out.

Besides, I John 2:7 says, "He that loveth is born of God."

That's something besides faith. Then I John 2:29 says, "He that doeth righteousness is born of God." Is a man born of God three times—once when he has faith, once when he loves and once when he does righteousness? Or does it take all three of them to bring about the one birth?

Rom. 6:3-4—"With reference to." "Baptized into Christ—with reference to Christ." Well, it's the same word in Romans 10:10—"believeth unto righteousness"—that is, "with reference to" righteousness already received, and on the basis of it—that which you have already obtained—you believe. That's the predicament of my friend.

I Cor. 10:1-3 speaks concerning the baptism of the Israelites. "Unto" Moses they were baptized. And he said, "There's your same word 'unto'." Yes, and he said they were delivered by the Passover—when the Passover lamb was slain they were delivered. Delivered from what? From Egyptian bondage? No. The first born was delivered from death. That's all. And there when the blood was placed upon their houses, and the angel of the Lord passed through to destroy, over those houses he passed, and the firstborn did not die. That did not deliver them from Egyptian bondage. My friend made this statement, and I copied it down as he made it, "They passed through the sea after their deliverance from the Egyptians." I am going to turn and see what Moses said and put them side by side. My friend says they were delivered from the Egyptians before they crossed the sea. Moses, what do you say about it? This is the language of Moses—not the language of Tingley: "But the children of Israel walked upon dry land in the midst of the sea," that's beginning with verse 29; "and the waters were a wall unto them on their right hand, and on their left. Thus the Lord saved Israel that day out of the hand of the Egyptians." My opponent says, "They were saved, they were delivered from the Egyptians, before they reached the sea." Moses says when they crossed the sea "the Lord saved Israel that day out of the hand of the Egyptians." Now, which do you want? Here it is. It reads in your Bible just like it does in mine, unless you have cut it out. Go home and read it for yourself. Moses says, "When they crossed the sea, they were saved out of the hand of the Egyptians." My friend says, "No, they were saved out of the hand of the Egyptians before they got to the sea, and they crossed the sea after they were delivered from the Egyptians." Take your choice. I'll take my stand with Moses.

Then he came to the scholars and said H. T. Anderson, a scholar in the Church of Christ, found the word "for" 119 times in the New Testament, and that two times he tried to make it mean "in order to" and had found that in only eight cases could he translate it that way. Well, how many times did he find that he could translate it "because of"? How many times did any scholar find that he could translate it "because of"? Tingley, will you bring the translation that gives "because of". If some of them are translated that way, let us see them. Now, the fact is it occurred many more than 119 times in the New Testament—hundreds of times—and my friend is wrong even about that. But it is not translated "because of". Let him produce the passage that says so.

John 3:5—"born of water." He said, "Now I'm going to operate on that like I did on I Pet. 3:21." Well, we saw how he operated on I Pet. 3:21—just cut part of it loose. (I guess that's when he's going to take out my "differential"). We will see how he does the operating. John 3:5—"Except a man be born of water and the Spirit, he can not enter into the kingdom of God." Of course, I will have no chance to reply to what he says, but I will tomorrow night. But I am going to say that this expression does involve water baptism, and then let him do his operation, and I will see how his operation works.

Rom. 3:24. He said, "We are justified by faith in his blood. No baptism about it." I am going to turn and read that. I can quote it, but I want to read it. Rom. 3:24—"Being justified freely by his grace through the redemption that is in Christ Jesus." Now, the very verse introduced said redemption is in Christ. Well, Paul, you say redemption is in Christ—how do you get into Him? Gal. 3:27—"As many of you as have been baptized into Christ have put on Christ."

He came to Eph. 3:17 and said, "Here's the passage that tells us how we get into Christ." Well, I'll turn and read that. Maybe I have been overlooking something sometime. So I'll just read that. Eph. 3:17—"That you may get into Christ by faith." Well, I wonder how I have missed that all these years. "That you may get into Christ by faith." Have you brethren been missing that, too? I have missed that all this time. Well, let's see. I believe I misread it. "That Christ may dwell in your hearts by faith." Not a word said about getting into Christ in the passage. The poker gets into the fire, you know, before the fire gets into the poker. Well, we're going to see more about that.

Then to John 3:36—he quoted that. "He that believeth not shall not see life." The Revised Version translates it, "He that obeyeth not shall not see life." That covers the speech that was just made. I have a little time left and I want to reaffirm just a little on these matters. How much time do I have?

Mr. Nichols: Three minutes.

Mr. Porter continues: Three minutes. All right.

Now, I have called your attention to a number of scriptures showing that baptism is placed before salvation. Mk. 16:16 said, "He that believeth and is baptized shall be saved; but he that believeth not shall be damned." Remember the train ride that my friend took to Atlanta last night and how I wrecked that train. He has not tried to get it back on the track either. I wonder why he didn't? Maybe he will in this next speech. "He that enters the train and sits down shall go to Atlanta. You can go to Atlanta whether you sit down or not; so entering the train is the essential thing." All right; he said, "He that believeth and is baptized shall be saved." "Sitting down is equivalent to being baptized—they are unnecessary. Faith is equivalent to entering the train—they are the essential things to bring us to salvation and to Atlanta." My opponent says, "He that believeth is saved already before he has time to be baptized." "He that enters the train is already in Atlanta before he has time to sit down." Remember that Jesus said not, "He that believeth is saved and may be baptized" but "He that believeth and is baptized shall be saved." He places the salvation after both the belief and the baptism.

Why didn't my friend deal also with "He that believeth not shall be damned" in harmony with the illustration which I gave? "He that eats no food and does not digest it shall starve."

Then, I showed from Acts 2:38 that Peter said, "Repent, and be baptized for the remission of sins." My opponent said, "Repent" is second person plural; 'be baptized' is third person singular; and they can not be joined together—joined to the same predicate." I read from both Liddell and Scott's Lexicon and Thayer's Greek-English Lexicon where these scholars say that they can be joined and oftentimes are. Why didn't he say something about that? Maybe he will in his next speech. If he does I will attend to the gentleman tomorrow night. And so we have those things standing.

In I Pet. 3:21, remember that Peter said, "The like figure whereunto even baptism doth also now save us." My friend, I insist that you tell us what's the difference between the statements "Baptism doth not save us" and "Baptism doth save us not". Will you tell us the difference? If you don't, I'll put it in writing for you tomorrow night.

Thank you, Ladies and Gentlemen:

FOURTH NIGHT — TINGLEY'S SECOND SPEECH

Mr. Chairman, Gentlemen Moderators, Worthy Opponent, Ladies and Gentlemen:

I would call your earnest attention to this fact that in regard to the quotation of Mk. 16:16 and Acts 2:38 when introducing those scriptures to the audience, he did not repeat all of them. That is what I said last night. I did not hear him repeat all of them at any time later. The record shows at some time later in his speech he did repeat all of them. My worthy opponent led you to believe that when he first spoke that he repeated all of them. Ladies and Gentlemen, that is a sample of the tactics of my worthy opponent.

He has asked me about these two sentences on the board.

"Baptism doth now save us."
"Baptism doth not save us."

Neither one of them is scripture. He knows they are not scripture. I know they are not scripture. If I take "Top not come down" and put it on the board, that's not scripture. The words are still in the Bible. They are not scripture. Any verse taken out of its setting or any portion of a verse taken out of its setting is not scripture—they are merely words. I appeal to you to let your heart be honest in the matter. "Baptism doth now save us," is not scripture. When I erased the lower part, he was dumbfounded. When I added the one word—he was more dumbfounded. That's the first time that ever happened to him. He won't do that again to another debator for fear it will happen again. He is hung on his "not" and he can not get off! (Laughter.)

The scripture is, "The like figure whereunto even baptism doth also now save us not the putting away . . . " and the rest of the verse—the whole thing is scripture. I will deal with it a little more but lest I forget it, neither one of them are scripture. He knows it. You know it! They are words! Some of them he lifted out of their place in the Bible. They are just words. He knows they are not Bible. That's what I mean when I charge him with misquoting.

Col. 1:9-13—the seat of the whole business is right here. "For in him dwelleth all the fullness of the Godhead bodily. Now ye are complete in him which is the head of all principality and power in whom also ye are circumcised with the circumsion made without hands in putting off the body of the sins of the flesh by the circumcision of Christ." I would ask my worthy opponent —for I do not want to introduce any new matter at all in this speech as it is against the rules of debating, I have tried will try to observe carefully all the rules of debating and conduct myself strictly as a Christian gentleman—I would ask my worthy opponent tomorrow night, since he has already introduced the matter, he can answer tomorrow night, does he accept circumcism? Is baptism the New Testament for circumcision? Does it stand for the circumcision of the Old Testament? "In putting off the body of the sins of the flesh by circumcision of Christ buried with him by baptism wherein also ye are risen with him." How? What is the agency that does not bring the full force—the full force is not brought by baptism in the new or by circumcision in the old but they are pictures of it. "In him dwelleth all the fullness of the Godhead bodily. Ye are complete in him." How do we get into Him? What is baptism a picture of? "Through the faith of the operation of God." Is baptism an operation of God? It is not. It is an operation of a minister and a believer. And through faith in the operation of God who raised him from the dead. That's the power that makes a man a newborn creature in Christ, of which baptism is a beautiful symbol and circumcision was a symbol in the Old Testament.

Now, my worthy opponent did not again answer those questions. Ladies and Gentlemen, I asked plain and square; and he refused to answer them, and refused me, and was facetious in his answer. He said I could not get into the Baptist Church without being rebaptized. I happen to know that I can. If anybody questions that why I can prove it to you very quickly if he wants to follow that up. I want to know—my worthy opponent if his proposition that he has signed, "Baptism is essential to salvation", he said that—if that is so then every Methodist and Presbyterian and every person that has not been immersed is going to hell. Listen further, Moody, Finney, Sankey, Billy Sunday, Wesley, Whitfield, Luther are all in hell if my opponent is right. Why doesn't he stand up here and be man enough to say they are in hell. He hasn't the courage to stand by his convictions. He has to dodge. I tell you what I believe, Ladies and Gentlemen, frankly and honestly. Let him ask me. I'm happy to answer him.

Listen again. For instance he asked me in regard to Mark 16:16 would I accept the poison if he accepted the snakes. I accept all of Mark 16:9-20. My worthy opponent stands here and says, "Well, if he will do one thing I will do the other." I accept it all. Every bit of it. Completely and entirely. Now my worthy opponent dare not say he accepts it because he doesn't accept it. He only accepts the one verse he wants to. He accepts the 16th verse and only the first half of that. Ladies and Gentlemen, I defy him tomorrow night to say he accepts the 17th through the 20th verses for people today. I defy him. With all that is within me—I believe that's his statement—I defy him.

Listen, Gal. 3:26-27—and he used a simple illustration thinking it was attractive and clever and perhaps it was but again he gets hung on his "not". He says "You are not in your clothes until you put them on." That's a glaring example of the inconsistency of my opponent. What is the subject? Clothes? No. My worthy opponent has betrayed his own position and the position of all who stand with him. To every one of them—salvation is only a matter of an outward form. It's only a matter of a baptism. It's only a matter of something outside. They don't believe that an individual can know he is born again by the witness of the Spirit. That's the issue, Ladies and Gentlemen. My worthy opponent betrays his position. He says, "You can't be in your clothes until you put them on" as if putting on clothes is Christianity. He misses the whole business. Again, he didn't read the 26th verse. What is the subject? "For ye are all the children of God by faith in Christ Jesus." The subject is not putting on the declaration—or putting on the badge of discipleship, or putting on the uniform. The subject is becoming a child of God.

And you get that by faith in Jesus Christ. My worthy opponent then betrays his hand by saying that all Christianity is, is putting on clothes—like you put on Christ—your act, your honor, your glory—you and the minister—that's all. God isn't in it. Ladies and Gentlemen, our God is an infinitely greater God than that. He can take and has taken with briny tears on this altar hundreds and thousands of men and women who had their nature changed by the power of God and they became children of God by faith in Jesus Christ. And they were born again and now they were children and they grew and God opened their eyes that they ought to follow him by putting on the badge of discipleship and they put on Jesus Christ by being baptized into Christ. That's what that verse teaches. And the verse before it: first, the nature is changed, second, the man puts on the clothes. That's exactly what it says. Read it yourself. Gal. 3:26-27.

Now, he said distinguish the difference:

"Baptism doth not save us."
"Baptism doth save us not."

There actually isn't any difference except that the way I arranged it on the board is truer to the scripture than the way he arranged it—I got more scripture there than he had. (Laughter.)

My worthy opponent said in his explanation of the dying thief that a will is not in force until the testator dies. He says: "From the death of Christ then baptism is in force." Therefore the dying thief was saved just before Christ died. Didn't he say that? Ladies and Gentlemen, that's not so. He knows it is not so. He didn't think so when he said that. I call this audience to witness if he didn't say that. Christ died before the dying thief died. How long before we don't know. When the soldiers came around they found Christ already dead. In order to kill the dying thief they broke his knees and legs with a hammer. And some hour or hours after Christ already was dead—and according to my worthy opponent the new covenant was in force —then the dying thief died and is in hell according to my opponent. Because he died after the death of a testator. Now, I'm just taking his theology. Trotting out his horses.

He said I said the Holy Ghost fell on Cornelius when he was a sinner. I did not say that. I challenge him to go back and listen to the record. I was careful what I said. He asked me, was Cornelius a sinner? I said, "Yes, all have sinned and come short of the glory of God." He was saved and the Holy Ghost fell on him. The Holy Ghost fell on him after he was saved. He was saved when he believed or when he believed the word; the Holy Ghost fell on him; then he was baptized reluctantly by Peter.

Now, my worthy opponent entered John 3:5, "Verily, verily I say unto thee except a man be born of water and the Spirit he can not enter into the kingdom of God. That which is born of the flesh is flesh, That which is born of Spirit is spirit. Marvel not that I said unto thee ye must be born again." Now I'm very thankful he is very agreeable. I appreciate that. Now the issue we are debating is: Is baptism essential to salvation. "Verily, verily I say unto thee", said Jesus, "Except a man be born of water and of the Spirit he can not enter the kingdom of God." Listen to this verse. That was said before Pentecost. And that was said before Jesus died. That was said before the new covenant was in effect. The man to whom that was told needed to be born again and was born again and so far as we know never was baptized—Nicodemus. And it was said some time before my opponent said this baptism business came into effect. Now, he said it—I didn't I have been anxious for him to put his finger on it. If a will is not in force until the death of the testator, therefore the dying thief entered into the grace of God before the death of Jesus—Jesus said that before His death but the dying thief died after the death of Jesus. Listen, mark it, remember that. He's got himself up one of his blind alleys now. He is hung on a "not".

Second, if that means baptism, if that verse means baptism then baptism is before belief or the birth of the Spirit—and my worthy opponent's position is that belief comes first and baptism after. He is correct in order but not in design. Listen again, if John 3:5—remember this, he will be backing down on that position before this is over. He will be as silent as the tomb. If "born of water" means baptism then the word "born" carries the phrase water and of the Spirit. The preposition "of" occurs only once in the qualifying phrase and does not occur in connection with the Spirit. Go read your Bibles. Ladies and Gentlemen, mark down the scriptures and go home and read your Bibles and see whether these things we say are so or not. That's good for my people and that's good for Church of Christ. Read your Bible and don't believe either one of us. Both of us are under pressure, we're liable to make some statements that we don't quite agree with. He's going to get out of that death of Christ tomorrow night—if he does not he is hopelessly lost. Very fortunately I have been extremely careful. I have not so far as I know made any statement that I will back off the slightest iota.

Wait a minute: read your Bibles and see if that second "of" in the expression "of water" is in italics. Therefore the text enders it "Except a man be born of water and of the Spirit he can not enter the kingdom of God." This clearly shows that the action of the new birth—whatever water means—takes place at the same time "born of the Spirit" occurs. Therefore, my opponent can find no comfort in "born of the water" meaning baptism. Beyond question this scripture is interpreted by Eph. 5:26 that he might sanctify and cleanse it with the washing of water by the word as James tells us, "Of his own will begat he us with the word of truth that we should be a kind of first fruits of his creatures." Christ sanctified and cleansed it with the washing of water by the word. That's Eph. 5:26, James 1:3, "Of his own will begat he us with the word of truth." 1 Pet. 1:23, born again not of corruptible seed but of incorruptible by the word of God. Now, water there unquestionably means the word and the Spirit.

Now, let me turn around and cover every argument that he presented last night and tonight.

(1) Instead of I Cor. 1:12-13 teaching baptism is essential to salvation, the whole passage which my worthy opponent did not read last night until I made him read it; and then he dodged it completely since that time except for one time tonight when I pressed him unduly. Listen, the whole passage must be taken together. Paul says, "I thank God I baptized none of you." Now, the question is not at all about Paul being crucified or Cephas being crucified, the question is the question of division in the church at Corinth. Some of them were saying "Here, I'm following Paul." Some of them, "I'm following Cephas" and some of them, "I'm following Apollos" and some of them, "I'm following Christ." And in that divided church so seriously divided, the apostle Paul says, "None of us actually wrought anything in the sense of divine power or might. All we were was messengers; we brought the message—that's all. Just mouthpieces to declare we weren't crucified for you, none are divided, Christ isn't divided. Now, "I thank God I didn't baptize any of you." Now let me call your attention to this: Paul was saved on the road to Damascus, when he saw the Lord. He said he was not disobedient to that vision. He confessed Jesus as Lord and the apostle Paul three days later was baptized. He says in I Cor. 15:8 that he saw the Lord and when he saw the Lord he was born. Here the apostle Paul again runs absolutely counter to the position of my opponent and the apostle Paul here minimizes baptism to my

way of thinking far more than I would ever want to. "I thank God I baptized none of you lest you should say I baptized in my own name; I baptized the household of Stephanas besides I know not whether I baptized any other for Christ sent me not to baptize but to preach the gospel not with words of wisdom lest the cross of Christ, should be made of none effect." Paul says in I Cor. 4:5 "Though ye have ten thousand instructors in Christ ye have not many fathers in Christ Jesus I have begotten you through the gospel." He begat all of them. The word, Ladies and Gentlemen, is not conceive but that word is begat in the sense that I brought you through to birth. It is the same word as used born in other places. He begat all of them but did not baptize all of them. If a person cannot be born again without baptism then Paul lied when he said he begat them but thanked God he did not baptize them. Therefore: I Cor. 1:12-13 teaches that baptism is not essential to salvation for baptism has nothing to do with a birth because Paul brought them through to birth

(2) Paul explains the mission of ministers of grace in I Cor. 1:17—we are sent not to baptize but to preach the gospel, therefore baptism is not essential to salvation.

(4) My worthy opponent makes much of Mark 16:16 and yet he denies the balance of the chapter having to do with miracles. I dare him to say he accepts it. Mk. 16:16 does not show baptism is essential to salvation. It shows believing is essential to a salvation and refusal to believe is the only cause for damnation, therefore: it does not teach baptism is essential to salvation.

(5) Mk. 16:16 is a work of righteousness as recorded in Matt. 3:15. Concerning thhe baptism of Jesus. The Savior said unto. him, "Suffer it to be so now for thus it becometh us to fulfill all righteousness, then he suffered him." Jesus said baptism is a work of righteousness. The Bible says we are not saved by works of righteousness—Titus 3:5, "Not by works of righteousness which we have done but according to his mercy he saved us by the washing of regeneration and the renewing of the Holy Ghost," therefore Mark 16:16 can not teach that which is contrary to Matt. 3:15 and Titus 3:5.

(6) Mark 16:16 contrasts salvation and damnation on the basis of believing. It pronounces no damnation on the unbap-

tized believer, therefore: Mk. 16:16 teaches that believing is the essential to salvation and baptism is an act of obedience for saved believers.

(7) In Acts 2:38 it can mean either way. I was perfectly honest with you. I have tried to be honest, Ladies and Gentlemen. I must stand before God some day. I would not knowingly lead a soul astray for the world. I never have sold out to an organization or a movement. I want to know the truth of God. I have used my days and years and hours industriously. Jesus Christ saved me from sin one day. It was many days later, many months later, I was led to the truth of baptism. I followed Him in baptism. The Holy Spirit witnessed in my heart and witnesses today and I know I have passed from death unto life. I have never had to sell out to a movement or follow a certain form of doctrine. I believe if there is the slightest reason in my opponent's position, I'll tell you so. Acts 2:38 is the only leg he can stand on and then it's a cracked leg.. (Laughter). Listen, it can mean either way and the only scripture in the whole Bible that's true of. The preposition "eis" can mean "in order to" or second, "with reference to" or third, "because of". Now this is a sample. Matt. 12:40, "they repented at the preaching of Jonah," or "at the preaching of Jonah," or "because of the preaching of Jonah." Take your choice. It can mean any of them. They repented "with reference to the preaching of Jonah." They repented "because of the preaching of Jonah." Which makes the most sense? Jonah preached once before they repented, they did not repent in order to the preaching of Jonah, they did not repent for the preaching of Jonah but they repented because of, in reference to because they had heard the preaching of Jonah. "Repent and be baptized everyone of you for" or "because of" "in reference to" because your sins have been remitted, "the remission of sins and ye shall receive the gift of the Holy Ghost." Therefore: Acts 2:38 does not teach baptism is essential to salvation but it is because of salvation.

(8) My worthy opponent said that I said a second person plural number and a third person singular number could not be joined together. I did not say that. I said that that unusual Greek grammar construction would not sustain my worthy opponent's position. The words "repent" and "be baptized" are tied together with a conjunction. The word repent is in the sec-

ond person, plural number, therefore it is a direct command to everyone. And the Greek for "be baptized" is third person singular and not a direct command. That's what I said. That's what I say tonight. Therefore: Acts 2:38 can not mean baptism is essential to salvation. A man is electrocuted "for murder"—not in order to commit murder but because he already committed murder. "Baptised for the remission of sins," not in order for sins to be remitted but because they have been remitted.

(9) Instead of Acts 9:6, Acts 22:16, teaching that baptism is essential to salvation, it proves just the opposite. Paul said in 1 Cor. 15:8, "Last of all he was seen of me also as one born out of due time." He was born when he saw the Lord. Since he was not baptized until three days later, therefore, baptism Paul says is not essential to salvation. Paul confessed Jesus as Lord on the Damascus road. Listen I Cor. 12:3 says "Wherefore I give you to understand that no man speaketh by the Spirit of God calleth Jesus accursed. No man can say that Jesus is Lord but by the Holy Ghost." Paul said Jesus was His Lord. Since that confession was made three days before his baptism, therefore: baptism was not with Paul and is not today essential to salvation.

(10) Now Acts 22:16, "Now why tarriest thou arise and be baptized and wash away thy sins calling on the name of the Lord." Baptism is a symbol of salvation. Paul himself was told to wash away his sins. He washed them away by baptism according to this reading. Can a man wash away his own sins, I ask you? Can water on the flesh wash away sins of the heart? God alone can forgive sins. The blood of Jesus Christ alone can cleanse men. Therefore: Paul was symbolically to wash away his sins in the water of baptism.

(11) Baptism is a symbol of the reality, baptism is a figure of the death burial and resurrection of Jesus Christ. Baptism is only the shadow—not the substance. Baptism has no meaning unless there has been an actual remission of sins. Here in Birmingham at five points is a monument honoring Brother Bryan. The monument would be meaningless if Brother Bryan had not been first. Don't look for forgiveness or remission of sins in a tank of water. Baptism is outwardly to declare that our sins have been washed away by the blood of Jesus Christ.

(12) Contrary to the assertion of my worthy opponent,

Gal. 3:27 proves that baptism has nothing to do with salvation but is the next step after salvation for the verse before says we are children of God. Therefore, baptism is not essential to salvation. Baptism is a step signifying profession of Jesus Christ—growing up into Christ.

(13) Instead of I Pet. 3:21 teaching baptism is essential to salvation it teaches exactly the opposite. "The like figure whereunto even baptism doth also now save us not the putting away of the filth of the flesh but the answer of a good conscience toward God by the resurrection of Jesus Christ." It says baptism is a figure—"the like figure whereunto baptism." It says it is a figure of what saves us. Baptism is a figure of the death burial and resurrection of Christ we are told in Rom. 6. He says we are saved "by the resurrection of Jesus Christ." The last phrase and verse after the brackets, therefore: we are not saved by baptism but by a resurrection and baptism is not essential to salvation. It declares that baptism that saves us is not the actual putting away of the filth of the flesh, it declares that the act of baptism is the answer of a good conscience.

And I thank you, Ladies and Gentlemen.

PORTER-TINGLEY DEBATE

Fifth Session: 7:30 P. M., February 28, 1947

Birmingham Gospel Tabernacle, Birmingham, Alabama

Chairman: Emerson J. Estes — Birmingham, Alabama

Prayer: T. L. Marsden — Birmingham, Alabama

Moderators: Walter Hemingway, Bessemer, Alabama, for Mr. Tingley; Gus Nichols, Jasper, Alabama, for Mr. Porter.

Proposition: The Scriptures Teach that Alien Sinners Are Saved by Faith Alone Before and Without Water Baptism.

Glenn V. Tingley, Affirms
W. Curtis Porter, Denies

(Affirmative Address by Glenn V. Tingley)

Mr. Chairman, Gentlemen Moderators, Worthy Opponent, Ladies and Gentlemen:

My worthy opponent has been laboring under great physical difficulty. I, too, have been laboring under physical difficulty fighting a cold. I sincerely trust I will be able to complete tonight. I trust that I may have your interest and prayers. I will endeavor to hold my voice down so that it does not break.

The question has already been stated, "The Scriptures Teach that Alien Sinners are Saved by Faith alone before and without Water Baptism."

First there is no dispute between my worthy opponent and myself in regard to the fact that all Christians ought to be baptized but that they must be baptized in order to be saved is the point at issue. I feel that every Christian ought to be baptized. I believe that that is a plain command of the word of God to follow in obedience as well as a host of other commands for Christians.

"The scriptures"—the word of God, the sixty-six books of the Bible, "teach" is to show, to guide, to direct, to make to know how, to instruct, to cause to know, "alien sinners"—sinners who have never confessed Christ as Lord and Savior; "are saved"—that is justified, regenerated, converted, the sinner becomes a child of God "by faith alone" and "without water baptism." A word concerning faith. (Both my worthy opponent and myself are agreed as to the mode.) "Faith"—act or state of acknowledging unquestioningly the existence and power of a Supreme Being; the reality of the divine order. Historical faith is an assent to the truth revealed in the scriptures. Justifying faith is a saving grace wrought in the soul by the Spirit of God whereby one receives Christ.

A word or two concerning the matters that have gone before for this is, as my worthy opponent has already said, actually a continuation of the debate last night and the night before just reversed. I asked my worthy opponent some questions which he hedged on and refused to answer plain and open, free and frank. I insist that my worthy opponent answer those questions. You young ministers of the Church of Christ and members of the Church of Christ are taught these things and yet here is your exponent that refuses to state these things. He refuses to take his stand fairly and honestly and I challenge my opponent to give a fair and square, open answer to these questions.

First, are Methodists, Presbyterians and all Pedo-baptists lost and will they go to hell? I challenge him to answer that question. Let me pause a moment to say I believe every one—members of the Church of Christ, Catholics, Presbyterians, Baptists, Methodists—everyone with a church name or without a church name who has saving faith in Jesus Christ is saved and will go to heaven. I believe that with all my soul. My worthy opponent will not tell you if Methodists, Presbyterians and Pedo-Baptists are lost. I challenge him. For three nights I have challenged him and he never has met it squarely.

(2) Are Moody, Finney, Sankey, Billy Sunday, Wesley, Whitfield and all who have not been baptized by immersion lost and in hell?

(3) What baptism saves—Church of Christ, Baptist, Christian and Missionary Alliance?

(4) Will my worthy opponent accept one whom I baptize without rebaptizing him?

(5) Are those baptized by Baptist and Christian and Missionary Alliance preachers saved or damned? This audience has

a right to know what my worthy opponent believes and my worthy opponent dare not answer that question. He will have to hedge and twist and squirm and make you think he has answered it without ever answering it.

(6) Show me one scripture which states that a man is lost if he is not baptized.

(7) Is it true or not that a person has no chance to be saved who is not baptized into the Church of Christ of which he (my worthy opponent) is a member?

(8) I challenge my worthy opponent to tell this audience why Paul did not baptize a new convert every time he believed.

(9) What is the order of events in conversion? (10) What is faith? (11) Which comes first—faith or repentence in the conversion of the sinner?

My opponent said, in order to clear up a matter or two of last night, that the new covenant did not come into force until Christ died. Remember he said that. He quoted Heb. 9:16-17 and he said that in answer to my proposition in regard to the dying thief. He quoted "where a testament is of force there must also of necessity be the death of the testator for a testament is of force after men are dead; otherwise it is of no strength at all while the testator liveth." Now the dying thief died after Christ died. My worthy opponent said that the New covenant and baptism came into effect when Christ died. The dying thief died after Christ died. Jesus said he would be in Paradise. My worthy opponent said that he's in hell—if he had the courage to say it. His proposition says it. And he got himself in that hole. I didn't. I didn't expect him to get himself in that hole. He just fell in there.

In Luke 23:42-43 Jesus said, "Today thou shat be with me in Paradise." He died hours after Christ.

Now my worthy opponent has continually used the illustration of eating and digesting in order to keep from starving and he referred it to Mark 16:16 as being silly to say, "If he does not eat and does not digest he shall starve." In the field of physiology the act of eating is completed and then digestion comes as an aftermath. Every solitary thing he trots up proves my contention. If a man is saved by faith—he is saved. And baptism and everything else comes as naturally as digestion and assimilation and perspiration and elimination follow naturally. My worthy opponent only proves my point. He can't digest without eating; when he eats he will digest. Digestion is not a thing that nourishes though—it is assimilation that nourishes. Glucose can keep a man alive and it is never digested. Believing is the life giving element like eating is the lifegiving element. Salvation is not outward but inward—it's not of the body but of the heart. 2 Cor. 5:17, "Wherefore if any man be in Christ he is a new creature. old things are passed away behold all things are become new."

My worthy opponent last night and the night before got himself in another terrible hole. That hole is Gal. 3:27 in that he said: "put on Christ—you can not get into your clothes until you put them on. Putting on clothes is salvation. Those who are baptized into Christ have put on Christ." Now that's according to my worthy opponent and that's as far as he knows, that's as far as he goes. That's as far as his theology goes; that's the fundamental difference. He never reads the verse before. A sinner can put on Christ symbolically all he wants to and if there has not taken place before he ever puts on Christ the miracle called the new birth all the putting on Christ in the world does not amount to that much. (Snapping finger.) Verse 26 says, "Ye are all the children of God by faith in Christ Jesus." And "As many of you as have been baptized into Christ," you have put on Christ, you have put on the grownup garments. And they are children before they are ever dressed. They have to be born children of God before they can ever wear the symbol or badge of Christian discipleship. It is the difference between a fundamental change or an outward profession. I believe in a fundamental inner change wrought by the Holy Ghost whereby a person who was a sinner becomes a saint and a new creature in Christ Jesus. My worthy opponent does not believe that. He believes in putting on salvation like you put on a suit. I believe in being children of God by birth. In I John 5:10, "He that believeth on the Son hath the witness in himself." I ask my worthy opponent does he believe in the witness of the Holy Spirit within the human heart whereby an individual knows he is a child of God? He will not answer that.

"He that believeth not God has made Him a liar because he

believeth not the record that God gave of His Son." Col. 1:27—"to whom God would make known what is the riches of the glory of this mystery unto the Gentiles." Now what is the secret of this mystery? "Christ in you the hope of glory." Ladies and Gentlemen, I one day was a church member. I had been baptized; I was as lost as the devil. One day the gospel dawned on my heart by the Holy Ghost and I became a child of God by the Holy Spirit applying the word to my heart. I have the witness in my heart and I have Christ living within me and I am a born again child of God. If you do not know within your heart that kind of faith, my dear friend; that is for you, too. Eph. 3:17— "That Christ may dwell in your hearts by faith that ye being rooted and grounded in love"—no mention of baptism in any of these. Rom. 10:9-10—the great recipe of salvation, "But if thou shalt confess with thy mouth the Lord Jesus and believe in thine heart that God has raised Him from the dead thou shalt be saved, for with the heart man believeth unto righteousness and with the mouth confession is made unto salvation." Salvation is not by works. Eph. 2:8-10 says, "For by grace are ye saved through faith and that not of yourselves; it is the gift of God; not of works lest any man should boast for we are his workmanship" —He works on us. It is not of our works. "Created unto good works which were before ordained that we should walk in them." Rom. 5:19 says, "For as by one man's disobedience many were made sinners so by the obedience of one was many made righteous." Christ's work does the whoe work. You can't add to it or take from it—you accept it and the Spirit of God will make it real in your heart. Now, the Bible says that baptism is a work of righteousness and the Bible says that you can not be saved by works of righteousness. Matt. 3:15 regarding Jesus' baptism says, "suffer it to be so now for thus it becometh us to fulfill all righteousness" and "he baptized Him". Titus 3:5-7 says, "Not by works of righteousness which we have done." Then baptism didn't save Jesus, baptism can't save anybody. Faith in Christ saves them. We are "saved by grace through faith and that not of yourselves, it is the gift of God." Rom. 4:5 says "but to him that worketh not." The individual that works can not be saved while he is working. He has got to quit working and throw up his hands and surrender. "But to him that worketh not but believeth on him that justifieth the ungodly his faith is counted for righteousness." Sinners are saved by faith before water baptism.

A great body of scriptures tell us plainly how we get into Christ. My worthy opponent wanted me to tell him. Certainly he is ignorant of the matter evidently—so I'll tell him now. My worthy opponent quoted Luke 7:39 as proof that baptism is essential to salvation—now he got himself into that. Now that was before Calvary which he said last night was the point that the new covenant went into effect. I agree that the requirements of salvation are the same before Calvary as they are after Calvary. What it took to save a man before Calvary it takes to save a man after Calvary. Now listen to Jesus and the Holy Spirit on how a man is saved. I am only quoting a very small portion of each of the verses because of time.

(1) John 1:12—"Even to them that believe on His name which were born not of blood nor of the will of the flesh nor of the will of man but of God." No baptism there.

(2) John 2:11—"His disciples believed on Him." No baptism.

(3) John 2:23—"Many believed on Him." No baptism mentioned there.

(4) John 3:16—"Whosoever believeth on Him." No baptism.

(5) John 3:18—"He that believeth on Him." No baptism mentioned there.

(6) John 3:36—"He that believeth on the Son." No baptism there.

(7) John 4:38—"Believed on Him." No baptism.

(8) John 6:29—"Believe on Him." No baptism.

(9) John 6:35—"He that believeth on me." Not a word said about baptism there.

(10) John 6:40—"Believeth on Him." No baptism.

(11) John 7:5—"Believe in Him." No baptism.

(12) John 7:31—"Believed on Him." No baptism there.

(13) John 7:38—"He that believeth on me." No baptism there.

(14) John 7:39—"They that believe on Him." No baptism there.

(15) John 8:30—"Many believed on Him." No baptism there.

(16) John 9:35—"Believe on the Son." No baptism there.

(17) John 10:42—"Many believed on him." No baptism.

(18) John 11:25—"He that believeth in Me." No baptism there.

(19) John 11:45—"Believe on Him." No baptism mentioned.

(20) John 12:11—"And believed on Jesus." No baptism mentioned.

(21) John 12:42—"Many believed on Him." No baptism there.

(22) John 12:44—"He that believeth on me." No baptism.

(23) John 12:46—"He that believeth on me." No baptism there.

(24) John 14:1—"Ye believe in God, believe also in me." No baptism mentioned there.

(25) John 14:12—"He that believeth on me." No baptism in any of these.

(26) John 16:9—"Because they believe in me." John 17:20 —"Which shall believe on me through their word. (27) Acts 10:43—"Whosoever believeth on Him shall receive remission of sins." (28) Phil. 1:29—"Not only to believe on Him." (29) I John 5:10—"He that believeth on the Son of God." (30) I John 5:13—"That you may believe on the name of the Son of God." No baptism mentioned there. (31) I John 5:1—"Whosoever believeth that Jesus is the Christ is born of God." No baptism there.

I could go on. I could mention a hundred more scriptures or more than that to prove that baptism is not essential to salvation —that believing is essential to salvation.

(32) John 4:39-43—"Many of the Samaritans in that city believed on him for the saying of the woman which she testified he told me whatever I did. They said unto the woman, now we believe." No baptism there.

(33) John 5:14—"Afterward Jesus findeth him in the temple

and said unto him, Behold thou art made whole sin no more lest a worse thing come on thee." No baptism.

(34) Jesus said, John 5:24, "Verily I say unto you he that heareth my words and believeth on him that sent me hath everlasting life." If my opponent's position is correct, John 5:24 is a lie. "And shall not come into condemnation but is passed from death unto life." No baptism.

(35) Again Jesus said, John 6:29, "This is the work of God that ye believe on him whom he hath sent. Jesus said unto them, I am the bread of life. He that cometh to me shall never hunger. He that believeth on me shall never thirst; all that the Father giveth me shall come to me and him that cometh to me I will in no wise cast out." No baptism.

Now here's a question: if baptism had been essential to salvation as my worthy opponent says it is in Mk. 16:16 and Acts 2:38 and these others: Is it reasonable that God would give us 200 passages on how to be saved with faith and salvation linked together and not mention the act of baptism as essential to salvation? Do you think that that is reasonable with God? Not a bit of it. Ladies and Gentlemen, my worthy opponent found four verses where baptism and salvation are mentioned together. Four. I can give him more than 200 where believing and salvation are mentioned together!

Saving faith is a gift of God offered to all. There's historical faith. It's a speculative knowledge or assent to the truth revealed in the scriptures. Of this kind of faith the apostle James speaks then he says in James 2:17, "even so faith if it hath not works is dead being alone." That is not a mere profession of faith or assent to the truth that is not evidenced by the fruit of the Spirit and good works which proceed from faith and show it to be the right kind: that is not the faith that is the gift of God—saving faith, justifying faith. Historical faith is intellectual assent. I believe that George Washington lived. There is nothing saving about that faith—nothing changing about that, that's historical faith. There's justifying faith—that is saving grace wrought in the soul by the Spirit of God whereby we receive Christ as He is revealed in the gospel as our saving substitute and risen Lord, trust in and reliance upon Him and His righteousness alone for salvation. That faith begets a sincere obedience and consecration in the life of the believer.

Now let me show you that faith is a gift of God. Ladies and Gentlemen who follow my worthy opponent if these scriptures which I am to read to you are true then the position of my worthy opponent is absolutely untenable. Anyone who has not the witness in himself and anyone who has not received the gift of faith from God is damned from God to a devil's hell.

(1) Eph. 2:8—My worthy opponent does not believe in faith as a gift from God, my worthy opponent does not believe in a miraculous faith that changes a person's life wrought by operation of God in the individual making him a new creature. My worthy opponent does not believe that. He will explain his belief to you if I can only get him to do it clearly as Alexander Campbell did. I can make him do worse than even his arguments did on the blackboard last night. Listen, "For by grace are you saved through faith." Through faith—Do we have faith? "And that not of yourselves it is the gift of God." That's the message of the Bible. The faith that saves is God's gift. As I shall stand before God and as you shall stand before God, men and women if you have not received the gift of saving faith, you are lost no matter how you have been baptised. "For we are his workmanship"—that is, God works on us. "Created in Christ Jesus unto good works which God hath foreordained that we should walk in them."

(2) Mark 11:22—"Jesus answering said unto him, have faith in God." Look in the margin of your Bible. If you will look in the later translations—the American Revised, the American Standard or the one that came out last year that my worthy opponent quoted, look in that—it says "have the faith of God." It's not have faith in God in the original it's have "God's faith," that is the faith God gives and works in us.

(3) Gal. 2:20—"I am crucified with Christ, nevertheless I live yet not I but Christ liveth in me and the life which I now live in the flesh I live by what? "By the faith." By the faith of who? By what faith? "By the faith of the Son of God." "Who loved me and gave himself for me." The Bible says the Son of God gives me His faith which is saving faith. If you have it you can look the world in the face and say, "I know I am saved."

(4) Heb. 2:12 says plainly it's a God given faith. "Looking

unto Jesus the author and the finisher." Who produced this faith? "The author." Who is the author? "Jesus." Who will finish it? "Jesus." "Of our faith; who for the joy that was set before him endured the cross despising the shame and is set down on the right hand of the throne of God." Jesus is the author and the finisher, the perfector of faith for salvation. Listen, Jesus Christ is the only one who can give you faith that can save you. It's the personal truth apart from meritorious works. The Lord Jesus Christ was delivered for our offenses, raised for our justification.

Rom. 4:5, 23, 25. "But to him that worketh not." You can't work to be saved. If you work you can't be saved until you stop working and trust. "To him that worketh not." But does what? "But believeth on him that justifieth the ungodly, his faith is counted for righteousness. Now, it was not written for his sake alone that it was imputed to him." Now he's speaking about Abraham, "but for us also to whom"—what? "This faith," this believing, "shall be imputed". Get that word imputed? Imputed means you don't have it. We haven't got it naturally. Can't get it naturally; we can't develop it. "Imputed" the dictionary says is "to ascribe vicariously." Christ has to give it to us or we are lost. "If we believe on him that raised Jesus our Lord from the dead who was delivered for our transgressions and raised again for our justification." No works. No baptism. Salvation by faith.

(6)) John 1:12-13—"But as many as received him to them gave he power to become Sons of God even to them that believe on His name which were born not of blood nor of the will of flesh nor of the will of man but of God." How were they born? Were they born by their belief? No, they were born by God—they were born of God. They weren't born of man, they weren't born of their own will. My opponent will tell you it is your will. The Bible says it isn't your will. It says it's God's.

(7) John 6:29—"Jesus said unto them, This is the work of God that"—Lord what is the work of God? The work of God that He will work in the sinner's heart after he repents is "that ye believe on him whom he hath sent."

(8) John 20:31—"But these are written that you might believe that Jesus is the Christ the Son of the God and that be-

lieving you might have life through His name." Believing, we have life.

(9) Acts 3:16—"And his name through faith in his name hath made this man strong whom you see and know, yea the faith which is by"—whom? Jesus Christ. "By him hath given this perfect soundness in the presence of you all." Faith comes from God alone. Faith is by him.

(10) Rom. 10:9-10—"If thou shalt confess with thy mouth the Lord Jesus and believe in thy heart thou shalt be saved." Repentance comes first before faith. Here is where our fundamental difference will be. I want my worthy opponent to note this. Mr. Campbell, the founder of the so-called Church of Christ, says that faith is simple belief of the truth and never can be more or less than that. Faith, he says, is merely the intellectual acceptance of a fact and therefore repentance follows faith. Now the question does not say that Mr. Campbell taught that a sinner was saved from his alien sins by faith before and without baptism but the proposition says the scriptures. I have read to you the scriptures which says faith has to come from God, He has to give it to you. You can't be saved without it. If you work to get it you will never have it. Now, let's read Christ's word—Mark 1:15. "Saying the time is fulfilled, the kingdom of heaven is at hand, Repent and believe." My worthy opponent will say believe and repent. Jesus said, "Repent and Believe."

(11) Mt. 21:31-32—"Whether of them twain did the will of his father? They say unto him the first. Jesus said unto them, Verily I say unto you that the Publicans and harlots go into the kingdom of God before you. John came unto you in the way of righteousness and ye believed him not but the Publicans and harlots believed him and ye when ye had seen it—" What stopped you from believing? "Ye, when ye had seen it repented not afterward." Why? What is the result of repenting? "That ye might believe." You can not believe until first you have repented. Repent first, and then believe. That's the teaching of the word. Repentance and then faith put the Publicans and harlots into the kingdom of God but the priests and the elders would not repent, therefore, they could not believe.

(12) The apostle Paul said concerning his preaching in Acts 20:20-21, "I kept back nothing that was profitable unto you

testifying both to the Jews and also to the Greeks repentance toward God"—first—"faith toward our Lord Jesus Christ." He kept back nothing from them. His sermon and his message was repentance toward and faith toward our Lord Jesus Christ. Not a solitary word about baptism.

(13) The writer of the book of Hebrews said, Heb. 6:1-2, "Therefore leaving the principles of the doctrine of Christ, let us go on to perfection not laying again the foundation of repentance from dead works and faith toward God." Repentance and faith. Repentance from dead works and then faith. Repentance from dead works and then saving faith. Repentance was and is prior to faith.

(14) Peter stood before the apostles and elders to make this point in Acts 15:8-9, "God which knoweth the hearts bear them witness giving them the Holy Ghost even as He did us and put no difference between them and us purifying their hearts by faith." Faith purifies the heart. Saving faith always brings purification of heart. If faith does not follow repentance but if faith comes ahead of repentance, then my opponent has men with pure hearts before they have ever repented. Could there be anything more grossly expounded than that? Faith precedes repentance? Faith comes after repentance.

Mr. Campbell placed, as do the so-called Churches of Christ, faith before repentance. Christ said repentance and then faith. Mk. 1:15, "The time is fulfilled, Repent and believe." Paul summarized it by saying, "Repentance and faith." The book of Hebrews says, "Repentance and faith". Peter said, Acts 15:9, "Purifying their hearts by faith."

Now, Ladies and Gentlemen, the fundamental difference in this debate, right now we have reached the key point: is an individual saved within by faith?

I thank you.

Fifth Night—Porter's First Speech

Mr. President, Gentlemen Moderators, Worthy Opponent, Ladies and Gentlemen:

I am glad to come before you again at this time and in the negative of the proposition which my opponent has been affirming for the past thirty minutes. "The scriptures teach that alien sinners are saved by faith alone before and without water baptism."

I just want to mention, in the first place, the last argument that my friend made, and then I shall go back and review the other matters. That was with respect to the order of repentance and faith in the plan of salvation. He gave us a number of statements in which repentance was mentioned first, as Mk. 1:15; Mat. 21:32; Acts 20:21. He reasoned from all of these that men must repent before they can believe the gospel, or before they can believe in the Lord. He wants to know which comes first, repentance or faith. That comes in the questions presently. But I will just state here, for his consideration, that repentance does come before the degree of faith that saves is reached. And not only is that so, but even baptism comes before that degree of faith that saves is reached, friend Tingley. So you can be thinking of that while I come to other matters and get back to it a little later on.

Now, I have some questions for my friend. You know he said the other night that when men ask questions they are in desperation. So it seems that my friend, even though he is in the affirmative tonight, is in desperation and comes back with a lot of questions. At least, I was not in enough desperation that I gave him a lot of written questions while I was in the affirmative, but I don't mind that at all. He is the man who said it represents desperation; and so we'll just let it go that way. But here are my questions for him:

1. Where are the scriptures in the New Testament that contain the expression "faith alone" or "faith only"? I hope my friend will be "brutally honest" and give us the passages.

2. What is the difference between faith and repentance?

3. Is it any worse for a good, honest Methodist or Baptist to be lost than it is for a good, honest Jew to be lost?

4. What translation gives "because of" as the rendering of "eis" in Acts 2:38?

5. Does the word "for," from the Greek word "gar," in Gal. 3:28, mean "to introduce the reason," as the lexicons say?

6. Since you say the statement made by Paul that "Christ sent me not to baptize" proves that baptism is not essential to salvation, then if he had been sent to baptize, would that prove that baptism is essential?

7. If such expressions as "He was decorated for bravery" and "He was electrocuted for murder" were translated into Greek, would the preposition "for" be translated into the Greek preposition "eis" found in Acts 2:38?

8. Is an alien sinner saved by a living faith or by a dead faith?

9. Is faith alone—faith without works—living or dead?

(At this point Mr. Porter handed the questions to Mr. Tingley who said, "Thank you.")

Now, then, before I reply to the things that have been said and answer his questions I have just a few negative or counter arguments that I wish to introduce, showing, in the first place, that there is something required in addition to faith.

In James 2:14 James said, "What doth it profit though a man say he hath faith, and not works? Can faith save him?" Or as the Revised Version reads, "Can that faith save him?" Speaking of faith without works he said, "Can that faith save him?" In James 2:17 we are told that faith without works is dead being alone. James 2:26 says, "As the body without the spirit is dead, so faith without works is dead also." In James 2:24 we have the statement made, "We see then how that by works a man is justified, and N-O-T—not by faith only." My friend is going to get wrecked on the "not". James says "a man is justified by works and n-o-t—not—by faith only." My friend's proposition says a man is saved by faith alone or by faith only. But the Book of God says that a man is not justified by faith only. You can just take your choice as to which you are willing to believe.

We are not denying that men are justified by faith. Certainly, I believe that men are saved by faith. But when my friend puts in that word "alone" or "only" that's a different proposition altogether. There is not one single, solitary passage in all the Book of God that says a man is saved by faith alone. The only verse is all of God's Book that speaks about it in those terms is the one I have just given, and it says "N-O-T—not—by faith only."

All right. Again, in John 11:12 we are told that Jesus "came to His own, and His own received Him not. But as many as received Him, to them gave He power to become the sons of God, even to them that believe on His name." Here believers are given power to become the sons of God. If they were sons of God just the moment they believed, then they would not be given power to become the sons of God. That shows there is something in addition to faith.

In John 8:31-34 we find certain people who believed on Christ, and yet they were said to be the children of the devil. I'll get to some more of that presently.

In John 12:42-43 many of the chief rulers "believed on Him" but would not confess him, lest they be put out of the synagogue, for "they loved the praise of men more than the praise of God."

In Acts 11:21 we are told that a great number believed "and turned to the Lord." There was a thing referred to as belief, and there was something that followed that which is called "turning to the Lord." They believed and turned to the Lord. My friend's proposition insists that just as soon as they believed they had already turned to the Lord, and there can not be any such thing as "and turned to the Lord."

In the second place, we have salvation depending on repentance. In Luke 13:3 Jesus said, "Except ye repent, ye shall all likewise perish." In Acts 3:19 Peter states that repentance is that "sins may be blotted out." In Acts 17:30 all men everywhere are commanded to repent, said Paul. Acts 11:18—God hath to the Gentiles granted "repentance unto life." And so, on through Acts 26:20 and 2 Cor. 7:10 and 2 Peter 3:9 and many other passages that we might use to show beyond a doubt that men can not be saved without repentance. I'm telling you, my friends, that faith alone is not faith plus repentance. If sinners are saved by faith alone, you can save sinners without repentance, because faith alone means faith to the exclusion of everything else. Tingley, do you believe a man is saved without repentance? Will you contend that a man does not have to repent to be saved? Certainly, you are not going to do without repentance, are you? Well, is faith alone faith plus repentance? or is it faith to the exclusion of repentance? Now, you can see where my friend is, to begin with, on this proposition. "Faith alone" means faith without anything else. If there is anything else, it is not faith alone. So "faith alone" means faith without repentance. If there is repentance involved in it, then it is not "faith alone," and my friend must give up his proposition. If his proposition is true, men are saved without repentance, because it says they are saved by faith alone. We will pass, then, from that.

I come to his questions next. I am amused at my friend. He gave me all of these questions—or practically all of them—just this way when I was in the affirmative and the record will show that not a single, solitary one of them was skipped—not one. But he asks them simply for the purpose of gaining sympathy and trying to create prejudice—that's all. There is not another reason beneath the stars for those questions that he asked except to try to create prejudice against me and the position which I maintain. Suppose that all of these things do result—does that disprove what the Bible says? Suppose some body does go to hell, does that set aside the divine record? Are we determining the truth of a proposition by the number of people that may go to hell as a result of it or by what's stated in God's Book? What's our standard anyway?

Now, as I said the other night, you can turn the same thing right around on him. There is only one theory taught in the religious world today against which it can not be urged, and that's the theory of universalism. If a man is going to preach that everybody is going to be saved, why, then, of course, you could not create any prejudice against him. But according to friend Tingley's position, there are hundreds and thousands and millions of people who will not be saved, though they are good and honest and upright people in many ways—pay their debts and are good to their neighbors and all of that, morally clean and things of that kind—and yet they do not believe in Christ. They are going to hell. Well, it comes right back to him. He says they can not be saved unless they believe. So if because the position I hold sends somebody to hell proves it's wrong, then the position he holds does the same thing—it proves he is wrong. Did somebody say "sauce for the goose is salad dressing for the gander"?

Now, then, the questions:

"Are Methodists, Presbyterians and all Pedo-Baptists lost and will they go to hell?" Everybody is lost who fails to obey the word of God, the gospel of Jesus Christ, whether that includes Methodists, Presbyterians, Baptists, my friend, myself or anybody else. What will happen to us does not change what the word of God says. So you can see that he is simply trying to create prejudice. Well, I'm not afraid of it.

"Are Moody, Finney, Sankey, Wesley, Billy Sunday, Whitefield, Luther and all who have not been baptized by immersion lost?" I have already answered that question in the preceding one. Every person who fails to obey the gospel of Jesus Christ is lost—whether that's Moody, Finney, Sankey, Billy Sunday, Glenn Tingley, Curtis Porter or anybody else.

"What baptism saves—Church of Christ, Baptist or Christian and Missionary Alliance?" Well, he asked that the other night. I said, "The Baptism of the New Testament." That's the only thing I'm contending for. And certainly that answers the question.

"Will you accept one whom I have baptized without rebaptizing him?" I answered that the other night. Friend Tingley, certainly, I would not accept one baptized by you if he was baptized according to your teaching. (Laughter.) Now, it's possible that a man could be baptized scripturally by friend Tingley. But he could not do it and be baptized according to the teaching of Tingley. So that's what we are getting at.

"Are those baptized by Missionary Baptists or Christian and Missionary Alliance saved or damned?" It depends on whether they have done what the Book says or not. If they have followed teaching contrary to the Book, of course, they haven't done what the Book says. And that's answered in the one just preceding. It's just the same question over and over and over. It's just stated a little different each time, and includes somebody else each time, in an effort to create a little more prejudice. That's all in the world it's done for; and when men find themselves miserably lost and stopped and ruined in their contention for a proposition, then the only thing they can do is to resort to an effort to create prejudice. That's exactly what friend Tingley is doing.

"Show me one scripture which states that a man is lost if he is not baptized." I gave them the other night. My friend said that the same condition prevailed before the cross that did after, and I gave you Luke 7:30 in which we are told that those who rejected John's baptism "rejected the counsel of God against themselves." And Tingley says the thing is just as true now as it was then. Why, of course, the same thing would be true now. A man who rejects thhe baptism of Christ now would still be rejecting God's counsel. And can a man go to heaven who rejects the counsel of God? Tell us about that.

"Is it true or not that a person has no chance to be saved who is not baptized into the Church of Christ of which you are a member?" Eph. 5:23 declares that Christ is the Savior of the body. And there is no promise made in God's Book that He will save men who are out of the body.

"I challenge my worthy opponent to tell this audience why Paul did not baptize a new convert every time he believed." I can do it, friends. For the same reason that I don't. I haven't baptized a new convert every time he believes. Often times others did the baptizing for me, and I didn't do the baptizing at all. It was certainly just as true with Paul, because at Corinth, we are told in Acts 18:8, that "many of the Corinthians hearing, believed and were baptized." Paul didn't baptize all of them, but some of the others did.

"What is the order of events in conversion?" Well, I suppose he means what conditions come in conversion and what's their order? Faith in Christ, after hearing the word, repentance from sins, confession of faith and baptism for the remission of sins.

"What is faith?" Well, faith is a thing that has different degrees, but it resolves itself, of course, into trust in God or belief.

"Which comes first—faith or repentance—in the conversion of the sinner?" I answered awhile ago that from the standpoint of the degree of faith that saves men—even repentance is before that—but he will not say that in every sense repentance precedes faith, because even Tingley won't stand for that, as we shall see as the thing goes on.

Now, then, just a few things I want to notice in the closing speech last night—some new things introduced, and a number of them were introduced again awhile ago. So I'll take them up first, and then get on to the speech just made.

Col. 2:9-13 was given last night about the circumcision of Christ, the putting away of the body of the sins of the flesh, and being buried with Christ in baptism and raised through the faith of the operation of God who raised him from the dead. My friend wants to know: "Does baptism take the place of Old Testament circumcision?" No. That passage does not say, and Porter did not even intimate, that baptism is circumcision. The circumcision, I showed last night, was the cutting loose of the body of the sins of the flesh, which God does. He does it when a man is baptized. So God performs the operation; God does the circumcising. God is in heaven when he cuts loose the body of the sins of the flesh. But the baptism is merely a condition with which a man complies in order to have the remission of his sins or his sins removed.

He said that Baptists would take him in on his baptism. Well, I know some of them would, but I know some that wouldn't; and if that means anything against me, it is just as much against him.

Do I accept all of Mk. 16:9-20? Yes, I accept Mk. 16:9-20 just as I do all the rest of the word of God. Perhaps you want to know about the performing of the miracles here. Well, do you perform them, Tingley? My friend is very hoarse tonight. Looks like if he can do all these miracles, he'd have some of his brethren cure that hoarseness and let's get on. (Laughter.) Certainly, if the Lord is performing through him and through his brethren all these miracles here, such as taking up serpents, and drinking deadly poison, and things of that kind, and healing the sick, even raising the dead, why they could cure a little hoarseness in a man's throat. Certainly, that could be done, and the fact that my friend goes along through this debate with hoarseness is going to prove that he doesn't, and his brethren do not, possess the miraculous power that's mentioned here, or he would not allow it to continue. Incidentally, while he is at it, he might just relieve my blood malady, and I won't have to take any more atomic energy. (Laughter.) But I also believe, according to I Cor. 13:8-10, that the time was coming when those miraculous powers would be discontinued; and that time has come, and, therefore, I'm not trying to handle snakes and drink deadly poison.

Then to this argument—he made it again awhile ago, but since he made it last night I will come to it here—"Baptism is a work of righteousness—Matt. 3:21." Then he turned to Titus 3:5 where Paul said, "Not by works of righteousness which we have done, but according to His mercy he saved us." "Therefore," Tingley says, "we are not saved by baptism." And he said awhile ago when he quoted Matt. 3:16 that Jesus was not saved by baptism. Well, friend Tingley, was He saved by faith? Was Jesus saved by faith? If he's going to argue that Baptism is not necessary to salvation because Jesus was not saved by baptism, then, in order to make faith necessary to salvation, he would have to say that Jesus was saved by faith. And, of course, if He was saved by faith, then He was lost before He was saved. So we'll just wait to see. That thing proves a boomerang.

But, now, as to the works of righteousness—Matt. 3:16. Baptism is not the kind of works of righteousness referred to in Titus 3:5, referring to the works of man, to man's own devices and schemes and plans. Certainly, a man is not saved by that. Ps. 119:172 says, "All God's commandments are righteousness." Does my opponent mean to say that a man is not saved by the commandments of God? All God's commandments are righteous. In Acts 17:30 we are told that He commanded all men everywhere to repent. So "repent" is also an act of righteousness, and so is faith. These are God's commandments, and if he is going to eliminate all of that, why you will just have to save a man unconditionally and join the Universalists.

Acts 22:16—He came to that "wash away thy sins," and he said that cannot refer to baptism, because man is passive in that, but this is active—a man does it. Well, how about Rev. 7:13-14? John speaks about those who "have washed their robes, and made them white in the blood of the Lamb." I wonder if they did that themselves and just what that would have to do with his position here.

Then, he came back to Gal. 3:27 and said, "Now, Porter

talked about putting on clothes." And he said, "It doesn't mean a thing of that kind at all." Well, if it doesn't, he's the man that introduced it. I'm not the man that said anything about putting on clothes. He's the man who introduced that idea and said we put on Christ like we put on clothes. All right; you're not in your clothes until you put them on. And if you are not in your clothes until you put them on, and you put on Christ like you put on clothes, then you are not in Christ until you put Him on. Paul says you put Him on in baptism. So you are not in Christ until you are baptized. And if you are saved without baptism, you are saved out of Christ. Tell us, friend Tingley, can a man be saved out of Christ?

Then to the thief on the cross—and he came to that again awhile ago. Paul tells us in Heb. 9:16-17 that a testament is of force after men are dead. My opponent tried to make a little play on the idea that Jesus died before the thief did. Well, that's all right. The fact is that the will of Christ did not become effective before he died, and then was probated after He died. I did not say it became operative the very moment He died, but it was made valid by His death, and then probated in heaven. And, consequently, his little play on that is without any help to him whatsoever.

When he started his speech awhile ago he said, "We both agree there is no disagreement between us—about the fact that all Christians ought to be baptized." Yes, there is. Yes, there is. "We agree that all Christians ought to be baptized?" We don't do any such thing, Tingley. I do not find any place in God's Book where any Christian was ever told to be baptized. So he is wrong on that.

Now, he came to a number of scriptures here on faith. I John 5:1; Eph. 3:17; Rom. 10:9, 10 (and I want to call your attention to that). "If thou shalt confess with thy mouth the Lord Jesus, and shalt believe in thine heart that God hath raised Him from the dead, thou shalt be saved. For with the heart man believeth unto righteousness; and with the mouth confession is made unto salvation." Now, then, that's a very unfortunate passage for my friend, because my friend's proposition says a man is saved by faith alone, but this passage says, "If thou shalt confess with the mouth the Lord Jesus, and shall believe in thine heart that God hath raised him from the dead, thou shalt be saved." Paul mentioned two things and not one thing. So that passage doesn't even agree with his idea of faith alone. There are two conditions mentioned there.

Then he came to a whole list of them here about how to get into Christ, and he gave us John 1:12; John 2:11; John 5:23; John 3:16, 18; John 3:36; John 4:36; John 6:29, 35; John 6:47; John 7:38; John 7:39; John 8:30; John 10:42; John 11:25, 45; John 12:32; John 12:44; John 12:46; John 14:1; John 14:12; John 16:9; John 17:20; Acts 10:43; Phil. 1:29; I John 5:13; and I John 5:1. He gave all of these scriptures and said "No baptism, no baptism." Why, didn't you know you didn't give any scriptures at all, friend Tingley? You know he said last night when I wrote a passage upon the board there, because it did not contain the entire verse, that that's just words—that's not scripture at all. And Friend Tingley didn't quote one single, solitary one of these verses— he just made a reference to them and said "By faith—no baptism." Taking friend Tingley's own interpretation of it: Friend Tingley, that isn't scripture at all—that's just words. (Laughter). Why, the very idea.

Now, then, I want to show you what he did here. I may not get to every passage he introduced awhile ago, because I spent a little time dealing with last night, but we have all of tonight and all of tomorrow night So if there are a few that I don't get to in this speech, I will before the debate is over. So we are going to notice two or three he mentioned here.

One of the passages my friend gave to prove men are saved by faith alone was John 8:30. I wrote it down and put a parenthesis around it so I surely wouldn't forget it. This proves that men are saved by faith alone! I want to read it. Here we have John 8:30. Beginning with that verse the record says, "As he spake these words, many believed on him." That's salvation— they became God's children, according to Tingley. Let me read a little more. Maybe we didn't get enough to make it scripture. So we read the next verse, "Then said Jesus to those Jews which believed on him. If ye continue in my word, then are ye my disciples indeed; and ye shall know the truth, and the truth shall make you free." Then they engaged in a conversation with the Lord about it—back and forth they talked on down through the chapter until we come to verse 44, and Jesus said to those Jews who believed on Him, "Ye are of your father the devil." (Laughter.) "Ye are of your father the devil." They believed on him—didn't they? (Laughter.) Here are men who believed on him, and my friend introduced that passage to prove salvation by faith alone, but Jesus said concerning those very fellows, "Ye are of your father the devil, and the lusts of your father ye will do. He was a murderer from the beginning, and abode not in the truth, because there is no truth in him. When he speaketh a lie, he speaketh of his own: for he is a liar, and the father of it." There are some of the men that my friend Tingley introduced as examples of salvation by faith only. Jesus said they were of their father the devil. Tingley said they were God's children; they had their sins blotted out; they were saved; they were children of God; they were born again.

Mr. Nichols: Three minutes.

Mr. Porter continues: Three minutes. All right.

Another passage he gave was John 12:42. So we are going over there. In John 12:42 we have this statement. (I could quote it but I want to read it.) "Nevertheless among the chief rulers also many believed on him." My friend said that proves they were saved—salvation by faith only. Well, let's read a little more. Maybe we didn't read enough to make it scripture. "But because of the Pharisees they did not confess him, lest they should be put out of the synagogue: for they loved the praise of men more than the praise of God." Is that the kind of men that are saved? Men who loved the praise of men more than the praise of God? Why, he said those men were saved by faith only.

Then he gave us Eph. 2:8-10, being saved by grace through faith; that not of yourselves: it is the gift of God: not of works, lest any man should boast. Certainly, men are not saved by works that would enable a man to boast. If I could work my way into heaven independent of God Almighty, I'd have some reason to boast about it; but if I give up my will and vow to do God's will, and do what God commands me to do and get to heaven as a result of it, I have no ground for boasting. Certainly, not. This refers to man's work—man's devices and schemes and things of that kind that would give grounds for boasting—but if you are going to eliminate every kind of work, you would have to eliminate faith, for in John 6:29 Jesus said, "This is the work of God, that you believe on him whom he hath sent." They had just asked, "What shall we do, that we might work the works of God?" And Jesus told them, "This is the work of God, that you believe on him whom he hath sent." So even faith is a work—if he is going to cut out all kinds of works.

Then, he came to John 5:24, "He that heareth my word, and believeth on him that sent me, hath everlasting life." I want to ask my friend if John 5:24 contains the complete plan of salvation? Note that down, Friend Tingley, and tell us about it. Does John 5:24 contain the complete plan of salvation?

Well, with respect to all of these scriptures which he gave he said, "There is no baptism mentioned in them." Well, I can find other scriptures with no faith mentioned; in which also there is no repentance mentioned. He found a number of passages that mentioned faith, and in which nothing is said about baptism, but he didn't find a single one—not one— that said faith alone. But that's what his proposition says, and until he finds a passage that says "faith alone" or "faith only," he is left up in the air, hanging on the "not." It is a simple fact that I believe men are saved by faith, and I believe every passage that Tingley introduced that says men are saved by faith; and if he will introduce the one that says men are saved by faith alone, I'll accept that, too, or I will become an infidel, because I just gave you the passage awhile ago that said, "Ye see then how that by works a man is justified, and not by faith only."

Thank you, Ladies and Gentlemen.

Fifth Night—Tingley's Second Speech

Mr. Chairman, Gentlemen Moderators, Worthy Opponent, Ladies and Gentlemen:

I am very happy to continue the affirmative of the proposition the Scriptures Teach that Alien Sinners are Saved By Faith Alone Before and without Water Baptism.

My worthy opponent has challenged me to show one scripture which uses the phrase faith alone or faith only. If I could do that there would be no debate. Neither would there have been a debate last night if my worthy opponent could have showed any scripture which proves beyond a shadow of a doubt that baptism is absolutely essential to salvation. A subject in order to be debatable must have two sides to it and there dare not be in the scriptures or whatever authority you are looking to and depending upon a clear, positive statement of the words involved. Before this is done, by the end of tomorrow night, I will have given my worthy opponent plenty to show him, if he could open his eyes—that faith is the saving factor, the essential to salvation before and without water baptism.

Let me spend just a few moments on some of the propositions which he has been presenting. I gave you twenty-seven references in one book of John to show that belief is essential. He complains a great deal that I took the scriptures out of its setting. I did not take the scripture out of its setting and in no instance did I do any violence to the scripture. Neither did I misquote the scripture. I'd like to have some of you bring that blackboard and put up here the words of which my worthy opponent said was I Pet. 3:21 and then notice the difference between my taking the scripture in its plain, clear statement and my worthy opponent's twisting of the scripture. In every instance that I gave (I'll answer both of his objections to the scripture I gave in John 8, my worthy opponent was absolutely dead wrong; either he didn't know and has no right to debate or he purposely misled you; for what he said about both those scriptures in John is dead wrong—I'll prove it.)

(Blackboard)

Baptism doth now save us not

Baptism doth not save us

But my worthy opponent wrote himself on the blackboard, "Baptism doth now save us." That's what he wrote. He wrote that up there. That's not the way it reads in I Peter. But he said that was what I Pet. 3:21 said. But that is not—he left out a word in the midst of it—"doth also." He left out a statement which qualified it before—"the like figure." He left that out which changes the meaning. I challenge my opponent to take any of the twenty-seven scriptures, I read in John and take the portion before them or the portion after them and make them mean one iota different. Then all I did was just add one more word that is in the text and it upset him completely and he is still hung on his "not" and he can not get off and he is worried about it.

Now let me show you a sample of my opponent's misinterpretation of the Bible. He read to you John 8: I gave you 8:30 "As he spake these words many believed on him." That's the whole verse. Remember it's the whole portion that counts. "Then said Jesus to those Jews which believed on him, if ye continue in my words then are ye my disciples and ye shall know the truth and the truth shall make you free." I challenge my worthy opponent—both the American Standard Version and the latest version just issued, or to any other translation, or to his King James Bible that has the paragraph marks in it—and see if the next verse does not begin a new paragraph about people who didn't believe on Jesus. I challenge him to that. My worthy opponent misrepresented either through ignorance or deliberately. I can forgive him if it's ignorance, but he ought not to debate. If he did it deliberately, then my worthy opponent is misleading. There is a paragraph beginning with the 33rd verse. "They answered him, we being Abraham's seed." He was talking to them—people who believed in Him—"Ye shall know the truth and the truth shall make you free." In that crowd—read the whole chapter—there were some who did not believe and said, "We be Abraham's seed" and then Jesus gave them the balance of His judgment upon them. Let's turn to the twelfth chapter. He said that I read 42. That is correct. "Nevertheless among the chief rulers also many believed on him but because of the Pharisees they did not confess him lest they should be upt out of thhe synagogue for they loved the praise of men more than the praise of God." That's the truth. I'll give you two scriptures that—or rather two persons—that were two believers in Christ who were in that category. In other places the scripture names the people—one was Nicodemus and the other was Joseph of Arimathea. Both of them quietly worked for Jesus, spoke for him when they dared and could, and then with their loving hands took him down from the cross and buried Him. They were the ones who stayed inside the synagogue not making a public break but they believed on Him just the same in the synagogue or out of the synagogue. My worthy opponent wouldn't tell you about Nicodemus and Joseph of Arimathea. I did not not say or suggest—my worthy opponent says I said Jesus was saved at baptism. I did not say or suggest that Jesus was saved or had to be saved. He did not need to be saved—He was the Son of God. It was a work of righteousness which Jesus did. And the baptism of Jesus is stated as a work of righteousness.

My worthy opponent again misses the point entirely in regard to Galatians. He again says, "If putting on clothes is putting on Christ and if you put Him on by baptism that's the only way you can get into Christ." My worthy opponent can not get away from the fact there is a vital difference between being a person and being a person with a badge on, being a person with clothes on, being a person with a uniform on, taking a place as a disciple. "Ye are children of God by faith in Jesus Christ." That's how we get into Christ, that's how we become God's children. Then before the world of men, by profession and by baptism we take our position as disciples of Christ.

Remember again, I did not do violence to the scripture when I quoted it. I challenge my opponent to show one place where I did violence to the meaning as he did violence to the meaning of that scripture (Pointing to blackboard) leaving out a word in the midst of it and leaving out the qualification before it. I added one word—just the very next word in the verse—and it upset his applecart and he is hung on his "not".

My worthy opponent said he did not say that the new covenent went into effect at the cross of Christ. I'll have to let the record speak for itself. I do not want to falsely charge my opponent but my opponent did say here no less than six or seven minutes ago that it was valid when Christ died and was probated in heaven? Isn't that what he said? I copied the word down— "valid", "valid"—that's the word—v-a-l-i-d—valid. I looked up "valid". "Valid." He said, "Valid." He got himself into that —I didn't get him into it. And valid—in the dictionary right there—is "having legal force or authority." And the New Covenant then had legal force or authority at the death of Jesus—my opponent says that.

And the thief who died on the cross not being baptized couldn't possibly be in Paradise with Jesus—according to my opponent he'd have to be in hell.

Back to the questions that I asked my opponent. Did he answer them? My worthy opponent has not the courage to answer these questions with a forthright "Yes" or "No". He has not the courage.

Are Methodists, Presbyterians and all Pedo-Baptists lost and will they go to hell? Three times in his answer he said, "Everyone is lost who refuses to obey the gospel." "Everyone is lost who refuses to obey the gospel." Well, I would like to ask my worthy opponent: Does he regard Methodists, Presbyterians and Pedo-Baptists as having so obeyed the gospel as to be saved or are they lost? I'll put it that way if he wants it.

And the same is true for Moody, Finney, Sankey, Wesley, Billy Sunday, Whitfield, Luther. I am not appealing to prejudice. Ladies and Gentlemen, we want you to know the truth. What is the truth about the matter? Has my worthy opponent the courage to stand up here by his proposition and damn to hell everyone of them? He has to do it if his proposition is true and my worthy opponent—I warrant you—we will end Saturday without him having the courage to do that. He has not the the courage. He knows it isn't so.

I ask him what baptism saves—Church of Christ, Baptist or Christian Missionary Alliance. He said the church that baptizes with New Testament Baptism. I'll ask him, what church baptizes with the New Testament baptism? He wants it that way. I want to get this man on the spot where he can not wiggle and so we can put our finger on him and say, "There he is. We know where he stands." My worthy opponent twists and turns like an eel. He will not take a forthright position in regard to bothersome problems that embarass his theological error.

Again, in regard to the others, "Show me one scripture which states that a man is lost if he is not baptized." He said, "Well, Luke 7:30 — " he used that. I understood him to say—he can correct me if he desires—that John's baptism held true for salvation before the cross the same as Christian baptism holds true afterwards. Well, I'll wait on his answer.

Then I challenged my worthy opponent to tell this audience why Paul did not baptize a new convert every time he believed. He said, if they believed he does not always baptize them. Then let me ask him this—it has happened time after time—I don't know whether it has ever happened in his life or not, it has happened in mine. If they believe and the baptism is delayed, are they lost? There confessed Christ a family of five here one Sunday night. They were to come back to be baptized the next Sunday. The next Sunday they did not show up because one of the boys that confessed Christ as his Savior and had been born again was desperately ill. He died. I buried him the next Wednesday. Is that boy saved or lost? We have a right to have the answer.

My friends if baptism saved I would get every body to the creek the minute they confessed Jesus Christ. I'd keep the baptismal pool warm and full all the time. I'd get them into the water right now. My worthy opponent does not believe it. He won't admit these questions. If he believed them he'd frankly admit them. Ladies and Gentlemen of the church of Christ you ought to demand that he answer these questions forthrightly and fairly and squarely.

Now he pleased me by saying what is the order of events in conversion—faith comes first, repentance second, confession third and baptism fourth. That's exactly according to Alexander Campbell, founder of the Church of Christ. I am very happy that he stays with his founder. Now we can get some where, thank the Lord. Now I was talking about repentance when my time ran out. Now you see the Greek word in the New Testament translated "repent" means literally "to change one's mind." "Mind" has quite an inclusive sense. Matt. 12:41 is an example of repentance—he has asked me "What is repentance?" "The men of Ninevah shall rise in judgment with this generation and Ninevah repented. Here's an example of what repentance is. condemn it because they repented not at the preaching of Jonah and behold a greater than Jonah is here." Now the people of

Jonah 3:8-10, "But let man and beast"—here's what they did that's called repentance—"be covered with sackclothes, cry mightily unto God, yea let them turn everyone from his evil way and from the violence that is in their hand; Who can tell if God will turn and repent, turn away from his fierce anger that we perish not and God saw their works that they turned from their evil way. God repented of the evil that he would do unto them and he did it not." Repentance is that work in the soul by the spirit of God whereby a sinner is made conscious of his sin and is moved to turn from it.

II Peter 3:9—"The Lord is not slack concerning his promises as some count slackness, but is long-suffering toward us, not willing that any should perish but that all should come to repentance." Repentance of sin is such a sorrow for sins, such a change of mind that it leads the sinner to turn away from it. The sinner is made to see his sin; the sinner is made to see the holiness of God. The sinner hates his sin, he repent, he turns from his sin. Now my worthy opponent holds that repentance comes after faith. Ladies and Gentlemen, that is the fundamental error of Alexander Campbell and all who have walked in his footsteps since. That is the reason they do not believe in the direct operation of the Holy Spirit. That's the reason they do not believe in a heart-felt religion. That's the reason they do not believe in a dramatic change within the individual's heart. That's the reason, my friends, they teach repentance follows faith—faith comes first! Whereas the Bible says, repentance comes before faith. Now, if an individual says, for instance, that I can play baseball when I get in my junior year in high school it means that there are some things that have to come between the time they speak to me and the time I play baseball. Repentance comes before faith. An individual can not have faith without repentance—repentance precedes faith. I challenge my worthy opponent to show us in the Bible where repentance follows faith. I challenge him to show where repentance follows faith. I'll answer him with over two hundred scriptures in the Bible that puts faith as the prime and whenever repentance is mentioned in connection with it repentance always precedes it—it always goes ahead of it.

Now salvation comes by faith in Christ because everyone of the requirements in the word which have the negative statement are met by one who has faith in Christ. Faith can not come until one repents and turns from his sins. It is an utter impossibility. Because it is from God as I have already proven clearly by scriptures. I can not have love for the world and faith in Christ for they are opposite. Therefore, I must turn from the world, I must repent before I can possibly believe. Faith purifies the heart. My worthy opponent contends that men have pure hearts before they repent. That's utterly ridiculous reasoning in the things of God. How can a sinner have a pure heart before he repents? My worthy opponent says faith comes before repentance—repentance must come before faith can purify the heart.

Now in regard to these opposites. Listen. "He that believed and is baptized shall be saved, he that believeth not shall be damned." There's not one solitary word that suggests that not being baptized will damn you. No negative.

Acts 2:38—"Then Peter said unto them repent and be baptized everyone of you in the name of Jesus Christ for the remission of sins and ye shall receive the gift of the Holy Ghost." The man is paid for his work not to have the privilege of working, but because he already has worked. "For the remission of sins" a man therefore is baptized because his sins have been remitted.

Acts 3:19—"Repent ye therefore and be converted that your sins may be blotted out when the time of refreshing shall come from the presence of the Lord." The blood of Christ cleanses men from sin and the washing away is wrought by the blood of Christ and baptism is the declaration that has transpired. The faith we have is in the blood of the Lord. Listen to Rom. 3:25, "Whom God hath set forth to be the propitiation through faith in his blood to declare his righteousness for the remission of sins that are past through the forebearance of God. He that loveth is born of God. He that loveth not let him be accursed." Now note, please, the change is within. The operation takes place within and a man believes on Christ within his heart—he's changed inside. He is changed after he turns from the world and has faith in Christ—our faith is in the love of God. I John 4:5—"We have known and believe the love God has for us; God is love. He that dwelleth in love dwelleth in God and God in him."

Now everyone of these negatives is found in faith—every

last one of them. Baptism has not a solitary negative. Faith has a negative. Repentance because it precedes faith and can not be exercised, faith can not work until man repents therefore repentance and faith both have negatives. Baptism hasn't got a solitary one. Whenever an individual believes in Christ, he repents, turns from his sins and has faith in God, he believes in the love of God—that man is wholly born again.

Listen to Rom. 5:1. (I am giving you a host of scriptures setting a superstructure and showing you the position of the faith in the economy of God and, my friend, every argument that my worthy opponent has presented will be answered in due time—we will not dodge one nor will we quibble about a solitary one but we will answer fully and carefully and we will not dodge any issue. I challenge my opponent to frankly answer the questions I have asked him.) Now Rom. 5:1 — "Therefore being justified by faith we have peace with God through our Lord Jesus Christ." Faith brings peace with God. Either that's true or it's a lie.

John 3:36—"He that believeth on the Son hath everlasting life and he that believeth not the Son shall not see life but the wrath of God abideth on Him."

John 5:24—"Verily, verily I say unto you he that heareth my word and believeth on him that sent me hath everlasting life and shall not come into condemnation but is passed from death unto life." Ladies and Gentlemen, do you think that Jesus the Son of God would have said something like that if that were not so? If my worthy opponent is correct, then that isn't so! Jesus said, "He that heareth my word and believeth on him that sent me."

Listen, "Faith without works is dead." That's correct. Saving faith without works that follow is dead. That's correct. Listen, a baby is born. The baby doesn't breathe. It's a baby. Blood is coursing in its veins and to make it breathe, to make it work, to make it live, the doctor spanks its bottom. Waa.. aaa .h! Faith and works. Works are necessary and the individual who is born again will follow Christ. He will tell the truth, he will not steal, he will not go on drunks, he will not curse, he will be baptized, he will line up with God's people, he will go to work for Jesus Christ. In order to be a child of God? No! Because he is a child of God! A baby is born—it's a baby and it's just as much a baby when it's born and before it squals as it is five years later. It's just as much a human being and faith brings a man into the relationship whereby he is a child of God. Hallelujah, he is born again!

John 6:29—"Jesus said unto them, This is the work of God that ye believe on him whom he hath sent."

John 6:47—"Verily I say unto you he that believeth on me hath everlasting life. Jesus says, "He that believeth on me hath everlasting life." My worthy opponent says Jesus was mistaken —"He that believeth on me, repents, is baptized and is converted has everlasting life." My worthy opponent has not the courage to stand up here before you ladies and gentlemen and say that if an individual repents and believes like Methodists and Baptists and is not baptized by immersion; he has not the courage, he has proved it to you—to say that they are lost and they go to hell. I challenge him to do that. That's not prejudice! That's good debating and good reasoning. I challenge him is he honest in this. I question whether he believes in this or not himself within the depths of his heart. Jesus says, "He that believeth on me hath everlasting life." I believe that, hallelujah!

John 3:17-19—"God sent not his son into the world to condemn the world but that the world through him might be saved." Now how are we saved through the Son? "He that believeth on him is not condemned; he that believeth not is condemned already because he hath not believed in the name of the only begotten Son of God." Now how is a man condemned? By not being baptized? That's what my opponent says; that's not what the Bible says. The Bible says a man is condemned by not believing. The Bible says a man is saved by believing.

Acts 16:31—"Believe on the Lord Jesus Christ and thou shalt be saved and thy house."

Rom. 10:6, 9-10—"But the righteousness which is of faith speaketh on this wise say not in thine heart, who shall ascend up into heaven that is to bring Christ down." Now, the righteousness which comes by what? The Bible says not the righteousness of works, the Bible says Baptism is a work of righteousness. The Bible says you can't be saved by that. If you put that as a saving ordinance, that's not scripture, that's not right! Over and over it says, "Not that." That has its place but it always says, "The righteousness which is of faith." That's the righteousness which God wants. "If thou shalt confess with thy mouth the Lord Jesus and shall believe in thine heart that God hath raised him from the dead; thou shalt be saved, for with the heart man believeth unto righteousness and with the mouth confession is made unto salvation."

Rom. 11:20—"Because of unbelief they were broken off." Because they weren't baptized? No, because of unbelief. "Thou standest by faith."

Gal. 3:6—"Even as Abraham believed God and — " what? That "belief in God was counted to him for righteousness."

II Tim. 1:5—"Now the end of the commandment is charity out of a pure heart and of faith unfeigned." Now, that's the whole end of the commandment says God.

Acts 10:43—"To him gave all the prophets witness that through his name"—now through everyone of the prophets the Holy Spirit is saying giving witness to this fact, "That through his name whosoever believeth and is baptized and so on," my worthy opponent's position. But the Bible says "And everyone of the prophets say," the Holy Spirit said in Acts 10:43, "through his name whosoever believeth"—plus nothing, minus nothing—"in him shall receive remission of sins." That's the teaching of the word of God.

Eph. 3:17—"That Christ may dwell in your hearts" — How? "by faith that ye being rooted and grounded in love."

Now my worthy opponent last night brought Noah in on the scene. I will leave Noah for a little later.

The Scriptures Teach That Alien Sinners Are Saved by Faith Before and Without Water Baptism because—

First of all, the dying thief went with the Lord in Paradise and according to my worthy opponent died after the New Covenant was valid—that's his word tonight. He's changing all the time. He said valid tonight, by the death of Christ on the cross therefore salvation is by faith alone, salvation is not outward but inward, it's not in the body but the heart. Since baptism is an outward symbolic act, therefore, baptism is not essential to salvation—man's saved by faith alone.

2. Salvation is not by works and since baptism is a work of righteousness therefore a man is saved by faith alone before and without water baptism.

3. That sinners are saved by faith before water baptism is the clear teaching of more than two hundred New Testament passages on how to be saved that have not one word of baptism in them and since God is a reasonable God and a complete statement of scripture is that the believer is saved, therefore he is saved before and without water baptism.

4. Salvation is denied those who disbelieve. Since every negative is met by a positive statement in the gospel, therefore, no one can be damned for lack of baptism and individuals are saved by faith before and without water baptism. Salvation is by faith in Jesus Christ and that alone. Salvation is before and without water baptism.

5. The apostle believed people are saved by faith before and without water baptism for he said "by the foolishness of preaching to save them that believe." And he thanked God he did not baptize many of them, therefore, individuals are saved by believing the gospel before and without water baptism.

Thank you, Ladies and Gentlemen.

FIFTH NIGHT—PORTER'S SECOND SPEECH

Mr. President, Gentlemen Moderators, Worthy Opponent, Ladies and Gentlemen:

I am glad to appear again in the negative of the proposition which friend Tingley has been affirming for another thirty minutes. I am really amused at my opponent as he keeps on coming back with his questions. They have been answered outright and straight from the shoulder from time to time. It seems that my friend must have been asleep all that time and did not know what I was saying, or else he had his ears stopped and was not trying to hear.

Everyone knows that these questions are asked for the purpose of trying to create prejudice. He even brought it down to some one in this city, and some one in this autditorium, in order to try to create prejudice among his people in this auditorium against me—about some five who were "saved, regenerated, born again" at the altar and intended to be baptized the next Sunday, but one of them took sick and was never baptized. He wants me to tell whether he is in hell. Well, he's simply trying to create prejudice. We are not here discussing dead men in this community, or anything of that kind; we're discussing what the scriptures teach. In Mark 16:16 Jesus said, "He that believeth and is baptized shall be saved." I didn't say it. That's what the Lord said, and I'm just depending merely upon what He said. I suspect there have been people in this auditorium who intended to seek God at the mourner's bench and come through at the altar, but they died before they got to it; they put it off. Does that mean friend Tingley is wrong in insisting that they must believe to be saved? What has that to do with it anyway. Nothing but a plea for sympathy, and that's all in the world there is to it.

While he is raving and ranting and raging about the questions which he asked me, and which I have answered in a forthright manner on two or three different occasions, he entirely forgot the fact that he had nine definite, plain, specific questions handed him, and he said not one single word about them—not a word! I wonder what's the matter with Tingley? Ah, yes, he's great on answering questions, but you see how he did these. He got so worked up and so excited and so rattled about the whole thing that he actually forgot that he ever had any questions to answer. Well, we shall expect him to come tomorrow night and tell us somthing about them. No need to put them off. I demand that he answer them in his next speech tomorrow night, because if he waits until after that, then he will be putting if off until he knows that I will have no chance to deal with them as they ought to be dealt with. Friend Tingley, will you answer those questions in your first speech tomorrow night?

Mr. Tingley: I'll be glad to.

Mr. Porter: He will be glad to. Well, don't forget it, because you know that "forgettery" works so marvelously sometimes, and we want you to be sure not to forget it this time.

Now, then, just a few statements in his preceding speech that I didn't quite reach, and then on to the one that's just been made. He referred to faith being dead as a faith that is only an intellectual assent, or historical faith, and indicated that men could not be saved by a historical faith. Well, in John 20:30-31 John said, "Many other signs truly did Jesus in the presence of his disciples, which are not written in this book; but these are written that you might believe." I suppose that's a historical faith—it comes by what's written. He went on to say "And that believing you might have life through His name." So the very faith that come as a result of what was written was the faith that gave them life through His name.

Mark 11:22—"Have faith in God." Heb. 12:2—"Christ is the author and finisher of our faith." Rom. 5:1—"Justified by faith." Rom. 4:6—"faith imputed". John 1:12—"born not of the will of man." These are the passages he gave in the first talk tonight.

You noted the fact that when my friend came to the stand awhile ago he said, "No there's not a single passage which I gave that said 'Man is saved by faith alone.' " He agrees there is not one single verse that he has introduced—in fact, he agrees there is not a verse in all of the Bible that says, "Man is saved by faith alone." Yet that is what his proposition says. I believe every passage in the Book of God that says man is saved by faith. I'll affirm every one of them. I'll affirm a proposition with any man that alien sinners are saved by faith. I'll use the very same passages to prove it that he has used tonight, and they do say that men are saved by faith, but there is not one single one of them—and Tingley admits that it is so—that says, "By faith alone!" "Oh," he said, "if it said that, it would not be debatable." It would if Tingley were involved. Yes, it would, because the Bible does say in James 2:24, "Ye are justified by works and not by faith only." But that's debatable, because Tingley denies it. Now, the Bible plainly says, "Ye are not justified by faith only." Is that debatable? Why wouldn't it be debatable if it said, "Ye are justified by faith only?" If one's debatable, the other is. Tingley will not accept it when James says, "It's not by faith only," and yet admits there's no passage in God's Book that says, "It is by faith only." Well, James did not say a man is not justified by faith, did he? No. In fact, he implied that a man is justified by faith. He said, "Ye see then how that by works a man is justified, and not by faith only." That proves he is justified by faith. That's in perfect agreement with all the passages introduced by my friend. And it also shows at the same time that he is not justified by faith alone. By faith? Yes! By faith alone? No! Tingley has surrendered the whole thing when he said he can not find, in all of these two hundred passages that he introduced, one single statement, one single verse, that says "man is justified by faith only." He says, "Faith only is not there. It just isn't there." He admits that is isn't there! Well, I knew he could not find it when he signed his name to this proposition. Certainly, it isn't there. Since it isn't there he can not prove his proposition. There's nothing there that's even equivalent to it.

Oh, "But the passages don't say anything about baptism." No, and just numbers and numbers of them do not say a word about repentance. If that proves that baptism is excluded, it proves that repentance is excluded. They did not say a word about repentance, and that proves there's no repentance then, according to Tingley, because he said since not a word is said about baptism, that proves no baptism.

After all, I tried to get my opponent to tell me whether faith alone meant repentance. All these passages that say men are saved by repentance—or that repentance is necessary to salvation—disprove and upset the proposition that friend Tingley is contending for tonight. If it's faith alone, that's faith without repentance—"alone" means "without anything else." If a man is somewhere alone, that does not mean there is some one with him. If he's alone—that's all. If it's faith alone, that's faith without anything else. That makes no room for repentance; that makes no room for prayer, or anything of that kind; because if you have repentance, or if you have love, or if you have prayer at the altar, as he spoke of last night, and things of that kind, you have more than faith—it's not faith alone. He can not prove it. He knows it's not in the Book. He admits it's not there, and he is just simply assuming that because baptism or something else happened not to be mentioned in a particular passage, therefore, it's not anywhere. There are many other passages that do contain it, even though there are some in which it is not mentioned. You'll find many passages in which faith is not mentioned; and you'll find faith where repentance is not mentioned; and you'll find faith where baptism isn't mentioned; and you'll find baptism where faith isn't mentioned. I take them all. My friend takes only one of them.

Now, then he came to John 8. I was really amused at my opponent in John 8. I know he got hung up there, and he's going to stay hung up. He said, "Porter misrepresented this whole thing"—and that he hoped I did it ignorantly; he didn't want to think I did is deliberately. Well, I did what I did deliberately, friend Tingley. The act which I committed was premediated. There was no slip about it. I didn't just imagine, or come into this thing with my eyes shut and say something that I had never studied about. So if I misrepresent it, I did it deliberately, because I was deliberate in the things I said. Let's see if I misrepresented it.

John 8, beginning with verse 30, and on down through the following verses. Now, my opponent says—we'll just read it. John 8:30 says, "And as he spake these words, many believed on him. If ye continue in my word, then are ye my disciples indeed; and ye shall know the truth, and the truth shall make you free." Now, Tingley says they are already free, and I have not reached the paragraph yet—haven't even reached that paragraph yet. Jesus said to those men, before he got to that paragraph, that "Ye shall know the truth, and the truth shall make you free." Friend Tingley says they were already made free the moment they believed. Now, we come to the paragraph, and Friend Tingley thinks if you come to a new paragraph in a chapter somewhere, it's a different crowd altogether. I suppose he couldn't even write a letter to somebody and change paragraphs. If he did, why it would mean somebody else. The idea, Tingley! Don't you know paragraphs can change without the people involved being a different crowd altogether? Let's read it. I want to read it again and let you get the connection. "As he spake these words, many believed on him. Then said Jesus to those Jews which believed on him: If ye continue in my word, then are ye my disciples indeed; and ye shall know the truth, and the truth shall make you free. They answered him." Who answered him? Why, the crowd that wasn't there! This is the beginning of another paragraph and is talking about a crowd that had nothing to do with it! Jesus wasn't even talking to this crowd, but they answered! Why, the ones that answered were the ones to whom Jesus had spoken. To whom was Jesus speaking? "To those Jews which believed on him"—that's what the Book says. Jesus spoke "to those Jews which believed on him." —"they answered him." Who answered Him? Those Jews to whom Jesus had spoken—who believed on him. Why, certainly, that was deliberate, I didn't slip on that. Why, that was premeditated, friend Tingley. I knew you'd get into trouble. In fact, I knew you were already in trouble the moment you mentioned that verse. Doesn't that say that Jesus spoke "to those Jews which believed on Him?" "And they answered him?" Do you suppose the ones answered that Jesus had not spoken to? Who answered? They couldn't answer unless they were spoken to, could they? Can you answer a man if the man hasn't spoken to you? Why these fellows were the ones that Jesus spoke to. He said to those Jews—there's where He spoke to them—"to those Jews which believed on him" and "they answered him." Why, they are the same Jews that He spoke to. They are the ones that answered him, weren't they? (Laughter) If not, John, who wrote the Book was certainly wrong about it. He didn't know it because John says, "They answered him." If I answer a man, that means the man said something to me. But friend Tingley says, "No, the ones who answered him were the ones who hadn't been spoken to." Why, the idea! This whole audience can see the hole you are in, and you're going to stay there.

"They answered him." What did they say? I'm going to read it. We've got to these other passages from time to time, and we'll get to them more. We're going to deal with this while we are at it. "They answered him, We be Abraham's seed, and were never in bondage to any man: How sayest thou, Ye shall be made free? Jesus answered them"—the same ones who answered Him and the same ones to whom He had spoken—the Jews who believed on Him. "Jesus answered them, Verily, verily, I say unto you, whosoever committeth sin is the servant of sin. And the servant abideth not in the house forever; but the Son abideth forever. If the Son, therefore, shall make you free, ye shall be free indeed." And so on down through the chapter He goes—a conversation back and forth between them. And in verse 44 Jesus said to those Jews who believed on Him, the ones who answered him, the ones who were arguing the case with Him, "Ye are of your father the devil, and the lusts of your father ye will do." That's what Jesus said. These men believed on Him, and Jesus said, "Ye are of your father the devil"—the very ones who answered Him.

Then he came to John 12:42 about "Many of the rulers which believed on Him did not confess Him; they loved the praise of men more than the praise of God." He said, "Porter misrepresented that." No, I didn't. I just quoted the passage. I asked my friend to tell me, were these men saved who loved the praise of men more than the praise of God? Well, he brought up Nicodemus and Joseph and said, "Here's some of them." Well, this says "many of them." Many of those Jews believed on him, but they did not confess him. I want to know, were those men saved when they loved the praise of men more than the praise of God? Why didn't you tell us? They did not confess Him, and he gave a passage awhile ago in Rom. 10:9-10 which said men must confess Him to be saved. Rom. 10:9-10 said, "If thou shalt confess with thy mouth the Lord Jesus, and shalt believe in thine heart that God hath raised him from the dead, thou shalt be saved." Believe and confess—the passage he gave. This passage says they believed, but they didn't confess. Paul says, "Believe and confess" if you are going to be saved. So, according to his argument on the other, he cuts out the rulers of John 12:42.

Regarding Matt. 3:16 he said, "I didn't say that Jesus was baptized to be saved." No, I didn't say that he did. But what he said was that Jesus was not baptized to be saved. And he concluded from that that it is not necessary for us to be baptized to be saved. Well, I just showed the parallel. Jesus did not believe to be saved; and so that would prove that we don't have to believe to be saved. If it proves one, it proves the other.

Then back to Gal. 3:27. He said, "Now there is a difference between being a person and putting on clothes." "You first become the child, and then you put on the clothes." Of course, putting Christ on is putting the clothes on. Well, 1 Cor. 1:30 says "Christ is redemption and santification." So I guess if putting Christ on is putting the clothes on, then when we put on the clothes we put on redemption and santification. That's done, he says, in baptism. Now, then, the baby is born first, and then the clothes are put on. We put on the clothes, according to Tingley, when we are baptized. That's his illustration. So a Christian who has not been baptized is just a nude Christian, that's all. He hasn't put the clothes on yet.

As to the thief on the cross and Heb. 9:16-17, Paul said, "Where a testament is, there must also of necessity be the death of the testator. For a testament is of force after men are dead; otherwise it is of no strength at all while the testator liveth." I showed, and the thing that I contended for was, the promise that Jesus made to the thief on the cross was made before He died and before His will became ratified; before His will became effective. It could not go into effect while He lived. Paul said so. That promise was made to Him while Jesus still lived—before the death of the testator. If He wanted to save the thief on the cross without baptism, without repentance, without anything, that was His privilege; and the thief died some fifty-three days before the great commission recorded in Mk. 16:16 went into effect.

In Mark 16:15-16 Jesus said, "Go ye into all the world, and preach the gospel to every creature. He that believeth and is baptized shall be saved; but he that believeth not shall be damned." Luke records that they were told to tarry in the city of Jerusalem until they were endued with power from on high. On the cross Jesus said, "Today shalt thou be with me in Paradise." They died and that day went to Paradise. The body of Jesus went to the tomb. Three days afterward he arose from dead, spent forty days with His disciples, and over in the first chapter of Acts at the conclusion of that time, he gave the Great Commission as recorded by Mark and said, "Go into all the world, and preach the gospel to every creature." He ascended into heaven. On the day of Pentecost, ten days later, the Holy Spirit came to them—making a total of 53 days from the time the thief died and went to paradise until the Great Commission became operative. The thief on the cross died and went to Paradise fifty-three days before Mark 16:16 became operative. We are living since that time—since Jesus said—"He that believeth and is baptized shall be saved." You can not hold the thief responsible to the law of the Great Commission. He died before it was given. Tingley, you and I were born about 1900 years after it was given. We do not sustain the same relation to it.

Then, he came to repentance and the case of Jonah—about what repentance is—and he turned over to Jonah 3:8, in connection with Matt. 12:41, and showed me what repentance is. But he read too much. I am going to turn and read it to you. Remember this: If repentance is a condition of salvation, my opponent just as well surrender his proposition, because his proposition says faith alone. And "faith alone" is not faith plus repentance. Let us see. God pronounced doom upon the Ninevehites and here's the statement. They said, "Who can tell if God will turn and repent, and turn away from his fierce anger, that we perish not?" Here's where he read, "And God saw their works that they turned from their evil way; and God repented of the evil, that he said that he would do unto them; and he did it not." Tingley, when did God repent of the evil that He said He would do to them? "When he saw their works!" That's the wrong passage, Tingley; you must find one where He did is before He saw their works. This says God repented of the evil He was going to do them when He saw their works. They worked first, before God repented. You have the wrong passage.

Then, he talked about heart-felt religion. Yes, I believe in heart-felt religion. I believe all religions are heart-felt. And in Rom. 6:17-18 we have the statement made that shows there are a number of things involved with the heart. Rom. 6:17 says, "God be thanked, that ye were the servants of sin, but you have obeyed from the heart that form of doctrine delivered you. Being then made free from sin, ye became the servants of righteousness." Men, then, are made free from sin when they obey from the heart that form of doctrine delivered them. And that involves baptism. They are then made free from sin.

He talked about the pure heart by faith. Well, not only is the heart said to be purified by faith, but 1 Pet. 1:22 says, "Seeing ye have purified your souls in obeying the truth, see that ye love one another with a pure heart fervently."

Then he got back to Mark 16:16 and Acts 2:38—"No negative," he says, for Mark 16:16—"He that believeth and is baptized shall be saved."

(Blackboard)

Enter train — Sit down — Go to Atlanta
Believe — Be Baptized — Saved

Another passage he gave was John 5:24. The other night when I placed on the board "he that believeth and is baptized shall be saved," he came along with his train illustration and said, "You enter the train, and you sit down, and you go to Atlanta. It is necessary to enter the train but you go to Atlanta whether you sit down or not." So we mark that out—it is not necessary. (Marks out "Sit down") Parallel to that, "He that believeth and is baptized shall be saved." Baptism being parallel to sitting down, we'll mark it out. (Marks out "Be Baptized") We just have faith left there. Well, we'll give him another passage.

The one he gave awhile ago—John 5:24. Jesus said, "He that heareth my word, and believeth on him that sent me, hath everlasting life." There's you another parallel.

(Blackboard)

Enter train — Sit Down — Go to Atlanta
Hear — Believe — Have Life

Enter the train, sit down, go to Atlanta. Hear, believe, have life. But when you enter the train you don't have to sit down to go to Atlanta. So when you hear you don't have to believe to get life. Since you can go to Atlanta without sitting down we cross that out (crosses out "sit down" on new parallel) And it's parallel we cross out (crosses out "believe") Thus you have nothing but "hearing," and is puts him right back in that hole. A man is saved by hearing and no faith at all—faith is excluded by his own application and by his own illustration.

Now to Acts 2:38. In Acts 2:38 Peter said, "Repent, and be baptized everyone of you in the name of Jesus Christ for the remission of sins." Now, notice that. Peter did not say, "Repent, and you'll get the remission of sins." By the way, had you noticed that passage did not say anything about faith? Had you noticed that passage didn't say a word about faith? They cried, "Men and brethren, what shall we do?" Peter did not even say believe and, according to friend Tingley, that means they didn't have to believe, because there is no faith mentioned.

They said, "Men and brethern, what shall we do?" What did Peter say? Peter said, "Repent, and be baptized everyone of you in the name of Jesus Christ for the remission of sins, and ye shall receive the gift of the Holy Ghost." Not a word about faith. He gave some passages that said nothing about baptism; so he says "it's faith and no baptism." All right, here's a passage that mentions repentance and baptism but says nothing about faith. So it's repentance and baptism and no faith. The same argument that cuts baptism out of his passages cuts faith out of this one, because Peter did not say, "Believe;" he merely said, "Repent, and be baptized." Not "repent only;" not "be baptized only." He said, "Repent and be baptized for the remission of sins."

I have been trying to get my friend to tell me about those parallels he gave—those statements about being decorated for bravery and things of that kind—if they are really parallels. So you will have to get those questions tomorrow night and tell me.

Rom. 3:25—"through faith." Yes, through faith, "a propitiation through faith," but did you notice the fact that it didn't say "through faith only." "No baptism there." No, and no repentance there. Not a word.

All right, 1 John 4:6-7—he comes here and discusses the matter of love. Well, I thought your proposition said "Faith." You've turned now to prove that it's love. Love is not faith—that's something in addition to faith.

Then he comes to Rom. 5:1, John 3:36 and John 5:24 again. Rom. 5:1—"justified by faith." He said, "No baptism there." Well, no repentance there; no prayer there; no altar service. You cut them all out if you cut out baptism. I'll put baptism in just like you put the others in—in fact, a little bit "liker." (You may put that word in quotation marks).

John 3:36—"He that believeth not shall not see life." I called to his attention time and time again that the Revised Version reads, "He that obeyeth not shall not see life." Not a time has he even mentioned the fact.

Then to the baby being born. He says, "The baby is born but it doesn't breathe. The doctor spanks it, and it begins to let up a yell." So Christians are born—that is, men become born—they are new creatures in Christ, but they don't breathe. And you spank them by sousing them in the water; and then they start breathing, you see, as Christians. That's his idea. (Laughter). He makes baptism to the Christian parallel to spanking the babe. So the doctor spanks the baby and starts the baby to crying; and the preacher baptizes the Christian, and thus spanks him, and gets him to crying or doing something else—I don't know what. But the question is: Is the baby born out of Christ? That's the baby we are talking about here—the new creature in Christ, the new born babe. Is the baby born out of Christ? 2 Cor. 5:17 says, "If any man be in Christ, he is a new creature." All right, a new creature or a babe in Christ. How do men get into Christ? Gal. 3:27 says, "As many of you as have been baptized into Christ have put on Christ." So the baby is not born out of Christ.

Well, he said, "Now, according to Porter, 'He that believeth and repents and is baptized shall be saved'. The record said here, 'He that believeth shall have life,' but Porter says, 'No, it is he that believeth and repents and is baptized'." Well, according to Tingley, it is not, "He that believeth shall have life," but "He that repents and believes shall have life." Yet his proposition says there is nothing in addition to faith. It's just faith alone. "Faith only" can not include anything else—there'll be no repentance coupled with it whatsoever.

John 3:17—that we are going to be saved "through him." Yes, but can a man be saved by faith through Christ if he stays out of Christ? Gal. 3:27 says he is "baptized into Christ." How are you going to be saved through Christ if you stay out of Christ?

Mr. Nichols: A minute and a half.

Mr. Porter: Minute and a half. All right.

Acts 16:31 and Rom. 10:6-9. This gets me back now to faith again, and while it does not say faith only—my friend admits it does not—following Acts 16:31 we do find the jailer was baptized. Rom. 11:20—"broken off because of unbelief." Well, does that mean somebody was lost after he was standing by faith? What about that anyway?

2 Tim. 1:5—"faith unfeigned" and Acts 10:43—"through his name we have remission of sins." Yes, and Matt. 28:19 says we are "baptized into the name of the Father, Son and Holy Spirit." And Acts 19:5, in the Revised Version, says we are "baptized into the name of Christ." So that doesn't help him.

That gets back to the thief and then down to the final statement he made—"two hundred passages without one word of baptism in them." Yet in Rom. 16:26 Paul speaks about "the obedience of faith." Yes, there's faith and there's something that's called the obedience of faith God determined that that should be made known by the preaching of the gospel—"the obedience of faith"—to all, nations. So there's faith and there's the obedience of faith; and the faith must be coupled with obedience or it does not save. A faith that's dead, a faith alone, will not save men. James said in James 2:24—I gave it awhile ago—"Ye see then how that by works a man is justified, and N-O-T—not by faith only." That's found in the Book of God. Read your Bibles tonight when you go home. James 2:24 is the only place we have the expression just that way—"faith only"—and instead of saying that we are saved by faith only it says "Not by faith only." My friend said no one would debate it if it said, "By faith only," but he will dispute it when it says, "Not by faith only."

Thank you, Ladies and Gentlemen.

PORTER-TINGLEY DEBATE

Sixth Session: 7:30 P. M., March 1, 1947

Birmingham Gospel Tabernacle, Birmingham, Alabama
Chairman: Emerson J. Estes — Birmingham, Alabama
Singing Directed by: Claude McGee — Birmingham, Alabama
Prayer: William H. Lewellyn — Birmingham, Alabama
Moderators: Walter Hemingway, Bessemer, Alabama, for Mr. Tingley, Gus Nichols, Jasper, Alabama, for Mr. Porter.
Announcements concerning the printed debate: Dr. Glenn V. Tingley and George W. DeHoff.

Proposition: **The Scriptures Teach that Alien Sinners Are Saved by Faith Alone Before and Without Water Baptism.**

Glenn V. Tingley, Affirms
W. Curtis Porter, Denies

(Affirmative Address by Glenn V. Tingley)

Mr. Chairman, Gentlemen Moderators, Worthy Opponent, Ladies and Gentlemen:

I am very happy to take my stand again on the truth of God on the proposition, The Scriptures Teach that Alien Sinners Are Saved by Faith Alone Before and Without Water Baptism.

I would call your attention to a fact that my worthy opponent deeply ignored last night in regard to the matter of faith. My worthy opponent is a very splendid gentleman so far as following the eel in his tactics in debating. He is hard to corner at all. I have tried for five solid nights to get him to the position of Pentecost and last night to my utter delight I got him to finally put his feet on Pentecost. Now my worthy opponent passed over very lightly the fact that the matter of faith is a matter of great importance in the scriptures and that faith that a man is saved by is a faith that is in the scriptures. Justifying faith in the scriptures is a saving grace wrought in the soul by the Spirit of God whereby one receives Christ. I shall prove to you again tonight as I did last night.

My worthy opponent found a great deal of fault with my

questions. Well he might because he has been asked the same ones over and over and has hedged and sidestepped. Ladies and Gentlemen, I leave it to your fair judgment whether my opponent has answered the questions or not—if he has answered them fairly and honestly at all. My worthy opponent in a pulpit of the Church of Christ would not hesitate to say the things that here I suggest he say. He believes them. The Church of Christ ministers teach them and yet my worthy opponent has not had the courage not one time to face the questions honestly. He cries that I am appealing to prejudice. Here are the questions:

(1) Are Methodists, Presbyterians, and all pedo-Baptists lost and will they go to hell? Will my worthy opponent have the courage to honestly answer that question?

(2) Are Moody, Sankey, Billy Sunday, Wesley, Whitefield, Luther and all who have not been baptized by immersion lost and in hell? He teaches it in his pulpit—the preachers of the Church of Christ teach it—yet he hasn't the courage to stand here and teach it. I want him to stand solidly and squarely on this proposition. My worthy opponent for two nights stated—for two nights—that water baptism is essential to salvation. Last night and tonight we are debating on the proposition inverted: that faith alone before and without water baptism saves a man. Now, if a man has to be immersed in water to be saved, Moody, Finney, Sankey, Billy Sunday, Wesley, Whitefield, Luther and every Methodist, and every Presbyterian and every person that hasn't been immersed is in hell. Ladies and Gentlemen, that's so. My worthy opponent has not the courage to say that. His proposition stands or falls on that answer and I challenge him—I defy him—to stand up before this audience and stand on his proposition and honorably answer the question.

(3) What church baptizes with New Testament baptism?

(4) Will you accept those baptized by Missionary Baptists and Christian Missionary Alliance?

(5) Are they saved or damned?

(6) Show me one scripture that states a man is lost if he is not baptized.

(7) Is it true or not that a person has no chance to be saved

who is not baptized into the Church of Christ, of which he is a member?

(8) I challenge my worthy opponent to tell this audience why Paul did not baptize a new convert every time he believed.

Now my worthy opponent asked me some questions. I have not knowingly hedged, or dodged a single question. I have tried to answer them fully, freely and frankly. I am not ashamed of what I believe. Neither am I afraid to stand for what I believe. Now where these questions were asked—last night he said I said not a word about them. My worthy opponent might not have heard me but I did say I was asked some questions I will answer them in due time fully and completely. I did say something about them.

First, "Where are the scriptures in the New Testament that contain the expression faith alone, or faith only?" I answered that last night. I'll answer it again. If there were such a statement, the proposition would not be debatable. That's self-evident. But I will give my worthy opponent in the course of this message ample material to show him that the Bible says we are saved by faith alone.

(2) "What is the difference between faith and repentance?" Repentance is a change of one's life whereby a sinner turns from his sins toward God—a godly sorrow for sins, Paul says. Faith is a gift of God which saves a man after he repents.

(3) "Is it any worse for a good honest Methodist or Baptist to be lost than for a good honest Jew to be lost?" Now he has asked me the same question backed up. I will answer it fully and completely. I challenge my opponent to answer those questions I have given him to answer. If he says Methodists and Baptists are saved, then his proposition falls to pieces. If he says they are lost, then at least he is consistent and honest. My answer is: It is no worse for an honest Jew or an honest Methodist or Baptist to be lost than any other. **All who do not have faith in an adequate blood atonement in the Old or New Tetament are lost!**

The fourth and the seventh questions I will answer in a moment.

(5) "Does the word 'for' from the Greek word 'gar' in Gal.

3:27 mean to introduce the reason as the lexicons say?" Yes, it does. Certainly, frankly it does. I know that. He can't get away from Galatians. I am awfully glad he can not. We may actually get him right with the Lord and make an Alliance preacher out of him. If he stays in Galatians long enough, we sure can do something with him. Gal. 3:27—I challenge my worthy opponent to get any scholar in Greek to deny that a good translation of the "for", "gar", in view of the preceding verse and what follows states "Indeed, by virtue of being children as many of you as have been baptized into Christ have put on Christ." Now I have checked that with Greek professors today. That's a good English translation. It's true to the Greek word. Now what does it say? "For ye are all the children of God by faith in Christ Jesus for"—the Greek word means, so Greek professors say, "Indeed, by virtue of your being children," "As many of you as have been baptized into Christ have put on Christ." You can not put him on until you are born a child of God by faith. That's what that teaches. Wait a minute, that does not refer to water baptism. In my judgment or in the judgment of many scholars even of my worthy opponent's own persuasion for exactly the same expression in the Greek is used in I Cor. 12:13—"gar"—"for"—"by one spirit"—the same Greek construction so that all Greek testaments link these two together—"For by one Spirit are we all baptized into one body whether we be Jews or Gentile whether we be bond or free." It is the Holy Spirit baptism that takes the sinner and puts him into Christ. Now if my worthy opponent wants Gal. 3:27 to mean water baptism, I'll accept it as water baptism though I do not believe that's the meaning of it. But I'll accept it. Last night, he poked a great deal of fun at me having naked Christians. My worthy opponent is trying to dress up a hog of a sinner in the clothes of Christ and call him a Christian. He is trying to take a man with the nature of the devil in him and say by water baptism you put on Christ. That's all my worthy opponent knows about the New Birth. I have told you over and over he does not believe in the Holy Spirit changing a sinner whereby a man becomes a new creature in Christ Jesus and old things pass away and all things become new. Mark this, my friends, that's the fundamental issue. I'll stake the debate on that. Now, the apostle Paul said before you are baptized into Christ—"For ye are all the children of God by faith in Christ for as many of you as have been baptized into Christ have put on Christ." He said then, he's got Christians that are naked between the 26th and the 27th verse. We have had six children in our home. They are children of my wife and myself. My worthy opponent does not realize at all that the figure for conviction is the new birth. We have never had a youngster born in our house with clothes on yet. (Laughter). They are all born naked—every last one of them. After they are born they are children of ours—that's what that says! I'll accept the naked business. I'll accept it but they are children and then we clothe them. My worthy opponent takes people without having them born again by faith and clothes them, dresses them in Christ and they will be lost at the judgment day.

Sixth, "Since you say that the statement made by Paul that Christ sent me not to baptize proves that baptism is not essenital, if he had been sent to baptize would that have proved that baptism is essential?" It would confirm it. It's not a positive proof but it is corroborative proof. It would confirm it. If it had stated in First Corinthians that Paul was sent to baptize then that would confirm my opponents side. Otherwise it confirms my side.

I'll answer the seventh in a moment. The fourth and the seventh are two questions that go together.

(8) "Is an alien sinner saved by a living faith or a dead faith?" He is saved by a living faith—not a historical faith.

(9) "Is faith alone—faith without works—living or dead?" Living faith will produce works not to be or to prove that it is living but because it's living faith.

Now let me pause a moment and deal with the blackboard here. I want to give you an illustration of my worthy opponent's failure to use any sensible logic at all. I do happen to know some of the laws of logic. This what we call a parallelism and in any parallelism at all—in any one at all—parallels always must be kept parallel. That is, if you have, for instance, ten as one of the items that you are paralleling, you can not ever put ten in another (or the same item) in another column. They have always got to be parallel—they must be parallel. My worthy opponent wrote down belief plus baptism equals salvation. And my parallelism—Enter the train, sit down, reach Atlanta. Both of them are true. Primary things—it is necessary to enter the train. You'll get there whether you sit down or not. And so he crossed out those two. Then last night he proposed to you an intelligent audience hoping that I would not notice it and not thinking you would notice it that he had violated all the laws of logic. He said hearing and believing equals life. Wait a minute: believing is in the first column. Believing always must stay in the first column—in any law of logic in the world. And if we will take and erase this ("Hearing" from first column) and put believing here (Moving "believing" from second column to first) and put hearing any where he wants it, still believing will equal life on the basis of his own parallelism for, my friend, that is according to the laws of logic. That's a sample of how he meets my illustrations but he does not meet my argument.

(Blackboard)

Enters Train	— Sits Down	— Arrives Atlanta
Believes	— Is Baptized	— Is Saved
Hearing	— Believing	— Life
Believing		— Life

Now, turning to questions four and seven. By the way, his way of quoting scripture is not nearly as good as mine. Remember, he wrote "Baptism doth now save us," and said that was I Pet. 3:21, which it isn't. And then I decided that wasn't quite enough and I put the next word down. So I've got more scripture than he has—"Baptism doth now save us not." That's I Pet. 3:21 according to him, plus one word. "It saves us not," says the Word. Turn and read it if you don't believe it.

Question 4 and Question 7: Question 4 is, "What translation gives 'because of' as the rendering of 'eis' in Acts 2:38"? "If such expressions as he was decorated for bravery, he was electrocuted for murder, were translated into Greek would the preposition for be translated into the Greek preposition 'eis' found in Acts 2:38"? Now, in answer to Question 4, no translation gives "because of" for Acts 2:38. In answer to Question 7, "If such expressions as 'he was decorated for bravery,' and 'he was electrocuted for murder' were translated into Greek would for be translated 'eis'?" No! My worthy opponent is fully aware of the fact that the King James translation—now open your Bible and let me show you how he would trick you and not call your attention to this just to prove his point—open your Bibles to

Acts 2:38 and read and see if what I say isn't so. Mark this, Ladies and Gentlemen, I never would debate for judges, I would not debate for decision, neither to annihilate my opponent. He's a nice fellow. I rather like him. His coming over and shaking his finger in my face—I've tried never to look at him. That's good debating. You are ordered in good debating to address your audience and not your opponent. But I rather like to have it because it's very interesting. He has some fine facial expressions. I like to see his hair bob up and down. I really mean it, I'm sincere in saying it. I like it. I think it's fine, the only trouble with it, he's on the wrong side of the page. That's all.

But my worthy opponent in order to prove his argument will not tell you all the facts as they are. I frankly answered his questions. I frankly said that "because of" is not translated in any translation. I frankly said that, "no, that for would not be translated eis". Now, let me show you, "Repent and be baptized every one of you in the name of Jesus Christ," that next word is what? "For," you have a little letter beside it, and if you will notice in the center it says "unto". The King James translators themselves say that is wrong. H. T. Anderson of the Church of Christ, translated the New Testament two times and said it was wrong. Mr. McGarvey of the Church of Christ, one of your great leaders, said it was wrong. There isn't a scholar in the world that will say "for" is right there. If not, why not? Now those are the facts, ladies and gentlemen, "for" should be "unto" or "in reference to."

Now let me give you clearly as I can, the facts. Before the Lord I want to be honest. I'm being honest in my own heart. If I could get any new light I would accept it. One day I broke with orders and ceremonies and I wanted truth and Jesus Christ came into my heart and life, and I have had the time of my life because I know him as my Lord and Saviour. And you need not tell me there is no Holy Spirit that witnesses, and there is no reality in this business of prayer or healing or miracle working, because I know there is! Thank God.

Now the facts of Acts 2:38 are as follows, "eis" is used many times in the New Testament, and it is literally translated "in order to" or "with reference to" or "on the basis of" or "the ground of". That is the literal translation and they smooth it out into other words to keep the phonetics. An illustration of its use in the

New Testament Matt. 10:41: "He that receiveth a prophet in the name of a prophet shall receive a prophets reward." Now here "in the name of a prophet"—"eis"—cannot mean "in order to the prophet" but it must be considered "on account of," or "in reference to". Now, H. T. Anderson of the Church of Christ said that.

In Acts 2:38, the word "repent'" is in the second person, plural number, and therefore is a direct unequivocal command; and the Greek "be baptized" is the third person singular and therefore it's not a direct unequivocal command. Everyone is commanded to repent but not all are commanded to be baptized in this verse. "Eis" signifies "in reference to". Here is the true meaning of Acts 2:38: "Repent and be baptized every one of you in the name of Jesus Christ—'eis'—that is, 'in reference to', the remission of your sins." There cannot possibly be water baptism in reference to remission of sins without that the remission of sins has already taken place. The water baptism points to that which has transpired. A person has repented and they by faith have received remission of sins and because of that glorious fact, now "in reference to it", "in significance of it", "in reference to it", literally they are baptized because they have received remission of sins. That's the true meaning of Acts 2:38. Acts 2:38 therefore teaches that all should repent and receive remission of sins and because of this each individual should be baptized. Thayer's Greek Lexicon, highest authority in the world, gives that statement. A. T. Robertson, one of the greatest Greek scholars that ever lived, gives that statement.

Now, we're saved by faith alone. My worthy opponent said that you couldn't have repentance if you were saved by faith alone. Well, a man makes his living with watermelons alone. That's true. A clear statement. Man plows, plants the seed; he cultivates the plants; harvests the melons; he markets them. The fact that he's making his living from watermelons alone is the significant fact. Now, man's saved by faith alone. By faith we find there must be a man, there must be the God to have faith in, there must be contact with God, which is the basis of the blood, and is wrought through the Holy Spirit. The spending of money, the enjoying of money from the watermelons comes only after the watermelons are sold, after the transaction is closed. That's after he makes his living by watermelons alone.

What comes after conversion is the result of faith; and what comes before, must come before in order for there to be faith. My worthy opponent, knows as well as I do that there isn't a verse in the scripture that uses the word faith alone. If there was there wouldn't be any debate. But many scriptures would show that it is faith alone: Matt. 9:22; Jno. 1:12; Jno. 11:25-27; Acts 26:18; Rom. 1:16; "For I am not ashamed of the gospel for it is the power of God unto salvation to every one that believeth, to the Jew first and also to the Greek." Eph. 2:8,9, "For by grace are you saved through faith and that not of yourselves it"—that faith—"is the gift of God." Faith presupposes repentance, faith alone means all that precedes, including repentance.

My worthy opponent made a great to-do about John 8 last night. Well, turn to John 8. Ladies and Gentlemen, you need to follow the injunction of the apostle Paul. The Bereans were more noble that those of Thessalonica in that they searched the word daily to see whether these things were so or not. Now, Ladies and Gentlemen, I would gladly, I would gladly stand here and admit the truth of my opponent's position if there was any truth in it. My opponent is just as dead wrong about this as he was about that parallelism; as he was about baptism doth now save; as he has been about the other things because his fundamental premise is dead wrong. Now if you will turn to John 8—you'll find Jesus went to the temple, second verse; third verse, scribes and Pharisees brought a woman taken in adultery; now you see the reason in the sixth verse: "This they said tempting him that they might have whereof they might accuse him." They were after him, there was a great crowd of scribes and Pharisees continually after him. Here's a crowd; some of you would like to see termites pick me up and some think I am infinitely better than I could ever possibly be.

Well, "then spake Jesus again to them," this same crowd of critics and some friends; the Pharisees therefore said; Jesus answered and said; then said they unto Him: "Where is your father," accusing him of having no father according to propriety. These were spectators in the treasury. Then Jesus said again to them; twenty-second verse, "then said the Jews"; twenty-third verse, "He said unto them"; twenty-fifth verse, "They said unto him"—this great crowd; twenty-seventh, "They understood not that he spake"; twenty-eighth, "Then said Jesus unto them";

thirtieth, "As he spake these words many believed on him, then said Jesus to those Jews that believed on him, if ye continue in my words, then are ye my disciples indeed; and ye shall know the truth and the truth shall make ye free" and there's a paragraph. Then, the big crowd in which there were some who believed on him, Jesus answered them, 39th verse: "They answered and said 'Abraham is our father'." The crowd of critics, many of you are a crowd of critics of me, many of you are a crowd of critics of my worthy opponent, some of you are believing in my message, some came last night and said they would be here tomorrow not only to hear me preach but join the Tabernacle from the Church of Christ, some are being won, listen Ladies and Gentlemen, that was the situation here. Jesus said unto them; then they took up stones, 59th verse, to cast at him. Now I leave it to your judgment whether that was a crowd of critics and in that crowd of critics there were many that believed on Jesus. It was not a majority, it was just a certain number who believed in that big crowd.

Wednesday night he tied a "not,'" Thursday night he hanged himself up. Friday night he dug a hole in the ground, and now on this day he's fallen therein. Listen, my friend, he said that he did that by premeditation, he said that he did that with his eyes open. Ladies and Gentlemen, I leave it to you, read it, that's all I ask. Read it over and over and see if those three verses point to the crowd that believe on Jesus. Look in your Bible and see if there isn't a paragraph marking in there. There is one there, Ladies and Gentlemen, the scholar knew that was so! Adam Clarke said that was so; commentator after commentator said that was so. My worthy opponent stands up here and insults your intelligence when there isn't a commentator that will agree with him. Listen, he's in the hole and I'm afraid we had better bury him less the stench become too great.

Now, last night he dealt with a dying thief and Mark 16:16. Let's look at this method of exegesis of my opponent. Again, my worthy opponent put the baptism of John before the death of the cross as a matter of proving that salvation is dependent upon baptism. My worthy opponent makes baptism essential for salvation today. When my worthy opponent, brought fact to face with the dying thief, who was granted pardon and salvation by my Lord, my worthy opponent has wiggled now for three nights like an eel.

Listen, my worthy opponent quotes Mark 16:16, "He that believeth and is baptized shall be saved, he that believeth not shall be damned." He says that's binding for today. He affirms he must be baptized in order to be saved. But of Mark 16:17-20 which has no paragraph breaking; which no scholar will say is not for today; which every scholar says is for today with Mark 16:16. My worthy opponent says those signs and powers have passed away. There isn't even a chance to excuse him.

My worthy opponent makes everything that came before the cross as being under the old covenant. He wants to make everything coming after Mark 16:16 as being under the new covenant. He won't accept 17-29 for today; he's got fifty-three days in the middle there and I'm a little afraid he doesn't know in which covenant to place them. I'd like to have our worthy opponent tell us if John's baptism was necessary for salvation before the cross and if Christian baptism is necessary after Pentecot how in high heaven could the people be saved in the 53 days in between. His system is utterly confusion.

My worthy opponent in endeavoring to explain Paul's conversion three days before he was baptized said I Cor. 15:8 means before he became an apostle; that's the most amazing deception I ever head from any supposedly sane teacher of the Word. My opponent makes Paul an apostle before he ever gets him saved. Was Paul called an apostle before he was saved? I thank you, Ladies and Gentlemen.

SIXTH NIGHT—PORTER'S FIRST SPEECH

Mr. President, Gentlemen Moderators, Respected Opponent, Ladies and Gentlemen:

I come before you now in the negative of the proposition which my friend has been affirming for the past thirty minutes—that the sinner is saved by faith alone before and without water baptism.

(I would like to have this chart fixed up, please.)

Now, then, before I reply to the speech that has just been made, there are just a few things I want to call your attention to. In fact, there are three or four points I overlooked in my notes last night. One with respect to Gal. 3:27. My friend suggested something about the little word "are"—"Ye are the children of God by faith in Christ Jesus." Yes, the little word "are" is present tense of the verb—"Ye are the children of God by faith in Christ Jesus." The next verse says, "For as many of you as have been baptized into Christ have put on Christ." Or as the American Revised Version reads, "As many of you as were baptized." Ye are the children of God now because you were baptized in the past. So you have "are" present tense, when Paul writes and "were" past tense, referring to the time they were baptized. "Ye are God's children"—present tense—"because ye were"—past tense—"baptized into Christ." Or as the King James Version reads, "As many of you as have been baptized into Christ."

Then regarding Romans 4:5, Mark 11:22 and Hebrews 12:2—which my opponent said show that faith was imputed, that it was a gift of God, and that it was not something that man does. Mark 11:22—"Have faith in God." He said some translators give it, "Have the faith of God." Yes, if he will check, he will find that the article "the" is not in the original. But let that be as it may, he said this faith is imputed to him, but this passage Rom. 4:5-6—says faith is counted for righteousness; and that the righteousness is the thing that was imputed to man, and not the faith. Besides, "imputed" doesn't mean "given"—it simply means "counted." And if his position about that is correct, and man has nothing to do, but God simply gives these things, then if a man does not have faith, and he dies and goes to hell because of it, God is to blame, because man had nothing at all to do with it anyway. But in John 6:28-29 the people said to Jesus, "What shall we do that we may work the works of God" Jesus said, "This is the work of God that ye believe on him whom he hath sent," thus showing that faith, or belief, refers to what men do; it refers to their part. "This is the work of God that you believe." So men certainly must do the believing.

Then, also, in that same connection he calls attention to the fact that here was Abraham—and comparing us with him—having imputed to us righteousness by faith. If he will read on down through the chapter, in verses 11 and 12 he will find that that righteousness is imputed to those who walk in the steps of the faith of our father Abraham. Now, then, if Abraham was justified by faith only, his faith had no steps; but Paul talks about those who walk in the steps of Abraham's faith; and the blessing promised there is promised to those who walk in the steps of Abraham's faith. Men do not walk by simply taking one step.

Then, in the next place, John 1:12-13—about being born of God. "Born not of blood, nor of the will of the flesh, nor of the will of man, but of God." He said that if baptism were necessary, it would be the will of man—but that man's will is not involved in it. Again, I say if that is so, then if a man dies and goes to hell, he is not responsible for it—God just didn't force salvation on him. But in Rev. 22:17 we read, "The Spirit and the bride say, Come. Let him that heareth say, Come. Let him that is athirst come. And whosoever will, let him take the water of life freely." I ask my opponent if he intends to indicate by this that it is not up to man to accept, if men have no choice in the matter. If he has some choice in the matter, certainly he has some will in the matter, and that being true, he must accept or reject as the case may be. If this isn't true, then man is not saved because God doesn't force salvation upon him.

Then he asks the question, "Where is the scripture that puts faith before repentance." I mentioned last night that there is a degree of faith before repentance, and there is a degree of faith after repentance; but that the degree of faith which saves man is not reached until after repentance. But in Acts 2:36-38 we are told that Peter said "let all the house of Israel know assuredly, that God hath made that same Jesus, whom ye have crucified, both Lord and Christ." And since he said, "Let all the house of Israel know assuredly," the only way in the world they could know assuredly was to believe confidently. To those who thus know assuredly Peter said, "Repent, and be baptized everyone of you in the name of Jesus Christ for the remission of sins." Thus Peter placed repentance and baptism after faith—the confident faith—or the "knowing assuredly"—in that matter.

Now, then, just a few negatives here in connection with the chart.

My OPPONENT SAYS	THE BIBLE SAYS
The Scriptures Teach that Alien Sinners are Saved by Faith ALONE Before and Without Water Baptism	"Even so Faith, if it Hath not Works, is Dead, Being Alone." James 2:17 "Ye see then how that by Works a Man is Justified, and Not by Faith Only." James 2:14
HE THAT BELIEVETH AND IS NOT BAPTIZED SHALL BE SAVED.	"HE THAT BELIEVTH AND IS BAPTIZED Shall be Saved." Mark 16:16

I have a chart here that brings out **what we have** before us tonight. Over on this side (and I think perhaps you can read it from most parts of the auditorium) we have at the top, "My Opponent says;" and over on this side we have, "The Bible says." And here, my opponent says, "The scriptures teach that alien sinners are saved by faith alone before and without water baptism." Now, that's the proposition, word for word, which my opponent is affirming. Incidentally, you notice in asking these questions awhile ago the first question I gave was, "Where are the scriptures in the New Testament that contain the expression "faith alone" or "faith only?" He says, "There is no such statement." "There is no such statement!" The Bible does not say a single time that men are saved by faith alone. My opponent agrees that that is so. All right; here's what Tingley says (pointing to chart), and yet the scripture does not say it. There's not a passage in all of God's book that says it. He says, "You just can not find a statement that says men are saved by faith alone." He can find hundreds of them that say men are saved by faith, or words equivalent to that, but we agree with all of that. We preach it ourselves. But when he puts the little word "alone" in there, that's a different proposition. My opponent says he can not find in God's word a statement that says men are saved by faith alone! Well, he just as well erase it then, because that's what his proposition says.

I will tell you what he can find in the scripture. Over on this side (pointing to chart) we have some statements that are found in the scripture. All right; here is what the Bible says in contrast with his proposition. "Even so faith, if it hath not works, is dead, being alone." James 2:17. Now, take that and go home and read your Bibles for yourselves. If you have your Bibles with you, turn to it and read it. Here is what the scriptures say. Here's what the Bible says. "Even so faith, if it hath not works, is dead, being alone." Now, the book of God says faith without works is dead, that faith alone is dead. I asked my opponent a question here awhile ago: "Is an alien sinner" (that is number 8)—"Is an alien sinner saved by a living faith or by by a dead faith?" He says, "A living faith." All right, if it is a living faith, it can not be faith alone because James says, "Faith, being alone, is dead." Now faith, being alone, is dead—that's what James says. And my opponent says you can not be saved by a dead faith—that it is a living faith that saves the sinner. All right, then, if we can not be saved by a dead faith and it takes a living faith, it can not be faith alone, because James says, "Faith alone is dead." Now which of those do you want?

All right, that isn't all the scriptures say. Here's another passage—James 2:24—"Ye see then how that by works a man is justified, and not by faith only." That isn't what Porter said. I wonder if my friend will tell me whether this is scripture or not.

James 2:24—put this right over beside of what my opponent says and look at it. Here my opponent says that "sinners are saved by faith alone," but James says a man is justified "not by faith only." One says a man is saved by faith only; the other says a man is not saved by faith alone. My opponent says he is. The Bible says he is not. Now, just which one are you going to take? Well, we will have more on that as we go. (We'll get to this other at the bottom of the chart presently.)

I submit to you the fact that the expression "by faith" as used in God's word does not mean "by faith alone." For example, we read in Rom. 8:24 that a man is saved "by hope." Shall I put that down and say that means "by hope alone," that there is nothing in there at all except hope—that that's all there is to it? If "by faith" means "by faith only" why doesn't "by hope" mean "by hope only?"

Then in James 2:24, which we also have on the chart, James says, "A man is justified by works." Does that mean by works alone? Why, certainly not, but if "by faith" means "by faith alone," why doesn't "by works" mean "by works alone?" If it works in one case, it certainly works in the other.

And then remember this: the word "alone" has a certain meaning. "Saved by faith alone." That means faith to the exclusion of everything else. Along in my notes I have some statements he made about that. Now, get this: the book of God does declare that men are saved by faith—even some of these examples he gave also give the other side of it. Take Abraham, for example—he gave Romans 4—"Abraham was justified by faith." Yes, and if you turn to James 2:21-23, you will find James says, "Abraham was justified by works." I take them both. He takes only one of them.

Then in Heb. 11:21—Rahab, the harlot, perished not by faith, but in James 2:25 she was justified by works. By faith and by works, so declares the Book of God.

Then in Rom. 5:1 we are said to be justified by faith, but in James 2:24 we are also said to be justified by works. So it is by faith and by works, according to the Book of God.

Now, then, keep this in mind here. My opponent says he can not find this in the Bible (pointing to "My opponent says" on chart) but I can find this (pointing to "The Bible Says" on chart) And this is the direct contrast to that. They don't say the same. This says (pointing to chart), "Saved by faith alone," but the Bible says, "Faith is dead, being alone." This says, "Men are saved by faith alone." But this says, "Men are saved by works, and not by faith only." There's not a way on the earth that you can make those two statements read the same. They just do not read alike. I believe what the Bible says. If you want to believe what my opponent says, that's your privilege, but I will just stand with what the word of God says.

I want to notice some more about those answers to questions—regarding his questions. There are the very same ones he gave last night. He has introduced them all before, and they have all been answered. The only reason my friend has introduced them over and over is to try to create some prejudice because he sees the thing is going from him if he can not resort to a thing of that kind. So he wants to stir up a little prejudice, that's all. He says I have not answered any of them. Why, he said, "Porter, why don't you say that those who were not baptized have gone to hell?" I have said it over and over, according to God's book. Why do I have to keep on telling you over and over. Why, if the Book of God says a thing, suppose that sends me to hell, or it sends my friend to hell, or it sends everybody to hell that's in this audience. Does that change what the Book says? Why, he said awhile ago, "Porter's proposition stands or falls on this question." Now there is not a word of truth in that. "It stands or falls on this question." This question (as to who is going to hell) has nothing to do with the proposition. The proposition stands or falls on what the Bible says. The proposition says, "The scriptures teach." It does not say that "whether people go to hell or not teaches so and so." That has nothing to do with the proposition.

"What's the difference between faith and repentance?" He said, "Repentance is a change of one's mind; Faith is a gift of God." So they are not the same, and we'll have more to say about that later.

Then regarding number 3, he said, "It's no worse for one than another to go to hell." Well, all right then—"sauce for the goose is sauce for the gander."

Fourth, "What translation gives 'because of' as the rendering of 'eis' in Acts 2:28?" He says, "There is no such translation." I knew it. I kept telling him all of the time that he could not find it that way. Now, he comes and says, "There is no translation that gives 'because of' in Acts 2:38." If that's the meaning of it, all the scholars making the translations never did find that was the meaning of it in that verse. He said all scholars agree that the word "for" in Acts 2:38 is not a correct translation, that the word doesn't mean "for." Now, I read to you some translations last night, and I have them here again. I just want to notice a few of them.

First, the King James translation. He says no scholar will agree that "for" is the translation in Acts 2:38—all scholars deny that, he said. Well, was the King James translation made by scholars? Now you tell us. Tell us whether those forty-seven men that made the King James Translation were scholars.

Not only that but the Revised Standard Version, which is the latest translation in existence, being brought into print last year, made by a number of men who had part in translating the American Revised Version, translates Acts 2:38, "For forgiveness of sins." They put the word "for" in there, and I want my opponent to tell me, were those men scholars? He said, "Not a scholar will agree that 'for' is a correct translation of it." Why did they put it in, then?

And number 5: "Does the word 'for,' from the Greek word 'gar,' in Gal. 3:27, meant 'to introduce the reason, as the lexicons say?" He said, "Yes." All right, then. "Yes, it means to introduce the reason." Then Paul said, "Ye are the children of God by faith in Christ Jesus," and the reason is, "that as many of you as have been baptized into Christ have put on Christ." Friend Tingley says that's the meaning of it. Fine. That's what I knew all the time, but I had an awful time trying to get him to say anything about it. I had to put it in writing before he would say anything about it. Up until that time he never even mentioned the argument I made on that. He had mentioned Gal. 3:27, but he never did say a word about the argument I made on it—on that little word "for," or "gar," meaning " to introduce the reason." Now, he says, "It does mean to introduce the reason," but he said, "That's not water baptism. That refers to the baptism of the Holy Spirit. That's not water baptism." All right, then. Now, he says, "That's the baptism of the holy Spirit." Let us read it that way then. "Ye are all the children of God by faith in Christ Jesus for as many of you as have been baptized by the Holy Spirit into Christ have put on Christ." He has been arguing heretofore that men put on Christ—put the clothes on—in baptism. They are born first, then they put their clothes on, and they put their clothes on when they are baptized according to Gal. 3:27. So he has the man born, a new creature before he has the Holy Spirit baptism; yet he claims the Holy Spirit baptism is necessary to salvation. But now he has the Holy

Spirit baptism after he is a new creature, in order to put the clothes on. Why, you meet yourself coming back, Tingley! (Laughter). He has been arguing all the time that we put on the clothes when we are baptized—we put on Christ when we are baptized—just as you put the clothes on the baby that's born. But he says it is Holy Spirit baptism that saves us, then turns around here and says this baptism is Holy Spirit baptism that we submit to after we are born, in order to put on the clothes.

Number 6. "Since you say the statement made by Paul that "Christ sent me not to baptize" proves baptism is not essential to salvation, then if he had been sent to baptize would that prove that baptism is essential?" He said, "It would confirm it." "It would confirm it." All right, In John 1:33 we are told that John was sent to baptize. Back under John's ministry, John said, "He that sent me to baptize with water." Now, then, if that would mean that baptism was essential if it had been spoken concerning Paul, since it was spoken concerning John, it means baptism was essential under John's ministry—my friend being witness to it.

"If such expressions as 'He was decorated for bravery,' and 'He was electrocuted for murder' were translated into Greek preposition 'eis' found in Acts 2:38?" He says, "No." Then, why did you give those statements as parallel with Acts 2:38? In Acts 2:38 we have the Greek word "eis," and my friend says now these statements which he gave could not be translated into "eis" if they were translated into Greek. Well, the statement in Acts 2:28—"for the remission of sins"—if it were translated into Greek, would be translated into "eis" for the preposition "for." Since his statements could not be translated into that word, then the statements are not parallel. If they were paraellel, you could translate them both into the same Greek expression with respect to that preposition. Well, scholars say they are not parallel expressions at all, and my friend agrees to that.

I have read the eighth question and now the ninth. "Is faith alone—without works—living dead?" He said, "A living faith will produce works. It lives before it works." Well, if it lives before it works, it lives before it operates, then, doesn't it? If it lives before it works, it lives without works, but James says, "Faith without works is dead." My opponent says, "No, it lives without works, and then after awhile it works." But James says,

"Faith without works is dead." Now, you can take what my opponent says, or you can take what the Bible says. They are not the same, they don't even resemble each other. They are not anywhere close to the same.

I want to pass on now to some notes that I have taken.

Mr. Nichols: You have nine minutes.

Mr. Porter: Nine minutes. All right.

Regarding Acts 2:38, he said, "Holy Spirit baptism saves the sinner." He quoted 1 Cor. 12:13 in connection with it and thus insisted that the Holy Spirit must come before the sinner is saved. But Acts 2:38 says, "Repent, and be baptized everyone of you in the name of Jesus Christ for the remission of sins, and ye shall receive the gift of the Holy Spirit." My friend says we got all of that before we were baptized. Peter put that, whatever it is, after we are baptized. Then, not only that, but in Acts 8:14-16 there were certain ones in Samaria who had been baptized—who had believed Philip's preaching and had been baptized—had put on Christ, of course. They had believed Philip's preaching and had been baptized. Yet the apostles came there to lay hands on them because, the record says, "The Holy Ghost had fallen on none of them, only they were baptized in the name of the Lord." How did they get saved before they received the miraculous measure of the Holy Spirit?

The same thing in Acts 19:1-5. We have twelve men there at Ephesus, and the same thing occurred. They were baptized first and then the Spirit came upon them through the laying on of the apostles' hands.

Now we go back to the board.

MY OPPONENT SAYS	THE BIBLE SAYS
The Scriptures Teach that Alien Sinners are Saved by Faith ALONE Before and Without Water Baptism	"Even so Faith, if it Hath not Works, is Dead, Being Alone." James 2:17 "Ye see then how that by Works a Man is Justified, and Not by Faith Only." James 2:14

| HE THAT BELIEVETH AND IS NOT BAPTIZED SHALL BE SAVED. | "HE THAT BELIEVETH AND IS BAPTIZED Shall be Saved." Mark 16:16 |

Over on this side my opponent says, "He that believeth and is not baptized shall be saved." The Bible says, "He that believeth and is baptized shall be saved." I know the rest of the verse is, "He that believeth not shall be damned." We have discussed that. There isn't room for all of it here. Now we have this contrast drawn. "He that believeth and is not baptized shall be saved." Tingley, do you believe that? All right, now, Jesus said, "He that believeth and is baptized shall be saved." Notice the difference. "Is not" and "Is"! Are they the same? Or is my friend hung on his "not"? (Laughter). "He that believeth and is not baptized shall be saved." The Bible says, "He that believeth and is baptized shall be saved." Now, if you want to take my opponent for it, just help yourself. I'm going to take what Jesus said about it.

Now, in regard to his parallel about entering the train and his logic. We want to get to that. Just slip that out of the way just a minute. (The chart is removed, showing the blackboard).

(Blackboard)

Enters train — Sits down — Reaches Atlanta
Believeth — Is baptized — Shall be saved
Heareth — Believeth — Hath Everlasting Life

Now, he said regarding this, if you have "belief" over in this column (pointing to line 2, column 1), then you must have "belief" in it down here (pointing to line 3, column 1), because you must have a parallel. Well, who told you to parallel "entering the train" and "believing"? Where did you get your authority for that? Suppose we just erase this entirely (pointing to line 2). That's the parallel he made. (Porter erases all of line 2). And then just make a similar parallel down here like he made, and we'll have "hearing" under that (pointing to "Enters train) and "belief" over here (pointing to "Sits down"). Who gave him the authority to put "belief" under "Entering the train"? I have just as much authority to put "hearing" over here (pointing to column 1) and "belief" over here (pointing to column 2) as he had to arrange his parallel as he did. When we erase his line then we have no "belief" to contend with there (pointing to column 1) and we have "Hearing" first column, "Belief," second column, just as he had "entering the train" and "sitting down." So you can cut "belief" out just like he cut out "baptism." It is parallel with "Sits down," which is not essential. It cuts out faith on the same sort of parallelism. (After the erasure the blackboard chart appears as below):

(Blackboard)
Enters train — Sits down — Reaches Atlanta
Heareth — Believeth — Hath Everlasting Life

Well, he said he had more scripture than I did because 1 Pet. 3:21 said, "Baptism doth also now save us not." Yes, but when he read the word "not" there he changed the meaning of it entirely, because he ran right over a parenthesis and took a word from on the inside of the parenthesis and brought it to the front side—put it on the outside—and made a complete stop where there wasn't even any pause in the reading of the Divine Record. He changed the meaning of it entirely.

He said, "Well I like Porter. I like to see his hair bob up and down." (Laughter). Somebody else's hair may bob up and down as much as mine. (Laughter). He said the trouble is he is on the wrong side.

MY **OPPONENT** SAYS	THE **BIBLE** SAYS
The Scriptures Teach that Alien Sinners are Saved by Faith ALONE Before and Without Water Baptism	"Even so Faith, if it Hath not Works, is Dead, Being Alone." James 2:17 "Ye see then how that by Works a Man is Justified, and Not by Faith Only." James 2:14
HE THAT BELIEVETH AND IS NOT BAPTIZED SHALL BE SAVED.	"HE THAT BELIEVTH AND IS BAPTIZED Shall be Saved." Mark 16:16

Well, which side are you on? Here's the dividing line between me and Tingley (pointing to chart). He's one side (pointing to "My Opponent says" on chart), and I am on this (pointing to "The Bible Says" on chart). This is what he admits the Bible doesn't say (pointing to statements on left side of chart). He admits the Bible does say this (pointing to right side of chart). I'm on this side, and he's over there. Now make your own decision as to who is on the wrong side.

Now to Acts 2:38—the second person, plural, and third person, singular, again. I showed statements from the scholars last night that those words can be joined by the same predicate—that they can be joined to the plural verb as in the case of "Be baptized everyone of you." "Every one of you" includes just as many as "All of you." "Repent all of you, be baptized everyone of you." How many more are in one expression than the other? He said repentance was a command, and he sort of wanted to intimate that baptism was not, or at least, it did not seem to have as much force as the other. But in Acts 10:48 we have the statement written by Luke that "He commanded them to be baptized in the name of the Lord."

Then to the matter of making a living by watermelons. He said, "Yes, I believe in salvation by faith alone." Well, that does not include repentance. He said a man makes his living by watermelons alone. Now, he said, "You have got to have a man." Yes, if you are going to have a sinner saved, you have got to have a sinner, of course. No body is ruling out things of that kind. That has nothing to do with it. Certainly, there must be a sinner just as there must be a man. "And there must be a God," he said. Yes, there must be a God here. "And there must be money and there must be a sale for it—some body to buy," and all of that. But the man makes his living "by watermelons alone." Now, what does that mean? That doesn't rule out the fact that there is a man or that there must be somebody to buy or that there must be a God or anything of that kind, but it rules out anything else as a means of his living except watermelons. If I come along and say that "watermelons alone" means that you can also include pumpkins in it, you know that isn't so. If a man makes a living by watermelons alone, that doesn't mean watermelons and pumpkins. If a sinner is saved by faith alone, that doesn't mean faith and repentance, because you have parallel conditions just as you would have two kinds of products if you had watermelons and pumpkins. Man in all of it—certainly. God in all of it—certainly. But faith alone and watermelons alone—not faith and repentance and not watermelons and pumpkins. I can put pumpkins in that man's occupation and have him make his living by pumpkins as well—though it's by watermelons alone—and do it as easily as he puts repentance in his proposition where it says faith alone.

Now to John 8. How much time do I have?

Mr. Nichols: A minute and a half.

Mr. Porter: A minute and a half. Well, I'll read this—just a little of it—about those who believed on Him. Now notice this. Verse 30, "As he spake these words many believed on him. Then said Jesus to those Jews which believed on him, If you continue in my words, then are you my disciples indeed." We have not reached the paragraph yet. Verse 32 (and still we have not reached it). "Ye shall know the truth, and the truth shall make you free." That is spoken to the Jews, who believed on him, as though they had not yet been made free. Jesus said, "Ye shall know the truth, and the truth shall make you free." And then verse 33, "They answered him, We be Abraham's seed, and were never in bondage to any man: how sayest thou, Ye shall be made free?" My opponent says this was another crowd. John said it was the same crowd to whom he said, "Ye shall be made free," because they replied and said, "How do you say we will be made free?" My opponent says this was another crowd. John said they referred to the very thing that he said to them. He said, "Ye shall be made free." And they said, "How do ye say we shall be made free? We have never been in bondage." So the very ones Jesus spoke to are the ones who replied, and the replied concerning the very thing that He said to them—the matter of being made free. So it certainly stands, and all that he has said about it is wrong.

Thank you, Ladies and Gentlemen.

SIXTH NIGHT—TINGLEY'S SECOND SPEECH

Mr. Chairman, Gentlemen Moderators, Worthy Opponent, Ladies and Gentlemen:

My worthy opponent quibbled a good bit about faith alone—alone. And he ignores my answer that if there were such a statement in the Bible there would not be a debate. My worthy opponent admitted when I pressed him in regard to the question for the two nights previous—The Scriptures Teach that Water Baptism to a Penitent Believer of the Gospel is Essential to Salvation from Alien Sins—that there was not one scripture that said those words either. That's what makes a debate—a matter about which honest people can disagree—that makes a debate.

I was interested in the answers to the questions I gave him. And for the first time he almost said that Methodists and Presbyterians and people that have not been immersed are lost and in hell and that Moody, Finney, Whitfield and the others are in hell. I thank him for answering the question. Of necessity I must hasten for I do want to sum up the arguments that have been made. I want to make it clear to your mind the position that we have taken so that you will have something to think about but I must spent just a moment on the chart of my worthy opponent.

MY OPPONENT SAYS	THE BIBLE SAYS
The Scriptures Teach that Alien Sinners are Saved by Faith ALONE Before and Without Water Baptism	"Even so Faith, if it Hath not Works, is Dead, Being Alone." James 2:17 "Ye see then how that by Works a Man is Justified, and Not by Faith Only." James 2:14
HE THAT BELIEVETH AND IS NOT BAPTIZED SHALL BE SAVED.	"HE THAT BELIEVTH AND IS BAPTIZED Shall be Saved." Mark 16:16

Now, I believe in this particular statement very definitely. (Pointing to proposition on chart). I believe in this (Pointing to James 2:17 on chart). I believe in this (Pointing to James 2:14). I believe in this (Pointing to Mark 16:16). This is not scripture (Pointing to "He that believeth and is not baptized shall be saved").

I want to show you what I did to my worthy opponent's misstatement of scripture the other night, please. You remember he wrote:

"Baptism doth now save us"
"Baptism doth not save us"

and said, "Now you erase the one you do not believe." I utterly dumbfounded him by erasing the bottom one. And he still has not got his heart beating quite right because of the shock at that particular time. Then I just added one word, and that is the next word in the Bible giving a little more scripture. He left out a word—"also"—that should be in there and "figure" should be in front of it. Now that changes the entire picture and I would call the attention of my worthy opponent and the audience to the fact that several translations of scripture translate it that baptism is the figure—in those very words.

Now my worthy opponent came to the parallelism. All right, I'll let him go at this: Hearing plus believing equals salvation. I'll let him put that and then make the parallelism equal: Buying a ticket and Entering the Train—that's the important thing, entering the trains gets you to Atlanta. You can erase this (buying ticket) buy your ticket on the train and reach Atlanta but you have got to believe to be saved and you have got to enter the train to get to Atlanta. Ladies and Gentlemen, keep your parallelism equal. Do not allow him to mix up belief with htat which is not parallel.

Now a word about repentance. "Repentance, watermelons and pumpkins." That's the first time I ever knew that repentance is a pumpkin. Well, my worthy opponent says it, however. But listen to me carefully. Pumpkins are not necessary to watermelons. Repentance is necessary to faith. Pumpkins are not necessary to watermelons. No individual can have faith without repentance. Repentance is necessary to faith.

Now, turning to James 2. I am so happy my worthy opponent has dealt with it because I fully expected him to deal with it. Now let us deal with it. I believe in these words from the Bible, "Even so faith if it hath not works is dead being alone." A faith that does not produce works is alone and is dead and is not saving faith. That's true. I believe that with all my heart. "Ye see then how that by works a man is justified and not by faith only." I believe that with all my heart. Let me show you, though. You know that the second verse of the first chapter of James says, "My brethren count it all joy." You know that the first verse of the second chapter says, "My brethren have not the faith of our Lord Jesus Christ and the glory of God with respect of persons," You know that the third chapter says, "My brethren, be not many masters." Who is James talking to? He is talking to the brethren. He is talking to born again ones. There is not a word in here addressed to the unsaved. It is addressed to the saved—to the people who were saved by faith.

All right, now, let's notice this portion that he called our attention to—the fourteenth to the twenty-sixth verses, "What doth it profit my brethern, though a man say he hath faith, and have not works? Can faith save him? If a brother or sister be naked — ." What is he talking about? Ministering to the poor. My worthy opponent does not believe that giving to the poor will save. I do not either. But an individual who is born again will care for the poor of the Lord's house. "Even so faith if it hath not works is dead"—it's a dead faith—"being alone." That's what I am pleading against. I'm pleading for a living faith that produces works.

Listen again my friends, "Yea, a man may say, Thou hast faith and I have works: show me thy faith without thy works and I will show thee my faith by my works." Faith produces works. Works declare faith. There can be no works acceptable unless they are preceded by faith. "Thou believest that there is one God. Thou doest well." Now an illustration is given. All of those who believe without producing works, who believe without salvation. "The devils believe and tremble." They have faith and they tremble. "Was not Abraham our father justified by works when he offered up Isaac," and then to prove his point that works must follow faith he calls on Abraham to witness. "Ye see then how that by works a man is justified for as the body without the spirit is dead so faith without works is dead."

I wish I could spend my entire thirty minutes on it. Let me show you one or two things. Abraham, we are told in Rom. 4, believed God and it was counted to him for righteousness. Then he received the seal of circumcision and then Isaac was born and then he offered Isaac. Now listen, mark this, my friends, "The scripture was fulfilled which saith when he had offered Isaac his son upon the altar." Now when was Abraham justified by works? When he offered Isaac upon the altar. Ladies and Gentlemen, twenty-six years before, God had stood before Abraham and said, "Abraham your faith is counted for righteousness." And the scriptures said, "Abraham was a friend of God. Abraham believed God." For twenty-six years he had walked with God. Was he saved or lost in that twenty-six years? My worthy opponent says he was damned. God said he was saved.

And Abraham twenty-six years later—Romans and Genesis and other scriptures say God accepted him—twenty-six years later he went up and offered his son upon the altar. James and Paul both say if a man had living faith then that man with a living faith ought to produce works. One year, two years, twenty-six years—all his life he ought to produce faith.

Then he went on to say that I am contending for a living faith before works. I am. I plead guilty. I will stake the debate on that, that I am preaching a living faith before works. Did you ever see a corpse work? You can not possibly work until you have life. You never can work until you have life. You have got to have life before you can work. You have life, then you work. I believe in a living faith first, then works naturally result. A living faith for twenty-six years and if after twenty-six years James says that an individual who does not have works is still crying, "Faith, faith," that faith is dead, that is the faith of devils. That's not the faith that saves. He's not one of the brethren. I believe that with all my heart.

1. Now, I want to sum up what we have said. 1 Cor. 1:12-13, instead of teaching that baptism is essential to salvation and faith is not the essential, the whole passage teaches exactly the opposite. Paul said, in the next verse, "I thank God I baptized none of you but Crispus and Gaius lest any of you should say I baptized in my own name. I baptized also the household of Stephanas besides I know not whether I baptized any other, For Christ sent me not to baptize

but to preach the gospel, Not with words of wisdom lest the cross of Christ should be made of none effect." Therefore, an individual is saved by faith before and apart from water baptism.

2. Paul says in I Cor. 4:15—"For although ye have ten thousand instructors ye have not many fathers for in Christ Jesus I have begotten you through the gospel." Now he begat all of them but he did not baptize them. If a person can not be born again without baptism, then Paul lied when he said he begat them for he thanked God he did not baptize them. First Corinthians teaches that baptism is not the essential but that faith is the essential.

3. Paul explains the mission of ministers of grace in 1 Cor. 1:17—"Christ sent me not to baptize but to preach the gospel not with words of wisdom lest the cross of Christ be made of none effect." Therefore, man is saved by faith alone before and apart from baptism.

4. Paul was saved after Pentecost, is my fourth argument. He was saved before, he was baptized. He was the apostle of grace and yet declares that he was sent not to baptize, but to preach. He thanks God he had baptized a few. Therefore, Paul so minimized the act of baptism, then an individual can be saved by faith before and apart from any work of righteousness.

5. My worthy opponent makes much of Mark 16:16 for today but he denies the balance of the chapter having to do with miracles. And there is no paragraph there. Mark 16:16 does not teach baptism is essential to salvation. It shows that believing— our proposition tonight—is essential to salvation and it shows that disbelief is the only cause of damnation.

6. Mark 16:16 is a work of righteousness. Recorded in Matt. 3:15 corcerning the baptism of Jesus, Jesus said, "Suffer it to be so now for it becometh us to fulfill all righteousness." Then since we are not saved by works—Titus 3:5, "Not by works of righteousness" of which baptism is one, "which we have done, He saved us according to his mercy by the washing of regeneration and the renewing of the Holy Ghost." Therefore, Mark 16:16 cannot teach that which is contrary to Matt. 3:15 and Titus 3:5.

7. Since Mark 16:16 contrasts salvation and damnation

on the basis of belief but pronounces no damnation upon unbaptized believers, therefore, Mark 16:16 teaches that believing is essential to salvation and baptism is an act of obedience for saved believers.

8. In Acts 2:38 it can mean either way and is the only scripture in the entire Bible of which that can be said. The preposition "eis" can mean "in order to" or "with reference to" or rarely "because". A sample, "They repented at the preaching of Jonah." They repented "eis" the preaching of Jonah. They did not repent in order to the preaching Jonah. they repented "with reference to" the preaching of Jonah. They repented "because of" the preaching of Jonah. That, my friend, is a literal exegesis of it. Jonah preached once before they repented. They did not repent "in order to" the preaching of Jonah, but "because of" the preaching of Jonah. "Repent and be baptized every one of you in the name of Jesus Christ in reference to the remission of sins and ye shall receive the gift of the Holy Ghost." Therefore, Acts 2:38 does not teach baptism is essential to salvation but that one is to be baptized because he has received the remission of sins.

9. According to the Greek grammar Acts 2:38 will not sustain my worthy opponents position. The words "repent" and "be baptized" are tied together by a conjunction. The word "repent" is in the second person, plural number, therefore is a direct command in the Greek, while "be baptized" is third person singular and not a direct command. Therefore, Acts 2.38 can not teach baptism is essential to salvation. My friends, we are baptized "for the remisssion of sins"—not in order that they may be remitted but "in reference to" because they have been remitted, therefore I am baptized.

10. Acts 9:6 and Acts 22:16 giving us Paul's conversion instead of proving that baptism is essential to salvation proves just the opposite. Paul said in 1 Cor. 15:8 that last of all he was seen of men also as of one born out of due time, that he was born again when he saw the Lord. Since he was not baptized until three days later, therefore, baptism, Paul said, is not essential to salvation.

I must pause, and call your attention again to this. My worthy opponent said when Paul saw the Lord that was his apostleship. Then my worthy opponent said three days later he was saved. Do you mean God would confer apostleship upon an unsaved man? Of course He would not! You can not have apostleship until a man is saved.

11. Paul confessed Jesus as Lord on the Damascus road. 1 Cor. 12:3, "Wherefore I give you to understand"—Paul is the writer of this—"that no man speaketh by the Spirit of God calleth Jesus accursed and that no man can say that Jesus is Lord but by the Holy Ghost." Since Paul's confession of Jesus as his Lord was made three days before his baptism, therefore, Paul was saved by faith before and without water baptism.

12. Acts 22:16 says, "And now why tarriest thou, Arise and be baptized and wash away thy sins calling on the name of the Lord." Baptism is the symbol of salvation. Can a man wash away his own sins? Of course he can not. Can water on the flesh wash away the sins of the heart? God alone can forgive sins. The blood of Jesus Christ takes away sins. Therefore, Paul was told to symbolically wash away his sins in the water of baptism.

13. Baptism is the symbol of the reality. Baptism is the figure of the death, burial and resurrection of Jesus Christ. Baptism is the shadow—not the substance, therefore, baptism has no meaning unless there first has been an actual remission of sins. Here in Birmingham we have a statue honoring Brother Bryan. The monument would be meaningless if Brother Bryan had not been first. There is no forgiveness of sins in baptism. It is a monument.

14. Contrary to the assertion of my worthy opponent, Gal. 3:27—"As many of you as were baptized into Christ" proves that baptism has nothing to do with salvation but is the next step after salvation for the words before says, "Ye are children of God by faith in Jesus Christ." You have got to be children first before you can put on clothes. You have got to be a child of God before you can wear the badge of discipleship that's acceptable to God. Therefore, an individual is saved by faith.

15. Gal. 3:27 states that baptism is the step signifying the growing up, it's the badge, it's the Toga Virilis. Therefore baptism is not essential to salvation and a man is saved by faith.

16. Instead of 1 Pet. 3:21 teaching baptism is essential to salvation, it teaches just the opposite. "The like figure whereunto even baptism doth also now save us, (not the putting away of the filth of the flesh but the answer of a good conscience toward God)"—how are we saved? "By the resurrection of Jesus Christ." It says that baptism is a figure. It says it is the figure of what saves us. Baptism is the figure of the death, burial and resurrection of Jesus Christ. It says we are saved by the resurrection of Jesus Christ of which baptism is a figure. Therefore we are not saved by baptism but by the resurrection and baptism is not essential to salvation but a man is saved by faith in a resurrected Christ.

17. It declares that the baptism that saves us is not the putting away of the actual filth of the flesh. The act of baptism is the answer of a good conscience. This good conscience is obtained by the blood of Christ. Heb. 9:14—"Purge your conscience from dead works to serve the living God." Therefore, baptism, a figure, can not be and is not essential to salvation, but faith is essential to salvation.

18. Since sin can not be pardoned by ordinances and rituals, therefore, a man is saved by faith.

19. Since sin is not outward defilement but inward, not of the body but of the heart, and can only be purged by the power of God within a man, therefore, a man must be saved by faith and without baptism.

20. Since baptism is a badge of discipleship, a declaration of fact, therefore baptism is not essential to salvation, but all believers in Jesus Christ who are born again ought to be baptized.

21. Since no scripture condemns a man for not being baptized but declares that the subject for baptism must be a believer; second, the mode of baptism must be immersion; third, the design and purpose of baptism is to show forth the Lord's death and resurrection; fourth, it is a figure, an emblem, therefore, baptism is not essential but faith is the essential to salvation.

22. Since the only way of salvation is by believing in Christ and the scriptures damn those who do not believe and states that all believers are saved, therefore, faith is the essential of salvation because the dying thief went to be with the Lord in Paradise, according to my worthy opponent he died after the New Covenant became valid—that was his word last night—

and valid means authoratative. Mark it, my friend, and look it up in your dictionary. Since the New Testament became valid on the death of the cross—my worthy opponent's word, therefore, the dying thief violates his theory entirely and salvation is by faith alone.

23. Salvation is not outward but inward, it is not of the body but of the heart. Since baptism is an outward, symbolic act, therefore salvation is not by baptism.

24. Salvation is not by works. Since baptism is a work of righteousness, therefore a man is saved by faith alone before and without water baptism.

Listen, sinners are saved by faith before water baptism is the clear teaching of more than two hundred New Testament passages on how to be saved that have not one word of baptism in them. Since God is a reasonable God and the complete statement of scripture is that the believer is saved, therefore, he is saved without water baptism.

25. Salvation is denied those who disbelieve. Since every negative is met by a positive statement in the gospel, therefore, no one can be damned for lack of baptism, and an individual is saved by faith before and without water baptism.

26. Salvation is by faith in Jesus Christ and by that alone. Therefore, people are saved before and without water baptism. The apostle Paul believed that a man was saved by faith alone before water baptism for he said "By the foolishness of preaching to save them that believe." He thanked God he did not baptize them but he preached to them to save them. Therefore, individuals are saved by belief of the gospel before and without water baptism.

27. Since the scripture always presents repentance before faith and no individual can possibly have faith until he repents and, third, since faith purifies the heart a man must repent before he can have faith. My worthy opponent and his position will have men with purified hearts before they have repented. There, a man is saved by faith and faith alone following repentance.

28. Since a man is saved by faith and this faith is a gift of God, not of yourself, it is a gift of God and something infinitely more than historical faith or intellectual assent but

a vital life giving principle whereby a sinner becomes a child of God. Men and women, if you do not know you are born again in the name of our Great God why don't you turn your heart over to Him and yield to Him? Therefore, an individual is saved by this mighty force of faith alone and before, without water baptism.

29. Since the dying thief was saved according to the words of Jesus, he did not die until according to the words of my opponent the New Covenant was valid by Christ's death on the cross. He was saved by faith and faith alone without water baptism.

30. Since Cornelius, according to Acts 10, was saved and the Holy Ghost fell on him before and without water baptism and Peter very reluctantly consented to baptize him, therefore, Cornelius was saved by faith alone before and without water baptism.

31. Since faith includes all that precedes it such as a man, a God, sin, an atonement, conviction, repentance, which lead to faith therefore the man is saved by faith before and without water baptism.

32. My worthy opponent argued that 1 Pet. 3:21 made baptism essential to salvation. He went on to say that Noah was saved by water. This is true but when was Noah saved in God's sight? When did Noah become God's man and God's child? My worthy opponent always gets the works of faith mixed up with the act of faith that makes a man a child of God. Look where he has got himself. In Heb. 11 we read that by faith Noah built an ark. For 120 years his faith caused him to build an ark and according to commands of God thus he was physically saved from the flood by the work of his living faith. None could be saved from sure destruction unless they have living faith. According to my worthy opponent no one was saved until after the flood. God said he walked with God over 120 years before the flood because by faith he had believed in God. Therefore, a man is saved by faith alone before and without water baptism.

33. James is not writing to sinners. He is writing to Christians, his brethren. According to my worthy opponent a Christian is one who has already been baptized when he was a

sinner. James does not say that sinners are saved by faith plus works. A man is saved by faith alone before and without water baptism and he ought by all means to be baptized. He ought by all means to produce the works here outlined in James.

34. Christ always had been and was the Son of God when he was baptized. He is the Son of God. He is our example. Those who have been born again and who are children of God by faith are the ones who should be baptized. We become children of God through faith. Therefore, a man is saved by faith alone before and without water baptism.

In answer now as the time will allow to as many arguments as possible of my opponent's which might not be clear in some of your minds. He quoted in his last speech John said, "He that sent me to baptize" and said that, therefore, baptism was essential to salvation. What's he going to do with the dying thief? He is either under John's baptism or Christian baptism. Jesus said he was saved and with Him in Paradise and the man was not baptized. What's my worthy opponent going to do with him? He hopelesslly gets himself into terrible and awful fixes. My friends, Ladies and Gentlemen, our God is a God who saves men in a glorious and matchless way. He changes men's lives completely and utterly and will change your life.

Listen to this. My worthy opponent in his arguments—he is a very nice man and we have all had a wonderful time together. I have and I am sure that you have. Everything has been lovely—but in his method of argument he is as nimble as a monkey. He tried to swing himself through a forest of error until he found himself caught in the thick underbrush. Like a trained flea he has leaped hither and yon, landing everywhere but upon the argument or the plain simple questions—the questions I have asked him night after night. Even tonight he did not come right out and answer them like I did. Ladies and Gentlemen, if he wants me to answer any question plainer, I'll be glad to answer. But as for my worthy opponent, I have had to almost beg him to get a half-hearted answer out of him. Like a squirrel in a cage he has gone round and round running in circles always coming back to where he began which is somewhere under the Old Covenant or under the New Covenant—or during a period of fifty-three days in which he finds himself in between. I want him to tell this audience in his final argument how a man was saved in that fifty-three days between the cross and Pentecost. Having hanged himself upon a "not" of his own making, he has dug for himself a grave, now he finds himself buried beneath bare facts and plain hard truths, crushed by an avalanche of logic. What appeared to be a flash of atomic energy on the horizon has dissipated itself into the shades of ecclesiastical oblivion .

Ladies and Gentlemen, my closing word to you. I am serious and dead in earnest about this debate. I have not quibbled about particular definitions. I want to see men get to God. It's been my fervent hope and plea that men will find Jesus Christ as their living Savior and their living life within their hearts ere this debate comes to an end. I trust that the seeds sown will bring good fruit in your heart. I trust that you will read your Bibles. You have heard my worthy opponent tell you to read your Bibles. I plead with you to read your Bibles. Do not listen to what my worthy opponent says. I assure you he is dead wrong. But do not listen to what I say because, my friend, I want you to get it from the Word of God. You read the Word of God.. Ask God to open the eyes of your understanding that you might behold wondrous things therein. Do not follow any man. Follow the Word of God. Jesus Christ has sent into the world His Holy Spirit and lighteth every man that cometh into the world and God will make plain and clear to you the method of salvation, my friend. If you with an honest heart will seek the truth of God, Jesus Christ will beget you unto life and you will be born again a child of God by faith in Jesus Christ, then you ought to put on the garments of Christ. You ought to put on the badge of discipleship. You ought to like Abraham for twenty-six years or for 120 like Noah produce works because you have faith. You have got to have life before you can work.

Thank you, Ladies and Gentlemen.

SIXTH NIGHT—PORTER'S SECOND SPEECH

Mr. President, Gentlemen Moderators, Respected Opponent, Ladies and Gentlemen:

I am before you now for the closing of this discussion. This speech will be exactly thirty minutes long. When that is over the debate will be history, and you will make your decision in view of the judgment and eternity after awhile.

My opponent put on quite a little display in the closing minutes of his speech telling how the flash of atomic energy had failed to explode and things of that nature. How he had buried Porter with his arguments, and things of that kind, but I think he is finding that the corpse is proving to be about the most lively corpse that he has ever had hold of. Just somehow he cannot keep him buried, it seems, and so it is all in vain when he tells you things of that nature.

He talked about his squirrel cage and said that I had brought the same scriptures and had run around like a squirrel in a cage, from one step to another on the various steps in the squirrel cage —around and around and around and around. My contention is that he cannot even find one step to go in his squirrel cage, because there is not a single passage in all of God's Book that says what his proposition says. I do not demand that it contain the entire proposition just as it is written, but he cannot find the expression, "saved by faith alone," or anything that's equivalent to it. He can not find it in all of God's Book. It is not there.

My friend said awhile ago, regarding my upsetting his illustration with the pumpkin proposition, that it is the first time he ever knew that repentance is a pumpkin. Well, it is the first time I ever knew that faith is a watermelon. (Laughter). Now, you can see what the gentleman is doing. He is trying to cover up and not meeting the issue at all. Of course, no body said that repentance is a pumpkin. But I made the illustration in harmony with his illustration. He let the watermelon equal faith, and I let the pumpkin equal repentance, and they stand on exactly the same plane. If what I said meant repentance is a pumpkin what he said meant faith is a watermelon. My friend Tingley, can you not see an inch past your nose? It looks like he would know he was getting into things like that.

Now, he said Porter quibbled about this because he could not find the scripture that says an alien sinner is saved by faith before and without water baptism. He said if the exact words could be found, there would be no debate. He said he would not debáte if such a statement were found. Yes, you would. When the book said baptism saves us in answer to a good conscience you debate that——you say that is not so. So if it did not read exactly like you wanted it to, you'd still debate, regardless of what it said, in the same way you are proceeding with respect to these other matters.

Then he came back to his questions about all those who are in hell, and things of that kind, as though that had a thing on earth to do with the proposition. I have shown you from time to time that our question says—our proposition says—"the scriptures teach." It does not say the thing is taught by how many are sent to hell or how many are going to hell. That has nothing to do with what the scriptures teach. If every one of us goes to hell, that still does not change the scriptures. I am just trying to get before you what the scriptures say, and it matters not how many go to hell as a result of it. Let that be as it may—the scriptures say!

Then, he said, "Well, I tell you. I believe in all of them." You can believe this, or this, (pointing to chart) or you can believe this over here, but you just can not believe all of them. This says "Sinners are saved by faith alone" (pointing to chart). This says, "Faith alone is dead." Friend Tingley says sinners are saved by a living faith. That's right there (pointing to paper) in answer to a question awhile ago—that sinners are saved by a living faith. Well, if they are saved by a living faith, it is not by a dead faith; and if it is not by a dead faith, it is not by faith alone, because James says, "Faith alone is dead." We will have more on that later on in the speech.

Then he came to the board again. Someone move the chart from the board just a moment for me. We want to take care of his illustration again. (The chart is moved).

Enters train — Sit down — Reaches Atlanta
Believeth — Is Baptized — Shall be saved

Now then, "He that entereth the train and sits down shall reach his destination." "He that believeth and is baptized shall be saved." He makes it; "He that entereth the train shall reach Atlanta" and "He that believeth shall be saved." He cut out "sitting down," and he cut out "baptism" because he had made them parallel. Now, "He that enters the train shall reach Atlanta." But did you not know that a man could reach Atlanta without entering the train? Since he can reach Atlanta without sitting down, if that proves baptism is not necessary, then since he can reach Atlanta without entering the train, that proves faith is not necessary, because he has made them parallel. Can't you go to Atlanta without entering the train, friend Tingley? Is it true that you can't reach Atlanta without entering a train? Why, we had some folks to leave here last night for Atlanta, and they were not going by train. (Laughter). They got home and are already in Atlanta now but did not enter a train. They got to Atlanta without entering the train. You can go to Atlanta without entering a train. I can go without entering a train. So entering a train is not necessary. If you make that parallel to faith, then faith is not necessary to reach salvation. That saves a man without faith, without baptism—without anything.

He made his plea a while ago that he wanted you to turn to God. He wanted you to give your hearts to God, and he was pleading for you to do that. Well, why don't you? Well, according to him, the reason you do not do that is that you are just waiting for God to send you faith. You can not do anything about it yourself. You can not exercise the faith yourself. God must send it to you. Until God sends it to you you can not do anything about it. You will just have to sit and wait.

Then regarding baptism being a figure, he said, "Yes, it's a figure. 'The like figure whereunto even baptism doth also now save us'." He said I left out the word "also." That did not change the meaning of it. "Also" just means "in addition to." In the type Noah was saved by water, and we are also saved by baptism. The word "also" just helps my side. It does not help my opponent a bit. "But it's a figure!" Figure of what? Well, he has been saying it's a figure of salvation, but there is not a word in the passage that says anything about it's being a figure of salvation. The verse before said that Noah was saved in the Ark by water. "The like figure whereunto even baptism doth also now save us (not the putting away of the filth of the flesh, but the answer of a good conscience toward God)." Now, where's the figure? Noah and his family in the ark, borne on the bosom of the water, were transported from the old world to the new world. After a true resemblance, or in the anti-type, as many translations give it, baptism saves us—transports us from a state of condemnation to a state of justification. There's where the figure is. One is a resemblance of the other. Not a word said about baptism as a figure of salvation. That's what my friend reads into it, but it isn't there. He has to read it into the passage to get it there. It just is not there.

But he said, "It's not the putting away the filth of the flesh." Well, certainly not. Baptism is not a mere outward washing. It's not for the purpose of washing dirt from the body—certainly not. It has a meaning much deeper than that, and so it saves us. But my opponent says, "Yes, but it goes on and says it saves us by the resurrection of Christ." Well, certainly it does. Peter says, "Baptism saves us by the resurrection of Christ." My friend Tingley says, "The resurrection of Christ saves us without baptism." Now, are those two statements the same? One says, "Baptism saves us by the resurrection of Christ" and the other says, "The resurrection of Christ saves us without baptism." Now, you can see those are not anywhere related to each other.

I was really amused at him when he came to James 2 which said man is not saved "by faith alone." "These passages," he said, "are written to people who were already saved." He says that these passages can not apply to the alien sinner. Well, my opponent has been giving Rom. 4:3-5 about being saved by faith. Mr. Tingley, did you not know that was written to the saints at Rome? The very passage he has been depending upon was written to the saints in Rome. But because James is written to "my brethren" it can not refer to alien sinners. All right; this that is written to the saints in Rome can not then apply to an alien sinner. I'll just move over; he's taking a ride with me.

Not only that, but he gave 1 Cor. 12:13 about "by one Spirit are ye all baptized into one body," and applied that to alien sinners. Friend Tingley, did you not know this was written to the saints at Corinth? Didn't you know that? Now, you see where he has gotten himself.

"Well, but Abraham was justified by works," he said, "when he offered his son Isaac." "Yes," Tingley said, "but he had been a servant of God for twenty-six years before—he did not become a child of God when he offered Isaac upon the altar, because he had been a child of God for twenty-six years." He gave Rom. 4:3 about the scripture which said, "Abraham believed God," referring back to Genesis 15. But Abraham had been serving God at least seventeen years before Genesis 15, to which Paul referred to here. You make it refer to his justification, his salvation as an alien sinner, in Rom. 4:3. Yet Abraham had left his country and was brought out by faith and you can trace him by the smoke of his altars through those years before you come to that statement that Paul referred to. That was back there a number of years before the scripture referred to by Paul which you depended upon to prove salvation for an alien sinner.

We are both in the same boat again.

To 1 Cor. 1:12-13—"Christ sent me not to baptize, but to preach the gospel." I want to reaffirm the argument I made last night on that while I am at it—an argument that my friend has not touched to this day and can not touch while the world stands. 1 Cor. 1:12-13, Paul said, "Now every one of you saith, I am of Paul; and I am of Apollos; I am of Cephas; and I am of Christ. Was Paul crucified for you? or were you baptized in the name of Paul?" He had asked, "Is Christ divided?" Now note this. Paul shows that those men who were claiming to belong to him, and to be of him, that two things are necessary: First, Paul must be crucified for them. Second, they must be baptized in the name of Paul. And if Paul had not been crucified for them and they had not been baptized in Paul's name, they could not belong to Paul. And so with Cephas and so with Apollos. And the same principle comes right on to Christ. Christ must be crucified for you, you must be baptized in the name of Christ, to belong to Christ. Some said, "I belong to Paul." Some said, "I belong to Apollos." Some to Cephas and some to Christ. The principle shows those two things are necessary in order to belong to them. Christ has been crucified for us, but along with that, we must be baptized in His name in order to belong to Him. My opponent has not touched it to this good hour. The only thing on earth he has done is try to array scriptures against it. He tries to make on scripture deny what that scripture says, but that is not the way to answer an argument. No, the scriptures are not in conflict. They are in perfect harmony.

Further on you read where Paul said "I thank God I baptized none of you, except Crispus and Gaius; lest any man should say that I thought baptism was essential to salvation!" Is that the way it reads in your book? That's the argument he bases on it; that's what he's trying to get out of it. That's the conclusion he's drawing—that Paul thanked God he had not baptized but few of them because he did not think baptism was necessary. That is not what Paul said. There was division in Corinth, and they were calling themselves after men, and Paul did not desire them to call themselves after him; therefore, he said, "I thank God I baptized none of you, but Crispus and Gaius; lest any man should say that I had baptized in my own name." He did not say, "Lest any man should think it was necessary."

Then he said, "Christ sent me not to baptize, but to preach the gospel." According to Tingley, that proves that baptism is not essential. Well, I came to Birmingham not to baptize; I came to preach the gospel. That does not mean that I do not think baptism is essential—not at all. Then he agreed that if it had said he was sent to baptize, that would make it essential. I showed him where John said he was sent to baptize; so it was essential in John's day, then, according to my friend Tingley. He said, "Oh in that case what are you going to do with the thief?" Well, the thief on the cross had the promise made to him before Jesus died. He was the testator. If he wanted to set aside John's baptism and save the man without baptism, without repentance, without faith—without anything—he had a right to do it as a testator, because in Heb. 9:16-17, Paul said, "A testament is of force after men are dead; otherwise it is of no strength at all while the testator liveth."

Then to 1 Cor. 4:15, Paul said, "I have begotten you through the gospel." He said that is the same word as "born" in John 3:5; therefore, baptism is not necessary since Paul begot them (brought them to birth) but did not baptize them. Well, that word "beget" is the same one you find everywhere else. I called attention last night to the fact that people are begotten before they are born, and Paul merely said, "I have begotten you." Tingley said, "That's the same word that's used with respect to the Corinthians." Yes, and it's the same word that is used with respect to to a physical begetting. The very same word, but that does not mean that begetting does not precede birth. We all know that it does.

Mark 16:16—He said, "Porter denies the miracles." No, Porter does not deny the miracles. Neither my friend Tingley nor I will drink any deadly poison nor handle snakes nor raise the dead. Neither of us is doing that. Now, if my friend has done any of it lately, I have not heard of it. So if he has done anything of that kind, we have not heard of it. Neither of us is doing that. Why? Well, those miracles were for a definite purpose; and I showed from 1 Cor. 13:8-10 that Paul said the time was coming when those things would be done away. They were given for a definite purpose to confirm the word as I showed last night. And so neither my friend nor I work any such miracles today.

But regarding his "faith only," or his faith the only thing that condemnation rests upon here, he said, " 'He that believeth and is baptized shall be saved,' and that means the only thing he would have to leave off is belief—that would damn him. It didn't say, 'He that believeth not and is not baptized shall be damned'." No, and I showed last night that we might take a similar expression, "He that eats food and digests it shall have health, but he that eats no food and does not digest it shall starve." Now, you know that is not necessary. A man who eats no food will starve. You do not have to say, "And does not digest it." And a man who has not believed can no more be baptized than a man can digest food that he has not eaten. It takes both the eating and the digesting of food to bring health, but eating no food alone will bring starvation. It takes both belief and baptism to bring salvation, but unbelief alone will bring condemnation. You do not have to say, "And is not baptized."

Titus 3:5—"Not by works of righteousness". I called his attention last night to the fact that in Psalms 119:172 David said, "All thy commandments are righteousness." Then I showed from Acts 17:30 that God had commanded all men everywhere to repent. So repentance is a work of righteousness; and if that means we are not saved by obeying the commandments of God, that cuts out repentance. Now, Paul was not talking about doing the commandments of God. He was talking about a man establishing his own way and following his own system, and by doing that certainly no man could be saved.

Acts 2:38—He said the word "for" can mean it either way. "Yes, sir, here's one that might prove that baptism is necessary to salvation." It can do it, he said. He admits that that can mean that baptism is essential. "It can be either way." "You can be baptized for the remission of sins," He said, "It rarely means 'because of'." The fact is it never means "because of", and he found not one single translation in existence today that gives it "because of". He went to Matt. 12:41 to try to offset it by the statement made, "They repented at the preaching of Jonah"— the same Greek word "at". Certainly, and it conveys the very same prospective meaning, "They repented unto or into the preaching of Jonah." It does not mean "because of" at all, my friend says.

Then Matt. 26:28—Jesus shed His blood "for the remission of sins." The very same expression we have in Acts 2:38. You are baptized for the remission of sins; Jesus shed his blood for the remission of sins. Does "for" mean "because of"? If so, then Jesus shed His blood because men were already saved. The Greek grammar, he said, in this case has the second person, plural and the third person, singular. "Repent"—second person, plural; "be baptized", third person, singular. Well, he did not have to go to the Greek to ge that. That's so in English. I gave you an example of that. The principal of a school might say to the students, "Come ye, and be examined everyone of you in the name of the state for your certificate of promotion." Now, "come ye" is second person, plural; "be examined everyone of you" is third person singular. Yet they refer to the same group. The very ones who are told to "come" are the ones told to "be examined"; and both verbs joined together to secure the same result. So his quibble on that is not worth a dime.

Then to Saul. He said, "Paul said in 1 Cor. 15:8 that he was born again when he saw the Lord." Paul did not say any such thing. I want to turn and read that—1 Cor. 15:8—where my friend says that Paul declared that he was born again when he saw the Lord. Let us see if that is what it says. If it is, I have been mistaken all these years. "And last of all he was seen of men also A-S—as—one born out of due time." He did not say that he was born again. Not a word is said about being born again, but he said, "He was seen last of all by me as one born out of due time"—one prematurely born. The others had seen Him, but Paul had not seen Him until this time. He had persecuted the church of God and wasted it and felt his inferiority. So much so that he felt inferior as one would be inferior who was prematurely born when compared to one who was not thus born but had been born at the proper time. And so he said, "I am the least of all the apostles. I am as one born out of due time. I am inferior to the others." That's the way he felt about it. He had no reference to being born again. He did not say a word about being born again. When my opponent says that Paul said he was born again when he saw the Lord, he is reading words into the scripture that are not there.

I have placed on the board here the words, "Baptism doth also now save us." Not the entire scripture, because I did not have room for the entire scripture, but I did not misrepresent the meaning of it. I gave it exactly. "Baptism doth also now save us." He says that is not scripture, but he comes along and says, "Paul said he was born again when he saw the Lord." There is not any part of that found in the Bible—not any part of it; it's not there. But yet he calls it scripture—he calls it scripture!

"Porter said that Paul became an apostle when he saw the Lord." Porter did not say any such thing. Porter said that Paul was being qualified for an apostle, because an apostle must be one who has seen the Lord. I did not say he became an apostle there.

Then he said, "It's just a symbol." "Arise and be baptized and wash away thy sins" is only a symbol—just a symbol. "Wash away thy sins" would mean washing away his own sins, he claims, and since a man could not wash away his own sins, then baptism is only a symbol. Well, I gave him last night, Rev. 7:13-14. I wonder why he did not say something about it. Here John sees a multitude of the redeemed and said, "Whence came these and who are they?" And the answer came, "These are they that have washed their robes and made them white in the blood of the lamb." They washed their own robes then, friend Tingley, because it is just exactly like the other. That being true, then, according to my friend Tingley, the blood of Jesus Christ is only a symbol—it is not worth anything, because they washed their robes.

He talked about a monument too "Brother Bryan"—whoever that is—that the man had to exist first and then the monument could exist. Certainly so. But the man and salvation are different propisitions. If he can find where baptism is a monument of salvation, he will have something, but he can not find it. All these statements he makes about putting on clothes, and baptism being a badge, and things of that kind, are just statements that he has made, but they are not contained anywhere in the Book of God. They are just not there.

1 Pet. 3:21—" The like figure." I have dealt with that. Then he said it is a person who pardons. God is a person. "It is a person who pardons and not baptism." Well, faith is not a person; so that cuts out faith, too.

Then about the dying thief and about the will becoming valid and becoming authoritative. I showed that the promise made to this thief was made before the testator died. The promise, therefore, was made before the testament became effective, or became of force, or was made so that it could operate, by the death of Jesus Christ; but that following the death of the testator there must be the probating of it before the will becomes operative. So that does not help my friend a bit.

Then, the two hundred passages he said that contain faith and said nothing about baptism. Well, just about every one of them says faith but nothing about repentance. If that means no baptism, it means no repentance.

And 1 Cor. 1:21—"It pleased God by the foolishness of preaching to save them that believe." That shows that the believer was not already saved, because God was going to save them that believe, and not at the very instant they believed.

Then, "The gift of God." And I was amused at that. Here's where he asked men to turn to the Lord. "Faith is a gift of God. It is not what man does." So if you are waiting for God to give you faith, you can not turn to Him until He does.

Finally, he came to Cornelius again. And he said Cornelius received the Holy Spirit, and that proved that Cornelius was saved before baptism! On the first proposition my opponent introduced this passage to prove the direct operation of the Spirit on sinners—alien sinners. He said in this case the Holy Ghost fell upon an alien sinner in order to save him. But he came back here and said the very fact that the Holy Spirit fell on him proves that he was saved—that he was a child of God! You can not have both positions. It just will not work both ways.

Then to Noah being saved by water. He said, "Yes, I believe that," but he said, "He was God's man first. He was saved 120 years before he went into the ark." Well, this salvation referred to here was not 120 years before, because God is referring to the salvation from the flood. He was not from that until the flood came. Notice that Peter said, "Wherein," that is, in the ark, "eight souls were saved by water." My friend said he was saved 120 years before he built the ark! Peter said he was saved in the ark. Now, you can just take which one you want. Whose side are you on? My friend Tingley's or the apostle Peter's.

Back to James 2:14—"Though a man say he hath faith, and have not works, can faith save him?", or "can that faith save him?" Why, he said, "If a man lives twenty-six years after he has faith and does not do any work, of course, that kind of faith will not save him." Well, suppose he lives ten minutes? If he lives ten minutes, he still has faith without works, and James says, "Faith without works is dead." My friend says, "You can not be saved by a dead faith."

That covers the notes that I have here—how much time do I have?

Mr. Nichols: About three minutes.

Mr. Porter: Here we have a contrast between what my opponent says and what the Bible says.

MY OPPONENT SAYS	THE BIBLE SAYS
The Scriptures Teach that Alien Sinners are Saved by Faith ALONE Before and Without Water Baptism	"Even so Faith, if it Hath not Works, is Dead, Being Alone." James 2:17 "Ye see then how that by Works a Man is Justified, and Not by Faith Only." James 2:14
HE THAT BELIEVETH AND IS NOT BAPTIZED SHALL BE SAVED.	"HE THAT BELIEVTH AND IS BAPTIZED Shall be Saved." Mark 16:16

Here is the proposition word for word that friend Tingley has been affirming these two nights: "The scriptures teach that alien sinners are saved by faith alone before and without water baptism." That's what my opponent says. (Pointing to chart). All right; here is what the Bible says (Pointing to other side of chart). "Even so faith, if it hath not works, is dead, being alone." My friend Tingley can not be saved by a dead faith—it must live. All right, James says, "Faith without works is dead"—faith alone is dead! My friend Tingley says he is saved by faith alone. James says, "Faith alone is dead." All right; if faith alone is dead, you can not be saved by a dead faith. You can not be saved by faith alone. Friend Tingley can not find this in the Bible or anything like it (pointing to proposition on chart). No, but you can find this (pointing to other side of chart). He said, "No, and you can not find baptism saves in the Bible either." Oh, yes, we did. We gave him several cases. 1 Peter 3:21, Mark 16:16, Acts 2:38 and many others. So here he admits that he can not find his— not a time—not a verse of scripture that says saved by faith alone or anything that equals that. So there's what Tingley says (pointing to left side of chart), and there's what the Bible says (pointing to other side).

Again, James 2:24 says, "Ye see how that by works a man is justified, and n-o-t—not—by faith only." All right, faith only and faith alone mean the same thing. This says (pointing to proposition) "saved by faith alone"—that's Tingley. This (pointing to other side of chart) says "not by faith only," and that's James—the writer of the Book of James in the New Testament. Whose side are you on? Which one are you going to take? Are you going to stand with my friend tonight? or are you going to stand with the inspired book of God Almighty and with those who wrote that men are not saved by faith only—"not justified by faith only"?

Again, my friend says this is not the Bible (pointing to left side of bottom of chart). No, I know it isn't, but that is what friend Tingley believes. Friend Tingley, do you not believe that "He that believeth and is not baptized shall be saved"? If you do not, you had just as well shake hands with me and say that I'm right. Whenever you say you do not believe that the man who believes and is not baptized shall be saved, you give up your whole contention, because that's what you are contending for—

that the believer is saved whether he is ever baptized or not. Listen to this: (pointing to chart) "Before and without water baptism." Doesn't that mean "And is not baptized"? That's what he says right here in his proposition—"faith alone before and without water baptism." That means "not by baptism". The man who is not baptized is certainly the man who is "before and without water baptism." That's exactly what this is—"He that believeth and is not baptized shall be saved." That's what my opponent says; that's his position. "He says, "I do not believe that. It's not scripture." I know it. I do not believe it either. I'll shake hands with you on it.

Mr. Nichols: Half a minute.

Mr. Porter: Half a minute. Over here (pointing to other side of chart) Jesus said, "He that believeth and is baptized shall be saved." It's not, "He that believeth shall be saved," but "He that believeth and is baptized shall be saved." Thus we have the statements in contrast between the position occupied by my opponent and that stated in the Book of God Almighty. I'll take my stand with God's Book and stay there until I die.

I thank you, Ladies and Gentlemen.

www.ingramcontent.com/pod-product-compliance
Lightning Source LLC
Chambersburg PA
CBHW030137170426
43199CB00008B/95